Electra

A Gender Sensitive Study of Plays Based on the Myth

Final Edition

Batya Casper

Olympus Story House

CONTENTS

Preface

This study examines various dramatic forms of *Electra*, one of the recurring myths of Western civilization. It defines the nature of the mythical complex and, except for two examples which I have included to illustrate the modern writer's need to break with the myth (as with the guidelines of our rigidly hero-oriented, Western culture), it will include only those plays which conform to the same mythical deep structure.

In these plays, as in our culture so far, the hero is essentially male and will be referred to throughout, in the masculine. I attempt, throughout, to keep my language gender sensitive so, throughout the text, when using the word "man," I am referring, not to humankind, but to people of the male gender. Thematically, the feminine and the masculine, in this work, are presented as dramatic metaphors for contradictory impulses that rage within the human soul: impulses for creativity, passion and freedom versus the drive of the "civilized" human being toward control, reason and order.

This book has allowed me to examine theater for what I believe is its authentic purpose: the dramatization of the human's deepest concerns and the inescapable confrontation of them with society.

In this second edition, I have added Aeschylus' *Agamemnon* to the other two plays of the *Oresteia*—in so doing, completing his trilogy. I have expanded the quoted texts of all three plays, both to bring you the thrill of this particular translation and to highlight the kinds of questions we might ask as we journey from ancient to modern times: In this trilogy, is Clytemnestra a heroine, a demon, or a victim? How sensitive is she to the suffering of Athens' enemies? As queen and woman, is she loyal to her people? To the plight of their enemies, the people of Troy? To what extent does she—the queen—play the party line when imagining their plight? How similar or different is Clytemnestra the woman from us?

What about her feelings for her husband? Do they ring true today? Can we identify with her?

Will the Clytemnestra of these plays be the same woman we will encounter in other Greek plays? Why? Why not? How about the other characters? What function do they perform—for the playwrights? The spectators? Ourselves?

How does the chorus figure in these plays? Who do they represent?

What relationship exists between the chorus and royalty? Between royalty and their people? Between the people and the gods? What function do the heralds perform? In *Agamemnon*, what feelings does the herald have for his fellow soldiers at Troy?

To what extent (if any) does the status of women differ from that of men? Are we different from those characters?

How much do we learn of fifth-century Greece from the Greek plays?

In this edition, an argument will be made for a more in-depth reading of gender-sensitive issues and the influence that socio/sexual behaviors have had over society. The French expression, "Tout ca change, tout c'est la même chose" will accompany us from ancient Greece to our own world. To what extent is it true that the more things change, the more they stay the same?

I wish to thank the Department of Special Studies at the University of California–Los Angeles Library for making its resources available to me. I thank Carey Perloff for having furnished me with what was, at that time, an unpublished script of Ezra Pound's *Elektra*, together with the press releases for the world premiere of that play which she directed.

I reserve a special place in my heart for Professor Henry Goodman of UCLA Theatre Department, who has since left us for a better place, for having inspired me, so many years ago, with his profound knowledge and with that open, friendly manner—his trademark. My gratitude to Donald Cosentino, for having set me on my journey through the mysterious world of myth; to Carl Mueller, renowned for his translations and his teaching, who furnished me with some of the most exhilarating hours of my life; and to Anna Krayevska for her profound knowledge of the original Greek texts.

Introduction

And why should it be that whenever men (and women) have looked for something solid on which to found their lives, they have chosen not the facts in which the world abounds, but the myths of an immemorial imagination—preferring even to make life a hell for themselves and their neighbors, in the name of some violent god, to accepting gracefully the bounty the world affords?[1]

The issue raised in the above quotation will be the focus of this book, which examines in its various dramatic forms a recurring myth found at the very source of Western civilization. It will benefit us to bear this quotation in mind as we work our way through the plays, each with its unique language, and its different—often challenging—historical, political, and social perspectives.

But first things first: Before attempting to assess the theatrical forms of Electra, we will need to address ourselves to the nature of myth.

Claude Lévi-Strauss claims that the oral tradition, which was the original transmitter of mythical material, is like the work of *bricolage*.[2] Like bricolage, it is often the result of a closed system in which the artist is forced, over and over, to reuse the same materials. So, in folktales and in myths, songs, refrains, and specific lines are used repeatedly in different forms, each time with a new dramatic intent. The oral tradition, like bricolage, takes objects already imbued with meaning through interactions they have had in other contexts and, with them, constructs new formations, thereby creating yet again new arrangements of meaning. The results of bricolage and myth are similar to the results of theater. Medieval performances, for example, by means of the naïve and spontaneous participation of acrobats, jongleurs, and devils, together with the interaction of all the above with the audience, produced theater that had a far different and greater impact than had been foreseen by the church-writers at the outset.

Writers often assume—often mistakenly—that their readers have the background, causes, and ramifications of their subject matter at their fingertips before even beginning to read. I am anxious not to make any such assumption. Therefore, at the opening of this work, I have set a brief list of those gods and goddesses who figured in the Greek Creation Myths and who are most germane to the myth and plays of Electra—our subject matter. The mythical characters, in our list, served as precursors for the myths and plays of Electra and for the deeds that have made them either famous or infamous. In fact, those characters' stories reflect the arduous journey that was made by Western civilization from chaos and almost constant cruelty to reason, law and order. Some grasp, however elementary, of how the ancient Greeks evolved, of how they interpreted the world they lived in; some understanding of the pre-classical and classical Greek world-views will, I believe, enable us to understand the betrayals, murders and acts of revenge that transpire in the plays we will read.

We will question how particular each play is to its culture, or how universal; and how alike it is to our own, modern world.

Just as we have set the background of the Creation gods at the opening of our study, so too, we have set the history of the House of Atreus immediately before the plays of that trilogy. It is no more than background information for whoever wants it. With all the plays in this study, we will question how characteristic each is to its own particular historical period, and what relevance, if any, each play has to our own day. Is our world less violent? Less racist? Less sexist? Less self-aware? Less questioning? How different is modern Western culture from that of our precursors?

The plays in this study stretch from the Classical Greek plays of the three great fifth-century tragedians to those as late as the twentieth century.

Lévi-Strauss maintains that a myth is comprised of all of its variants including its latest interpretation. [3] Again, the significance lies in the bricolage effect. Each new form of the myth is encrusted not only with the legacy of the past and the special significance it had for its initial audience, but with the specific relevance and social commentary that it has for the present. The post–Freudian world is incapable of understanding the ancient Greek myths in the way that the Greek world had; rather, we comprehend it in a way that combines what we believe was the fifth-century BCE Athenian understanding of the myth with our own Freudian and post–Freudian perspectives.

Myth is part of the oral tradition and as such its nature depends on its fluidity, its essential changeability from performance to performance, and its independence of the written form. The magic of the Electra myth consists in this very fluidity, in the fact that it is never trapped in any specific dramatic form, but appears again and again, each time with a different face, and for a different effect.

Isis Suckling the Child Horus, from Egypt, Late Period (332–64 BCE), bronze statuette, 6 × 6.7 × 8.5 cm, h 23.5 cm (without peg), Inv. ÄM 8286 (bpk Bildagentur/Aegiptisches Museum und Papyrussammlung/photograph by Sandra Steiß/Art Resource, New York).

Oral tradition, which constituted the original conveyor of the myth, was and is to this day Aristotelian by nature. It is mimetic, an imitation of reality. But the myth that it conveys deals simultaneously with the real and the ideal. In his definitive work, *Sacred Narrative*, Theodor Gaster claims that myth "transforms the social into narrative, the punctual into the durative, the diachronic into the synchronic." It exists in two simultaneous time spaces: at the moment of presentation and for all time. Prime examples of this duality can be found in the myths of the Passover and the Easter stories. Gaster sees myth as interdependent with ritual and, as such, as a form that has a close affinity to drama. [4] Indeed, we see this to be the case with the ceremonial enactments of the Easter and the Passover myths. However, the tale in which the myth is couched is always based on the immediate and the specific, fabricated as with bricolage from the structure and complexities of contemporary society. Gaster defines myth as "any presentation of the actual in terms of the ideal." [5] T.S. Eliot also maintained that all our realities are founded in concretes and it is up to us to come up with interpretations. [6] This view of myth coincides exactly with the understanding of theater that will be explored in this book, a theater that is after all the conveyor of a myth in its multiple forms. The universal is derived by theatergoers from the tangible, the particular, and the specific.

Gaster describes the evolution of the mythical in the following way: first is the "primitive stage" in which "the story is the direct accompaniment of a ritual performed for purely pragmatic purposes. It serves to present the several features of the ritual, ... as incidents in a transcendental situation." Today we might consider the Passover ceremony or the Easter Mass, in which myth and ritual are intrinsically related, as examples of this stage. Second is the "dramatic stage" in which "the ritual or cultic performance has been toned down into an actual pantomimic representation of the story," such as the Mystery Plays that are no longer myths. Then comes the "liturgical stage" in which the story no longer parallels the ritual, but is simply a recitation, a religious ceremony, such as the medieval Christian hymns, which are only part of the ritual. Finally, there is the "literary stage ...a mere tale, severed altogether from any ritual observance." [7]

Gaster gives the Homeric hymns and some of the Hebrew psalms as examples of this stage. Regardless of its relationship to ritual, myth operates both synchronically and diachronically, as does the theater we shall observe in this study.

Electra is one of the most recurring myths of Western civilization. This book will attempt to define the nature of its mythical complex and illustrate how all the plays under examination—except those whose deviations from the structure I regard as a deliberate attempt on the part of the playwright to change the myth—are comprised of the same mythical deep-structure.

Myth became incorporated into Western theater for the first time in fifth- century BCE Athens, when both the mythical content and the dramatic form constituted a reflection of the contemporary social structure and a record of the changing ideologies particular to that society. In Jacobean England—two thousand years after the Greek period—a mythical complex that conforms to the deep structure of the Greek Electra myth can, I believe, be discerned (though in a very different theatrical form) in Shakespeare's *Hamlet*. It is the resurfacing of the Electra in a social structure that bears uncanny points of resemblance to that of classical Greece. Yet again, in twentieth-century Europe, we shall see the myth reappear and flourish as the result of an intellectual impulse akin to that which had given rise to the plays of classical Greece.

Claude Lévi-Strauss claims that, though the surface structure might differ radically from presentation to presentation, myths can be classified and recognized as belonging to the same group by means of the invariable pattern of their deep structure. [8] In such a way, though the surface structure, the theatrical treatment, and the ensuing sociopolitical messages, differ drastically from play to play, the deep structure remains invariable throughout all the Electra plays within this study—except for those plays we will examine as deliberate attempts on the part of the playwrights to change the mythical structure.

The plays we will be examining as typical of the myth share all of the five central characters. They all present an Agamemnon figure that has been replaced in some way by Aegisthus, and they all have an Aegisthus who has usurped the position of Agamemnon both in the political arena and in the affections of the Queen. In all of these plays there is a Clytemnestra figure whose affections are diverted from her children and directed toward the current ruler. Electra is always the unmated, the imprisoned, and the vengeful; while Orestes is, in all the plays, the son and heir of Agamemnon and the would-be avenger of his father's murder.

In the myth, Orestes always approaches the action from a separate physical or psychological space than that of the other characters. He is always forced to take a stand against the establishment. The focal point of action is always the meeting of the old (Agamemnon) with the new (Orestes) and the play is always propelled into action by the meeting of the male (Orestes) with the female (Electra). Electra represents filial loyalty, Clytemnestra is "tainted," a mother manquée, and Aegisthus is characterized by a lack of idealism or any sense of the spiritual.

In the *Myth of the Eternal Return*, Mircea Eliade [9] describes archaic times as a period of a-historicity in which men and women, unequipped to rationalize the harshness of human suffering in terms of history and human cause and effect, used ritual as a safeguard of time as circular, static, and recognizable. Ritual celebrations of the cycle of seasons of death and rebirth always reenacted the same point in time, and always brought men and women back to the pattern of life and death that has always been and will never change.

Eliade claims that the ancient Hebrews were the first to propel men and women into a sense of history with their belief that political and social defeats and victories were caused directly and deliberately by divine intervention.

Whether Eliade's claim is correct or not, Aristotelian logic soon replaced the more primal cycle of the eternal return with the cause and effect (i.e., history) of a homocentric world.

Only in post–Hegelian times have people become disenchanted with history. Only with Nietzsche did thinkers begin to question the validity of the Judeo-Christian heritage, for with them western culture began to hark back to static, pre-patriarchal times and to the myth of the eternal return as an alternative to the masculine, the causative and the destructive.

Nietzsche sensed that the twentieth century (not to mention the twenty- first) would have to question. He foresaw that his future would herald in a period of constantly revolving, often antithetical, conflicting and struggling ideologies.

The Electra myth, I believe, originated out of an archaic myth of eternal return. The purpose of this book is to examine its adaptation from myth into the early patriarchal system, to examine its transformation from its earliest theatrical forms in Aeschylus, Sophocles, and Euripides, and to observe its manipulation in the hands of subsequent writers.

The Greek plays always took place at the festival of Dionysus, a theater dedicated specifically to the celebration of the cyclical myth of return; for just as early Christians in the Middle Ages clung to pagan images and ideals, so early Greek patriarchs found it hard to fully relinquish archaic concepts of ritual and static time.

Geza Roheim, in *The Gates of the Dream*, identifies two sources of mythology: the "dream" and the "problem of growing up." [10]

Ancient Greek mystery rites were ceremonies that led the adolescent through a symbolic death and rebirth as preparation for adulthood. Anthropological sources for many cultures testify to the fact that adolescent boys were—and in some instances still are—removed from the comfort of the maternal into an all-male society beyond the confines of the homestead. Only when fully initiated into the rites of manhood can they return as beneficial members of society. In all the plays included in this study as those that conform to the deep structure of the myth, the audience witnesses the rebirth of Orestes. He is an adolescent returning to his community from a separate space. As such, he is similar to the actor, the prophet, and the hero. All such figures return from an off-stage space; all such figures grapple with their vision and are ultimately snared, on their return, in the too close ties of their own homes.

This journey is exclusively a male journey. In this context, the hero is always male.

In all the versions of the Electra myth studied in this work, there has been an artificial separation of the male from the female. At times, it seems almost as though the plays of Sophocles and Euripides were wake-up calls— deliberate dramatizations of the harm that the artificial divorce of the feminine from the masculine, both in the individual and in Athenian society, was causing their culture.

An enormous contradiction existed between the secondary status of women in fifth-century BCE Athens—women who were bought as child brides away from their mothers' homes and left voiceless and without status from that point on inside an enclosed and separate women's house—and the larger- than-life amazons of classical Greek mythology. This contradiction might indicate an exaggerated fear held by men of that period toward women and female sexuality, and an overwhelming desire on the part of men to suppress women.

It is not surprising that such a fear and opposition of the sexes should surface as part of the inner structure of the Electra myth. I believe that in archaic times this myth had enacted the murder of the male by the matriarch and the incorporation of his body into Mother Earth in order to ensure fertility and the return of vegetation each spring. Later, in patriarchal hands, the focus of the murder switched. It became primarily that of the female (mother) by the avenging male (son), itself the story of what many believe was the patriarchal takeover of earlier female goddesses. The story then became that of the repressed female (Electra) as emblem of the repressed emotional life of a people and its desperate attempt to be liberated and incorporated into some vision of the future. More than likely, Sophocles and Euripides were both warning their generation of violence that would ensue as the result of an artificial stifling and/or separation, of male and female principles inherent in each individual male, and in Athenian society as a whole.

In its outlook and treatment of women, the Jacobean period (1603–1625 England, reign of King James) bears striking similarities to fifth-century BCE Athens. Texts from the Jacobean period record the accepted societal policy regarding women: the necessity that they be modest, acquiescent, temperate, pious and chaste, and that they have no voice in politics, religion, or the education of their children. Yet, as with the Greeks, the women of the Jacobean theater are noted for their fiery temperaments, their intemperate sexuality, and their proclivity for lust, murder and insanity. The Jacobean period was also a period of vast expansionism, of rapidly changing ideologies and gross materialism; it is understandable, therefore, that a visionary such as Shakespeare could create *Hamlet*, a play which I believe adheres to all the aspects of the deep-structure of the Electra myth. It might be argued that Shakespeare was almost consciously writing during England's adolescence (in which case the theme and structure of the Electra play would be particularly appropriate) and warning England both of its enormous potential for idealism—the Hamlet/Orestean vision—and the danger that it succumbs to the short-sighted materialism of its Aegisthean complacence.

The end of the nineteenth century sought an alternative to the patriarchal legacy of Western culture, and the task of the early years of the 20th century became for many the creation of a new history. In this work, we will examine the Electra plays of the 20th century as works that confront the status quo with the new, sometimes deliberately a-heroic, Orestean vision. We will examine the anticlassical, anti-tragic, antiheroic structure of modern theater and the expression of the ideology of each play in terms of its theatrical space, structure, use of images and language.

Lévi-Strauss describes the human need to stratify existence in terms of clusters of similarities and binary oppositions. [11] Western culture recognizes its own experience in terms of:

Male/female — logical/instinctual
Spiritual/material — night/day
Rational/emotional — repression/freedom

These oppositions are manipulated again and again in the theatrical configurations of the Electra myth. As previously noted, patriarchal history has become associated with action, Apollonian logic and masculine repression; whereas the female in the archaic world represents static acquiescence, nature, instinctual wisdom and patience. Does Electra fit into this characteristic of the female?

Perhaps not so much. Electra is heroic in her relentless loyalty to past values and if she is violent, ruthless and even insane, it is because she has become the hysterical call for deliverance of the imprisoned female and life force. As we read through this study, we will note how, already in the Greek plays, Electra evolves from the female priestess, instrument of ritual and renewal (Aeschylus), to the "insane" voice of the anti-establishment (Sophocles), to the pathetic call of the demented, imprisoned female spirit (Euripides).

Yet, where Orestes is the hope for the future, Electra is the only one who understands the values of the past and who clings tenaciously to them throughout the long centuries of patriarchal culture.

In the Greek plays of Athens' Classical age, we will see how Electra has retained some of the vengeful fury attributed to female priestesses of a much earlier, darker age. We will recognize Electra as a shadow, a last gasp of primal, Chthonic, mystery (i.e., secret to women) cults—which were still tolerated in fifth century BCE Athens and practiced by women.

The most archaic of moral codes, now relegated to the underworld, insists that patricide and matricide are the most abhorrent of sins, never to be tolerated. Ancient, foul-smelling hags (the Furies) guard the underworld. They serve Gaia, Mother Earth, first of the goddesses. At the beginning of time, Gaia's children, the Titans and the Hundred Handed, had risen up against her and her husband. From that time on, matricide, deemed more heinous than any other crime, will not go unpunished; it will evoke the eternal vigilance, the savage wrath and vengeance of the Furies. (We will encounter these Furies in Aeschylus' play of that name.) As mentioned, such hags have guarded the netherworld since earliest, archaic times, throughout the long dark centuries leading up to patriarchal Greek culture of the Classical period. Electra's fury is but a pale shadow of those prehistoric ghouls.

The ancient Greeks, the Jacobeans of 16th and 17th century England, and the twentieth and twenty-first centuries of the Western world can be characterized by their self-consciousness; their contradictory absolutist ideologies; warfare; violence; religious fundamental ideologies often based on superstition, ignorance, and sadistic practices; gross materialism; and periodic bouts of idealistic fervor.

The Orestean figure appears during periods of changing ideologies. He is the hero. It is he who struggles to liberate his generation from myopic and repressive materialism, as typified by Aegisthus, and lead it toward the ideal of the Orestean vision; and it is at this moment that the myth of Electra is re- examined.

It bears repeating that such a situation was dramatized when the religious confidence of the High Renaissance crumbled into the materialism and uncertainty of the Jacobean period. It is dramatized over and over in the changing and antithetical ideologies of modern times.

Peter Brook describes theater as that of "the invisible made visible."[12] The plays in this study manifest contradictions that are both inherent in and destructive of Western civilization—issues that were recognized by dramatists as early as fifth-century BCE Athens. For the duration of the theatrical performance, each play actualizes the imagined and the intuited into physical reality on stage. As such, each becomes a ritual binding of players and spectators in a shared materialization of abstractions that are germane to its respective time period.

As noted, these plays concretize the most seminal issues of Western society: the psychological and political rifts caused by the artificial separation of the male and female principles in the culture, and the violence that this has engendered; the development and progression of such concepts as honor, justice, patriotism and vengeance versus morality, personal suffering, and individual conscience; the development and gradual transformation of the community's understanding of the "tragic" and the "heroic" both in theatrical structure and in content; the understanding that "sanity" as a concept evolves into that of the masculine party line, while "insanity" becomes the voice of the female individual contradicting that of the establishment; the tragic hero as the harbinger of a new moral code, and these plays as the struggle of the hero to co-opt the world that is foisted on him toward his own revolutionary vision.

What relevance has the Electra myth for modernity? The end of the nineteenth century sought an alternative to the patriarchal legacy of Western culture, and the task of the 20th century and the early years of this century became for many the creation of a new history. In this work, we will examine the Electra plays of the 20th century as works that confront the status quo with the new, sometimes deliberately a-heroic, Orestean vision. We will examine the anticlassical, anti-tragic, antiheroic structure of modern theater and the expression of the ideology of each play in terms of its theatrical space, structure, use of images and language.

---

1 Joseph Campbell, Primitive Mythology: The Masks of God (New York: Penguin, 1987), p. 4.
2 Claude Lévi-Strauss, "The Structural Study of Myth," in Structural Anthropology (New York: Basic, 1963), pp. 207–31.
3 Lévi-Strauss, p. 217.
4 Theodor H. Gaster, "Myth and Story," in Sacred Narrative (Berkeley: University of California Press, 1984) pp. 110–36
5 Gaster, p. 112.
6 T.S. Eliot, "The Perfect Critic," in The Sacred Wood (New York: Methuen, 1920).
7 Gaster, pp. 125–128.
8 Lévi-Strauss, pp. 206–31.
9 Mircea Eliade, The Myth of the Eternal Return, or, Cosmos and History, trans. Willard R. Trask (Princeton, N.J.: Princeton University Press, 1974).
10 Geza Roheim, The Gates of the Dream (New York: International University Press, 1952) p. 401.
11 Lévi-Strauss, pp. 207–31.
12 Peter Brook, The Empty Space (New York: Atheneum, 1984), p. 42.

CHAPTER 1

PREHISTORY

F or the purposes of our study, I am glossing over a multitude of early Greek deities, and am setting the following synopsis of Olympian Creation Myths, in the briefest of terms, for reference, clarity—or simply to refresh a reader's memory:

Uranus: First Sky god, primal king of the gods.
Gaia: Earth, mother goddess and Uranus' wife.
Cronus: Second sky god, one of Uranus and Gaia's (giant) Titan children who overthrew their parents.

The reign of Cronus, characterized by chaos and anarchy, gave rise to the human race. During this earliest of periods, humans suffered greatly from ignorance, hunger, extreme exposure to the elements, predatory animals, and each other.

Zeus (meaning "sky"): Third sky god (third millennium BCE), son of Cronus. With the help of Hades, god of the underworld; Poseidon, god of the oceans; and other siblings, Zeus overthrew his father, Cronus, and established his place on the Olympian throne.
Prometheus, son of earth, fought valiantly to help Zeus overthrow Cronus, and establish Zeus as god of Olympian rule.

To reward Prometheus, Zeus invited him to feast on Olympus. Out of concern for the pitiable state of human beings of those primordial times, Prometheus stole a spark from the Olympian fire and brought it back down with him to earth. His gift of fire to humankind dramatically improved their living conditions.

Zeus retaliated for Prometheus' theft by sending Hephaestus, his fire-god, to Prometheus. Hephaestus bound Prometheus to a rock in the Caucasian mountains (subject of Aeschylus' play *Prometheus Bound.*)

Prometheus claimed to know of a curse that would bring about the downfall of Zeus if he were not forewarned. For a thousand years, Zeus kept Prometheus bound to his rock. For a thousand years, he tortured Prometheus for his secret—until, halfway through the second millennium, Zeus relinquished his anger and offered to free Prometheus in exchange for his secret. Prometheus' secret revealed that Thetis, a sea-nymph, whom Zeus was seriously courting, was destined "to bear a son greater than his father." Zeus heard the secret and broke off romantic relations with Thetis.

Instead, Zeus gave Thetis, in marriage, to Peleus, who had sailed with Jason on the ship Argo. (Prior to the Trojan War, around 1300 BCE, Argonauts had sailed with Jason on the Argo to Colchis to find the Golden Fleece—another story.)

All the Olympian gods were invited to Thetis' wedding—except **Eris**, goddess of strife. True to her job description, Eris went uninvited and, while there, threw a golden apple on the table as a wedding gift, engraved with the words, "For the fairest."

Hera, Mother goddess and wife of Zeus; Athena, goddess of wisdom and valor; and Aphrodite, goddess of passion and love, vied with each other for possession of the apple. To resolve the conflict, Zeus sent the three beauties to Paris, son of Priam. (Priam was king of Troy.)
Paris was the most beautiful of men. Eager to win the apple, the three goddesses bribed Paris—Hera, by promising she'd make Paris the greatest of rulers; Athena, that she'd make him the most powerful warrior; Aphrodite, that she'd give him the most beautiful woman in the world as his wife.

Guess whose bribe Paris chose? Aphrodite's of course. Aphrodite, goddess of fertility, love, and beauty, gave Helen to Paris. (Does this mean Aphrodite was the cause of the Trojan War?)

Without a doubt, the ancient Greeks were masters of human psychology.

In all the areas of the known world, from prehistoric findings to primitive sketches of today's preschool children, images of the circle, particularly of the snake swallowing its own tail, can be found. What is the significance of such a recurring motif? Erich Neumann writes:

The uroborus, the circular snake biting its tail, is the symbol of the psychic state of the beginning, of the original situation in which man's consciousness and ego were still small and undeveloped. A symbol of the origin and of the opposites contained in it, the uroborus is the "Great Round," in which positive and negative, male and female, elements of consciousness, elements hostile to consciousness, and unconscious elements are intermingled. In this sense, the uroborus is also a symbol of a state in which chaos, the unconscious, and the psyche as a whole were undifferentiated— and which is experienced by the ego as a borderline state.[13]

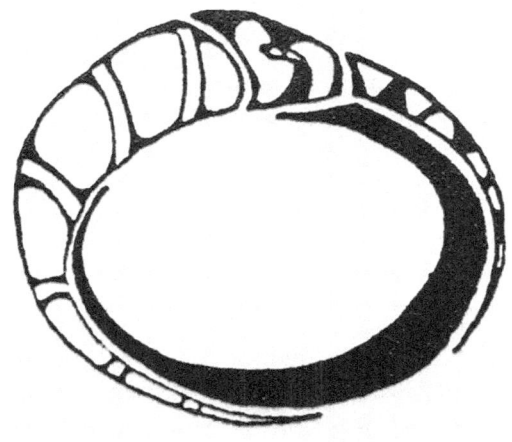

The Uroborus, the snake eating its tail (by Ilan Laks).

The earliest, preconscious state of the human being is symbolized for us by the historic image of the protective *uroborus*, the enclosed, womblike circle of the snake devouring its own tail—image of the eternal union of the male with the female. The *uroborus* is a state at rest. In it all oppositions coalesce. It is a state characteristic of the predawn of human history, and it is recreated with each nursing mother and child.

Despite its essential harmony of opposites, the *uroborus* is characteristically feminine in nature because it is the female state that is inert, elementary, and conservative. But with the growth of the human consciousness, the emerging individual experiences his or her earliest and most traumatic form of rejection, one that is brought about by the withdrawal of the lifeline: the milk and comfort of the mother.

With this sudden withdrawal of immediate comfort, all oppositions attack the consciousness. Hunger is experienced instead of food; want instead of comfort. More devastating than anything, loneliness is experienced where earlier the only sensation was that of containment and a centeredness characteristic of the "participation mystique." This state of loneliness and rejection is expressed, in myths and folktales, as exile, and as the lonely expanses of the desert. It is the essential precondition for consciousness and the human voyage toward maturation, both on an individual and on a societal level. I invite my reader to take a leap with me from where we stand now to accepting that the lonely expanse of the desert is where heroes and leaders, from Abraham, Moses, Jesus, and Mohammed, have realized their vision.

Throughout this study we will need to bear in mind that Western history was, until recently, a record of men and women—as perceived and portrayed by men—in a post-primitive, patriarchal world. Consequently, we have neither authentic women's emotions, nor any insights; no soul-searching of actual women from ancient times—and no account whatsoever of the spiritual awakenings of real ancient women warriors. All that we have of women's history are suppositions recorded by men. As Carol Gilligan writes in her book *In a Different Voice*, "It all goes back, of course, to Adam and Eve." "It" might be understood as meaning the problems caused by an all- male interpretation of human development. Gilligan says that, "if you make a woman out of a man, you are bound to get into trouble. In the life cycle, as in the Garden of Eden, the woman is the deviant."[14]

Erich Neumann claims, however, that the hero represents more than the individual male. "The hero," he says,

> *is the archetypal forerunner of mankind in general. His fate is the pattern in accordance with which the masses of humanity must live, and always have lived, however haltingly and distantly; and*

4

however short of the ideal man they have fallen, the stages of the hero myth have become constituent elements in the personal development of every individual.[15]

It is in the lonely regions of the desert that the emerging male first confronts his spirituality, a state that is the antitheses of the physical and the inert that have become so associated with the female. The female retains the characteristics of the Great Mother, container of all life. In such a way, she is depicted in early civilizations as the vessel, the dark interior of which is life- producing, nurturing—and threatening—by means of its mystery and its ability to hold, ensnare and destroy. The darkness inside the Mother Vessel is the night of the unconscious mind. Neumann makes the point that people still today talk of "inwardness" and of one's "inner," more reflective qualities. He maintains that this is because people have, from earliest times, projected themselves onto the "world vessel" by which they are encompassed.

Peering behind us down the dark hall of human existence, some believe that the earliest forms of human experience failed to distinguish between the masculine and the feminine, as all aspects of reality were subsumed at the predawn of human consciousness inside an obscurity akin to the preconscious state of the infant enveloped in the mother's womb. One of the earliest myths of ancient Egypt depicts the human being's first, tentative attempt at self- definition. It portrays the young hero "Shu" separating the sky from the earth. Ancient Egyptians regarded Nut—the sky—as feminine, perhaps because objective reality was still experienced as all-encompassing, because the human being still saw him or herself as an embryo held in a womb-like world.

On the other hand, an early Maori creation myth is one of many that identified the heavens as the masculine and the spiritual:

Tane-mahuta, the god and father of forests, of birds, and of insects, arose and struggled with his parents; in vain with hands and arms he strove to rend them apart. He paused; firmly he planted his head on his mother Papa, the earth, and his feet he raised up against his father Rangi, the sky; he strained his back and his limbs in a mighty effort. Now were rent apart Rangi and Papa, and with reproaches and groans of woe they cried aloud: "Wherefore do you thus slay your parents...? But Tane-mahuta ... regarded not their groans; far, far beneath him he pressed down Papa, the earth; far, far above him ... he thrust up Rangi, the sky ... so that they were rent apart, and darkness was made manifest, and light made manifest also.[16]

The "sleeping woman of Malta," Neolithic, 2nd millennium BCE (photograph by Eric Lessing/Art Resource, New York).

The separation of the world parents constitutes the birth of human consciousness and with it ensue the ambivalence and guilt of human experience:

> *In the view of cabala, original sin consisted essentially in this: that damage was done to the Deity. Concerning the nature of this damage there are various views. The most widely accepted is that the First Man, Adam Kadmon, made a division between King and Queen, and that he sundered the Shekhina from union with her spouse, and from the whole hierarchy of the Sephiroth.*[17]

In early consciousness (to be distinguished from the human being's preconscious state) earth is experienced as the all-encompassing Mother Nature. The human creature is tied to Mother Nature for life, for nurture and for sustenance. The sky, on the other hand, represents a "masculine" world of aspirations and of strife that is essential for the maturity and the self-differentiation of the individual. Spirituality as part of the masculine (sky) experience becomes recognizable in the maturing male adolescent, as in the early development of civilization, only after the essential wrench from the womb-like, nurturing, but ultimately stifling Earth Mother has been initiated.

It is believed that for several thousands of years the human being failed to make the connection between copulation and fertilization. Consequently, in many areas of the world, women were worshipped as the divine producers of life and, as such, as the sole force of immortality. Even after man's function in the process of reproduction was understood, the woman's ability to carry, bear and nurture human life accorded her a position of veneration among the community of men. We see from prehistoric art and totemic practice (even from art as late as some of the early representations of the Virgin Mary) that women were believed to have conceived by means of totemic (or divine) spirit. In fact, the original meaning of the word "virgin" did not refer to a chaste woman but to a woman who was emotionally independent of men, who, while perhaps physically fertilized by human sperm, was spiritually impregnated by a life-engendering force. In her book, The *Woman's Encyclopedia of Myths and Secrets*, Barbara G. Walker claims that

> *Mary's impregnation was similar to Persephone's. In her Virgin guise, Persephone sat in a holy cave and began to weave the great tapestry of the universe when Zeus appeared as a phallic serpent, to beget the savior Dionysus on her. Mary sat in the temple and began to spin a blood-red thread, representing Life in the tapestry of fate, when the angel Gabriel "came in unto her" (Luke 1;28) ... Gabriel's name means literally "divine husband."*[18]

Prehistoric notions of earth as the source of life and death were closely related to the human experience of vegetable life and its succession of seasons. Prehistoric art and ritual suggest that people at the dawn of human history saw a connection between the fecundating powers of blood in the woman's menstrual cycle and in pregnancy, and the need for the fertilization of nature. According to this theory, it seems that early mother goddesses needed human blood to fertilize the earth in order to ensure the rebirth of nature each spring. Primitive art testifies to early rituals in which the mother goddess sacrificed her physical partner after having become impregnated by him. The same art also demonstrates a symbolic connection between the mother goddess and the bee (the queen bee also kills the male after coitus). Archeological findings indicate the existence of prehistoric annual kings who were slaughtered each winter and whose bodies were torn asunder and scattered over the dry earth, whose blood was poured into the earth to ensure the renewal of life in the spring. Early tombs with funnels inside them for the conveyance of libations to the bodies of the dead have been found. Possibly, these libations had a dual purpose. They functioned as blood and food—both essential for the rebirth of nature.

The infant is inseparable from the body of his or her mother, dependent on her for his or her life's blood (milk).

With maturity, it becomes essential for the child to make a psychological and physical break with the mother. So it was, that in the dawn of human consciousness, the human creature was at one with, attached and dependent on the great mother, Mother Earth. Early Egyptian findings quite clearly depict the young god as part of the mother goddess. She is his throne. He sits and rules on her. He is killed by her and becomes incorporated into her. He is physically and psychologically part of her. Osiris is murdered and buried in the trunk of a tree (causing Neumann to recognize the tree and the coffin as integral symbols of life, death, and resurrection) and is ultimately liberated from there by his sister-lover. Death and resurrection as enacted by the gods are the theme of nature itself.

Conversely, as we have already seen, early art and philosophy portray spirituality as the "father." What, we might ask, does the father represent? Father qua father represents the longed-for emancipation from the female, and as nothing short of the complete self-realization of the (male) human being.

In his analysis of human consciousness, Neumann makes a distinction between the personal and the "supra-personal" parents of the hero.

> *The fact that the hero has two fathers and two mothers is a central feature in the canon of the hero myth. Besides his personal father there is a "higher," that is to say and archetypal, father figure, and similarly, an archetypal mother figure appears beside the personal mother. This double descent, with its contrasted personal and supra personal parental figures, constellates the drama of the hero's life.[12]*

(Again, when referring to the maturation of the individual, or to the development of the hero as archetype, the scholar addresses him or herself only to the male child.) A boy's personal father represents tradition, reactionism, and authority. The hero is the adolescent who pits himself against the old values as represented by the personal father, inspired by the ideals, the liberal, visionary message of the forward-looking spirit, represented by the Supra or Transpersonal Father. In such a way, the successful hero undergoes two vital struggles before he embarks on his heroic journey to full manhood—the first against his earthbound, all-consuming, deadly, Terrible Mother; the second against the reactionary, tradition-oriented Personal Father. In the myth of Orestes from Aeschylus onward, the hero, moved by the spirit of his dead, supra-personal father, struggles first to destroy the murderous Clytemnestra, and then Aegishthus, the materialistic and oppressive imposter king.

In freeing himself from the Terrible Mother, the hero enfranchises himself from the earthbound and the regressive in his own personality. Only when the hero recognizes himself as a separate entity from the world around him is he able to dispel the threat of the feminine and the nurturing to his personal wellbeing. Consequently, it is at this stage in ancient myths that images of the friendly, sister-lover emerge. Electra is such a figure. She is the sister-lover of the young hero and represents corporal reality. Athena is also such a figure; she is a benign goddess and, as such, represents the realm of the spirit.

To my mind, the original myth of Electra was just such an expression of early man's struggle toward spiritual growth and independence, and the subsequent plays that built upon the myth have become re-examinations of that struggle in its different forms.

This might explain the prevalence of incest in many theatrical versions of the Electra myth. Because several of the plays depict the hero as one who is torn between the dualities in his own nature and the neurotically close family ties in which it is not always clear where one family member ends and the other begins. These plays dramatize Orestes, under various names, as a complex being and as an integral part of an all-too close social structure. When Aristotle maintained that the most tragic situations are those that involve close family members, he was describing blood knots that draw upon the deepest wells of the human unconscious.

The *Oresteia* might simply be Aeschylus' record of 15th century BCE Greek history when invaders from northern Europe had conquered the then primitive indigenous Greek tribes, constructed fortified cities, and imposed some system of law and order. It was these conquerors who had first established homesteads, i.e., lasting constructions capable of housing families over several generations.

Greek mythology or, to be more specific, the birth of Western Civilization as recorded by the Greeks, is an excruciating story of human violence, suffering, and recrimination; where humans turn to the gods as their only guide; the gods play ruthlessly, if not mindlessly, with human lives; and fate seems to be the sole determinant of their wellbeing. It is born, with the establishment of the gods, out of chaos into the darkest of times; then inches its way painfully from Prometheus' gift of fire to mankind, to fifth century BCE Greece— western civilization's birthplace and the age of Aeschylus (Sophocles and Euripides), of light, reason, and the stunning game-changing initiation of democratic rule.

Brief Background to the Oresteia

The direct line of the House of Atreus:

Atreus and Thyestes, brothers, vied with each other for accession to the throne.

Thyestes seduced Atreus' wife.

In revenge, Atreus murdered Thyestes' two young sons, invited Thyestes to a grand banquet, and served him the severed limbs of his sons as dinner.

Devastated, Thyestes went into exile taking his third and youngest son, Aegisthus, with him.

Eventually, Thyestes died in exile.

Aegisthus returned to Argos, became Clytemnestra's lover, and planned to avenge the wrongs done to his father.

Agamemnon, Atreus' eldest son, inherited the throne—and the curse—of Argos.

Menelaus, Agamemnon's brother, inherited the throne of Sparta from his father-in-law, Tyndareus.

(Zeus, in the form of a swan, had seduced Leda, Tyndareus' wife—another story.)

Leda and Zeus' union produced twin girls: Helen and Clytemnestra. Helen married Menelaus, while Clytemnestra married Agamemnon.

Helen was the most beautiful woman known to man, so exquisite that the leaders of Greece swore they'd unite and come to Menelaus' aid in the event she was ever stolen.

The Trojan War was the result of such an event.

King Priam of Troy sent his son, Paris, to Sparta. It was there that Paris met Clytemnestra' sister, Helen.

Menelaus, King of Sparta, was occupied elsewhere the day Paris arrived in Sparta (it is believed that Menelaus was not the smartest of men) which meant that Helen, the most beautiful of women and Paris, the most handsome of men, were un-chaperoned.

Whether it was to honor the oath they'd sworn, or because of an already existing rivalry between Greece and Troy, the Greek rulers responded almost unanimously to Menelaus' appeal for military help.

Agamemnon was appointed Commander in Chief of "a thousand Argive ships," but when all were ready, the winds failed them. Days turned into weeks, then months, and no wind. The men lost their lust for war, began to miss their families, wanted to return to their homes.

Calchas, the priest, claimed that Artemis, virgin goddess, needed to be appeased, that the winds would never pick up until Agamemnon sacrificed his youngest, virgin daughter, Iphigenia. So, under the ruse that he intended to marry Iphigenia to Achilles, Agamemnon ordered Clytemnestra to send Iphigenia to him. Iphigenia went to be married. Once there, she was brutally murdered, offered as sacrifice to Artemis.

The sacrifice worked. The winds picked up, and the men sailed off to war.

It took the combined Greek armies 10 years—plus the Trojan horse—to defeat Troy.

Paris died in the ninth year.

All adult males were killed, women and children were taken into slavery, Troy was burnt to the ground—enough to turn all of us into pacifists.

Most of the plays in which Clytemnestra features portray her as a strong and willful woman—or, to put it their way, as "a woman with the will of a man." In his absence, Clytemnestra did not remain loyal to Agamemnon. She governed Argos for the ten years of the Trojan War—her lover, Aegisthus by her side. For ten years she mourned and raged over the murder of her daughter, Iphigenia, and planned her revenge.

Classical Greece

The heyday of Classical Greece did not materialize until 490 BCE, some 800 years after the story of Troy. It was catapulted in, after years of warfare, by the Greek conquest of Persia at the Battle of Marathon. Though Sophocles was younger than Aeschylus and Euripides younger still, all three playwrights lived during the Golden Age that followed the conquest at Marathon. Aeschylus was born in 525 BCE to a noble family near Athens. He fought in the Persian wars. He struggled against civil unrest, infighting and tyranny at home, and he lived to be a nobleman in his own right. He also served, as did all his compatriots, in this war that catapulted Greece into greatness. He served as governor for his city-state, and he witnessed Greece's perhaps greatest gift to the western world—its leap out of an age of darkness, dependence on Fate, lore, superstition and tyranny, to its game-changing instigation of judge, jury, and democratic rule.

Indeed, as we shall see when we consider the *Libation Bearers*, third in this trilogy of Aeschylus, our playwright might well be manipulating the festival of Dionysus—sacred for its bacchanal, its release and celebration of the senses, of alcohol and orgiastic pleasures—to stage issues of common cause to all Greek patriots. Issues of human destiny: Is history determined by the gods, or is it manmade? Are humans capable of independent government? Of civil duties and democracy? Can we elect our own moral codes, or is it sacrilege to even entertain those thoughts? Here, history, religion, myth, and—for the first time—issues of government are set center stage, examined, questioned and, in many cases, found lacking. This is the age of Protagoras where "Man is the measure of all things." What weight, if any, have fate, the gods, religion, myth and superstition, on issues of morality, reason, security and government? How possible would it be to remove myth and superstition from government? From society?

In our first chapters, we shall question whether Aeschylus, in setting his plays on Athens' Bacchanal stage, was bringing into physical form our own central theme: The imposition of masculine, Athenian Reason over terrifying Passions and uncontrollable emotions associated, by Greek males of that period, with the female.

We will question the source of such emotions and question their manifestation in physical form.

Aeschylus: Agamemnon, King of Argos

I will expound more about the *Oresteia* than any other play in this collection because I regard it as the foundation of our two themes: chaos versus law and order, and male versus female. Understanding this trilogy, when reading other plays in this collection, we will know what to look for.

As was customary with the first play of each trilogy, Agamemnon has opened onto the very real darkness of pre-dawn. Apart from a few torches lit around the periphery of the stage, the watchman and the spectators are literally peering through the darkness.

The prominence of gods and their altars on stage make us immediately aware of the all-pervasive hold gods have over the world of this play.

> Dear gods, set me free from all the pain,
> the long watch I keep, one whole year awake...
> propped on my arms, crouched on the roofs of Atreus like a dog.
> ...
> and now I watch for the light, the signal-fire
> breaking out of Troy, shouting Troy is taken.
> So she commands, full of her high hopes.
> That woman—she maneuvers like a man.
> And when I keep to my bed, soaked in dew, ...
> and the good dreams that used to guard my sleep...
> not here, it's the old comrade, terror, at my neck.
> I mustn't sleep, no—
> ...
> I cry for the hard times come to the house,
> no longer run like the great place of old.
> ...
> Just bring him home. My king,
> I'll take your loving hand in mine and then...
> the rest is silence. The ox is on my tongue. aye,
> but the house and these old stones,
> give them a voice and what a tale they'd tell. ...
> I speak to those who know;
> to those who don't my mind's a blank.
> I never say a word
> [*The Oresteia* (New York: Penguin, 1977), p. 39].

Already, we are in a state of high drama. *Agamemnon* has opened on the roof of the royal house of Atreus. For a year, the watchman has kept his eyes glued to the night sky. For a year he has prayed for a flare on the mountaintop announcing Argos' victory over Troy and the return of his beloved king,

But to what terrors at home is the watchman referring? What evil has befallen this place since the king and all able-bodied men left for war? Why the secrecy? What is the source of his nightmares? Why his resentment against Clytemnestra? In which way does she maneuver like a man? Why is it bad for her to move like a man?

Suddenly, as the "light (of the actual Athenian sun) appears in the east," our watchman sees the much-anticipated flare on the mountain." He runs off stage to inform the queen. Already this play has taken us from the physical and symbolic darkness of an accursed house, to the light of dawn and hope.

Now, the chorus of men too old to have served in the war ("We are the old, dishonored ones / the broken husks of men") congregate. They remind the spectators of the bitter history of Argos, and the cause of the Trojan War.

CHORUS
two kings with the power of Zeus,
the twin throne, twin scepter,
Atreus' sturdy yoke of sons
Launched Greece in a thousand ships,
armadas cutting loose from the land,
Armies massed for the cause, the rescue—

…
the heart within them screaming for all-out war!
Like vultures robbed of their young

…
soaring high from the nest, round and round they wheel,
they row their wings, stroke upon churning
thrashing stroke, …

…
all for a woman manned by many
the generations wrestle, knees
grinding the dust, the manhood drains,
the spear snaps in the first blood rites
that marry Greece and Troy.
And now it goes as it goes
and where it ends is Fate.
And neither by singeing flesh
nor tipping cups of wine
nor shedding burning tears can you
enchant away the rigid Fury

As the chorus chant, Clytemnestra lights the altar fires and performs her rituals. They beg her to share her news. She is busy. She ignores them.

They tell of the great tragedy that befell Clytemnestra: the sacrifice of her daughter, Iphigenia, to the winds of war. Calchas cried,

'My captains, Artemis must have blood!' ...
and I still can hear the older warlord saying,
'Obey, obey, or a heavy doom will crush me!—
Oh but doom will crush me once I rend my child,
the glory of my house—
a father's hands are stained,
blood of a young girl streaks the altar.
Pain both ways and what is worse?
Desert the fleets, fail the alliance?
No, but stop the winds with a virgin's blood, feed their lust, their
fury?—feed their fury!—
Law is law! [Oresteia, p. 110].

Here we have it: The bedrock of theater: Tragedy in its fullest form. Human beings ripped apart by inconsolable ideologies.

And once he slipped his neck in the strap of Fate,
his spirit veering black, impure, unholy,
once he turned he stopped at nothing,
seized with the frenzy
blinding, driving to outrage—
wretched frenzy, cause of all our grief!
Yes, he had the heart
to sacrifice his daughter [Oresteia, p. 110].

The chorus chant their paean of sorrow over the history of the house of Atreus; chant of the kings; of

One will that hurled young Greece
And winged the spear of vengeance straight for Troy!

We latter-day readers learn about the Classical Greek worldview and its relevance to the world of the Oresteia through the concerns of the chorus and those of the herald who arrives from Troy to announce Aegisthus' return. The chorus leader bewails the inescapable nature of human misery; the part that the gods and fate play in human suffering; and the relentless, recurring cycle of human violence and revenge that has beset the House of Atreus. The leader of the chorus accepts that, in this world, only the gods escape misery and that it is for humans to suffer. Wisdom, he believes, is earned by means of suffering.

What comes next? I cannot see it, cannot say.
...
But Justice turns the balance scales,
... sees that we suffer
and we suffer and we learn.
And we will know the future when it comes.
Greet it too early, weep too soon [Oresteia, p. 111].

Finally, Clytemnestra completes her sacrifice and her prayers, and informs the chorus of the wonderful news: Troy has been vanquished.

I am relying on my readers to follow every word of the text. Aeschylus' writing is exciting, poignant, passionate, and exquisitely crafted; while Robert Fagles' translation is of rare beauty. Still, let us share a moment here as Clytemnestra's imagines the end of the Trojan war.

They are kneeling by the bodies of their dead,
embracing men and brothers, infants over the aged
loins that gave them life, and sobbing, as the yoke
constricts their last free breath,
for every dear one lost.
      And the others,
there, plunging breakneck through the night—
the labor of battle sets them down, ravenous,
to breakfast on the last remains of Troy.
Not by rank but chance, by the lots they draw,
they lodge in the houses captured by the spear,
settling in so soon, released from the open sky,
the frost and dew. Lucky men off guard at last,
they sleep away their first good night in years. ...
...

...
      And even if the men come home with no offense
to the gods, the avenging dead will never rest—
Oh! Let no new disaster strike! [Oresteia, p. 116].

Note how vividly, how sensitively Clytemnestra imagines these scenes of victory and loss; how astoundingly modern and anti-war they are. Clytemnestra's words might as easily be the reflections of yesterday's mother in Vietnam, or today's in Iraq, Afghanistan or

Syria. Do we today envisage the aftermath of war with such clarity, such compassion?

We have not forgotten that Clytemnestra paid the first and ultimate price for this Trojan War. Has the barbaric sacrifice, the murder of her own daughter, Iphigenia, sensitized her to reality—to the suffering that belies war's much publicized glory—in a way she might not otherwise have understood?

It is obvious that the chorus approves of what she says. This is their response:

> Spoken like a man, my lady, loyal,
> Full of self-command.

Now let's listen to a short section of the chorus' reflections:

> but now in place of men
> ashes and urns come back to every hearth.
> War, War, the great gold-broker of corpses
> holds the balance of the battle on his spear!
> Home from the pyres he sends them,
> home from Troy to the loved ones,
> heavy with tears, the urns brimmed full,
> the heroes return in gold-dust,
> dear, light ash for men; and they weep,
> they praise them, 'He had skill in the swordplay,
> 'He went down so tall in the onslaught,'
> 'All for another's woman.' So they mutter
> in secret and the rancor steals
> toward our staunch defenders,
> Atreus' sons [Oresteia, p. 119].
> ...
>
> ...
> The people's voice is heavy with hatred,
> Now the curses of the people must be paid

How authentic, how cynical are these reflections? How non-partisan? Nothing, it might seem to us modernists, has changed since ancient times. War was as absurd then as it is now, yet still we fight, country against country, repeating over and over an endless, meaningless cycle of misery, cruelty, and reprisal.

A moment of silence now indicates the passing of time to the spectator, after which the herald enters and kneels. He is the first to have returned, grateful, from the war, He gives thanks to the gods, and informs us that Agamemnon is alive and on his way home "He comes, he brings us light in the darkness / ... Agamemnon lord of men."

Now let us listen to our first actual, first-hand account of the war—the Herald's own:

A long, hard pull we had, if I would tell it all.
The iron rations, penned in the gangways
hock by jowl like sheep. Whatever miseries
break a man, our quota, every sun-starved day.
Then on the beaches it was worse. Dug in
under the enemy ramparts—deadly going.
Out of the sky, out of the marshy flats
the dews soaked us, turned the ruts we fought from
into gullies, made our gear, our scalps crawl with lice.
    And talk of the cold,
the sleet to freeze the gulls, and the big snows
come avalanching down from Ida. Oh but the heat,
the sea and the windless noons, the swells asleep,
dropped to a dead calm...
But why weep now?
It's over for us, over for them.
The dead can rest and never rise again;
no need to call their muster. We're alive,
do we have to go on raking up old wounds?
Good-bye to all that. Glad I am to say it.

Are we not struck by how vastly different in tone this post-war speech is from the self-righteous rallying cries that had sent Greek men off to war?

At this point, our attention shifts to the home front.

It is from the chorus and the characters that we glean whatever understanding we can of the Classical Greek world-view and its relevance to our play. We learn, for example, that humans are expected to walk humbly with their gods; yet the single, irrefutably God-given commandment in this text is that a murderer be murdered in return—itself a recipe for further violence, for a never-ending chain of retributions and bloodshed.

The chorus and the Herald recall the history of the House of Atreus—their dark tale, familiar to most Aeschylus' spectators, which began with Atreus' heinous murder of his nephews (Thyestes' twin boys), and grew even more egregious when he served them, as food, to Thyestes.

They tell us how Atreus later became the father of Agamemnon, while Thyestes went into exile taking his last and only remaining son, Aegisthus with him.

By this stage, it might have become clear to the spectator that, beyond the characters and story of this myth, the theme of the play they have gathered to watch is that of the regeneration of murder and revenge—a seemingly never- ending cycle of tragedy, violence, and human suffering.

Finally, Agamemnon arrives, victorious from Troy laden with spoils, his most prized trophy being Cassandra, seer and daughter of Priam—the now murdered king of Troy.

Clytemnestra welcomes Aegisthus home.

> Now for the best way to welcome home
> My lord, my good lord...
>   No time to lose!
> What dawn can feast a woman's eyes like this?
> I can see the light, the husband plucked from war
> by the Saving God and open wide the gates.
> Tell him that, and have him come with speed,
> The people's darling—how they long for him. And for his wife,
> May he return and find her true at hall,
> ......
> I have not changed [Oresteia, pp. 125–6].

Are Clytemnestra's words genuine? Is her joy authentic?

I will leave my readers to listen without me to the Chorus and the Herald, as the chorus hints further that something is painfully rotten in his home state; and I will pick up here with the victorious return of Agamemnon.

Agamemnon is greeted by the chorus:

> Come, my king, the scourge of Troy,
> the true son of Atreus—
> ...
> ...
> ...That day you marshaled the armies
> All for Helen—no hiding it now—
> I drew you in my mind in black;
> You seemed a menace at the helm,

> Sending men to the grave
> To bring her home, that hell on earth.
> But now from the depths of trust and love
> I say Well fought, well won—
> The end is worth the labor!

It seems to me that war, for men, is what giving birth is for women. While in labor, women's pains are so excruciating—all swear we will never have a second child. Yet, we become so engulfed in joy, so euphoric the moment our baby is born, that any memory, every last vestige of pain is erased from our brains. Consequently, women have umpteen babies, and civilization, such as it is, has wars.

Yet listen to Agamemnon's first words:

> First,
> With justice I salute my Argos and my gods,
> My accomplices who brought me home and won
> My rights from Priam's Troy—the just gods.
> ... Once for all
> they consigned their lots to the urn of blood,
> they pitched on death for men, annihilation
> for the city. Hope's hand hovering
> over the urn of mercy, left it empty.
> Look for the smoke—it is the city's seamark,
> building even now.
> The storms of ruin live!
> Her last dying breath rising up from the ashes
> Sends us gales of incense rich in gold.
> For that we must thank the gods.

Agamemnon is all too conscious of the violence, the cruelty he has inflicted on the soldiers and citizens of Troy. He might well be weeping for his victims while uttering these words; yet the hold we humans have over our fate is tenuous. Our destinies lie in the hands of the gods, and Agamemnon cannot but celebrate the gods for delivering him from death's jaw.

> For their mad outrage
> Of a queen we raped their city—we were right.
> The beast of Argos, foals of the wild mare,
> Thousands massed in armor rose on the night
> The Pleiades went down, and crashing through
> Their walls our bloody lion lapped its fill,
> Gorging on the blood of kings.
> ....Our thanks to the gods.

21

Is this what Shakespeare meant, some twenty-one hundred years later? Was Hamlet referring to this when he sarcastically lauded armies for waging war over eggshells?

Let us bear in mind: tragedies were not presented merely for entertainment; they were also the playwright's opportunity to stage issues of vital social importance.

Is it innate to the human condition—now, as then—that we act, and allow others to act with brutality? Does being human mean that we follow brutality with thanks to the gods? Has our twenty-first century not progressed at all with regards to brutality and the nature of the gods?

The Greeks of 5th century Greece were nothing if not thoughtful. There are no complete villains, no pure saints on this stage, because no one is void of compunction. Humans are complex beings. Tragedy is the revelation on stage of brutality and remorse, evil and compunction, warfare and our reckoning with the gods, contradictory impulses, opposing ideologies—and the havoc they cause.

It might behoove us to take a second look, here, at Joseph Campbell's query, quoted at the introduction to this work:

And why should it be that whenever men (and women) have looked for something solid on which to found their lives, they have chosen not the facts in which the world abounds, but the myths of an immemorial imagination— preferring even to make life a hell for themselves and their neighbors, in the name of some violent god, to accepting the bounty the world affords?"

As for domestic unrest: Agamemnon, warrior, hero and statesman, returns home and calls for a national tribunal. Reverence to the gods, law, and order—if necessary of the harshest kind—should restore Atreus to its former glory.

AGAMEMNON
We must summon the city for a trial,
found a national tribunal. Whatever's healthy,
shore it up with law and help it flourish.
Wherever something calls for drastic cures
We make our noblest effort: amputate or wield
the healing iron, burn the cancer at the roots
[Oresteia, p. 134].

I have chosen Robert Fagles' translation of the Oresteia because of the beauty of his language, and because of how close he brings the plays to our own, contemporary sensitivities. Humanity has not changed. Nevertheless, I suggest that my readers study several other translations before settling on Fagles'. The Greek language lends itself to a choice of meanings. Different editions often seem like entirely different plays.

We might find it odd that Clytemnestra addresses the chorus before approaching Agamemnon. Perhaps she is nervous? Perhaps she needs to watch him for a while to test his mood? Despite—or perhaps because of—the resentment against her that we have already witnessed on the part of the Chorus, she addresses them in the most human of terms:

CLYTEMNESTRA
Old nobility of Argos
… I love the man (Agamemnon). I am older,
… I am human.
… when a
woman sits at home and the man is gone,
the loneliness is terrible,

…
and the rumors spread and fester

Yet, when Clytemnestra turns to Agamemnon, it is with an agenda:
And so,
Our child is gone, not standing by our side,
The bond of our dearest pledges, mine and yours;
By all rights our child should be here…
Orestes.
…
…
what if the people
rise up howling for the king, and anarchy
should dash our plans?
… Our child is gone. That is my self-defense
And it is true.

Before long, she changes her tone. She wants him to stride with royal (or, as we learn from Agamemnon's response, blasphemous, god-like) pride, the arrogance of the conqueror, along the scarlet carpets her women are laying down for him:

> Come to me now, my dearest,
> Down from the car of war, but never set the foot
> that stamped out Troy on earth again, my great one.
> Women, why delay? You have your orders.
> Pave his way with (crimson) tapestries.

Fawning, and coaxing, she approaches her husband. Agamemnon sees through her. He asks: "what am I, some barbarian peacocking out of Asia? Never cross my path with robes and draw the lightning. Never—only the gods deserve the pomp of honor/and the stiff brocades of fame. To walk on them ... it makes my pulses stir/with dread" *(Oresteia, p. 137)*.

Clytemnestra perseveres. Still playing on his ego, she persuades Agamemnon to disregard his qualms regarding modest behavior vis-à-vis the gods—to disregard the very real jealousy of the gods—and to walk like a conqueror, god-like into the palace over the scarlet carpets she has laid out for him.

"The old men" of the chorus, we are told, "huddle in terror."

Clytemnestra emerges from the palace a second time, first to persuade, then to order Cassandra out of the carriage reserved for Agamemnon's spoils and into the royal house.

Cassandra won't budge.

Clytemnestra gives up on Cassandra and returns to the house. She has a task to perform.

Here, Cassandra, the seer, has her frenzied vision, her oracle of what fate has in store for Agamemnon; indeed, of the murder that is being committed that very moment off stage, inside the House of Atreus.

In a frenzy, Cassandra rambles on, telling us her story, fighting against her fate. Finally, with full knowledge of what awaits her, Cassandra strips herself of her royal cloak and walks toward the palace. Again, she pauses. Recoils. She smells death—her own and Agamemnon's. Then she opens the doors and exits into the palace.

We hear Agamemnon's death cries—once, twice. The leader of the chorus pulls open the palace doors to reveal Agamemnon dead in his silver bath, covered by the still warm body of the now murdered Cassandra.

We will examine Clytemnestra's victory speech later; enough here to notice the cunning, the determination, and the tenacity with which this queen has avenged Iphigenia, her murdered daughter.

Clytemnestra exults that she has played her part in the curse of the house of Atreus. She regards herself as a necessary instrument in this cycle of murder and revenge, of male killings carried out in the name of the gods. In short, she believes that, with the necessary murder of her husband, she has brought about an end to her own suffering, and to that of the royal house.

We have already noted how in the Greek world of this period, he who murders, must, in turn, be killed.

The chorus is male, condemning of Clytemnestra and loyal to Agamemnon.

CHORUS
the people cast you off to exile,
broken with our hate.

CLYTEMNESTRA
And now you sentence me?
You banish me from the city, curses breathing
down my neck? But he—
Name one charge you brought against him then.
…
…
but he sacrificed his own child, our daughter,
the agony I labored into love
to charm away the savage winds of Thrace.
Didn't the law demand you banish him?—
hunt him from the land for all his guilt?
But now you witness what
I've done and you are ruthless judges.
…

By the child's Rights I brought to birth,
by Ruin, by Fury—the three gods to whom
I sacrificed this and—I swear my hopes
will never walk the halls of fear so long
as Aegisthus lights the fire on my hearth,
Loyal to me as always, no small shield
to buttress my defiance.

Is it possible that, despite her rage, all Clytemnestra wanted was a normal life with her daughter and a man who was loyal to her? Now, only now, after Clytemnestra has carried out her heinous deed, Aegistheus her lover, emerges. He too is exultant. He struts about the stage, boasting that it was he who'd schemed Agamemnon's murder; and that, in so doing, he has avenged the wrongs perpetrated against his father. He too mentions the Furies.

Now at last I see this man brought down
In the Furies' tangling robes. It feasts my eyes—
He pays for the plot his father's hand contrived.

Twice now, we have heard talk of the Furies. Take note, for these furies will yet rise from the dead to haunt us.

The chorus mocks Aegisthus. It was Clytemnestra who'd manifested the "masculine" gall necessary to carry out their act of revenge. Aegisthus had remained home, protected by a woman— in a woman's palace—rather than fight the Trojan War with his countrymen. He was absent even when the acts of revenge took place. In short, Aegisthus, according to the male world of this play, is all words, timid, worthless.

Here, at the final moment of the play, there is a twist. The chorus defies Aegisthus. Aegisthus threatens them. Though Aegisthus himself is not brave enough to act, he sets his thugs on the old men of the chorus. The thugs draw swords; the old men of the chorus defend themselves with sticks.

CLYTEMNESTRA
No more, my dearest,
No more grief. We have too much to reap
...
... No bloodshed now.

Aegisthus acquiesces to Clytemnestra's appeal; yet still he squabbles with the old men. He is the ruler. He has servants and power. He snarls at the chorus that he can crush them and anyone else who defies him. In short, we now see what had weighed so heavily on the chorus earlier in the play: Aegisthus, is no king. He is the most dreaded and despised of rulers: a tyrant.

Aeschylus: The Libation Bearers (458 BCE)

Aeschylus' Clytemnestra bears an uncanny similarity to the many prehistoric mother goddesses who sacrificed their partners to their magical powers of fertility and destruction and were virgin-like in their independence of their mates. Aeschylus could be deliberately manipulating his audience's memories of such rites as a way of drawing them under the spell of his theater. Let us keep *Agamemnon* in mind, as we move into *The Libation Bearers*. As the first play of the Oresteia, *Agamemnon* would have played immediately prior to *The Libation Bearers*: What did Clytemnestra say there, when she appeared to the spectators drenched in her husband's blood after she had murdered him?

CLYTEMNESTRA
So, he goes down, and the life is bursting out of him—
Great sprays of blood, and the murderous shower
Wounds me, dyes me black and I, I revel
Like the Earth when the spring rains come down,
The blessed gifts of god, and the new green spear
Splits the sheath and rips to birth in glory! [20]

Aeschylus' Agamemnon is reminiscent of ancient fertilizing god-kings who were sacrificed and buried in order to ensure the rebirth of nature. In addition, Orestes' actions, in *The Libation Bearers*, are those of the universal youth determined to rid himself of the dragon of maternal oppression and in so doing to liberate Electra, the life force imprisoned in his psyche.

Aeschylus provides an easy way out for such adolescent rebellion. In this trilogy, which deals with oppositions intrinsic to human experience—the male, the female, the spiritual and the physical conspire to bring about both psychological harmony and political balance. Was Aeschylus deliberately manipulating the hedonistic ceremony of the Dionysian festival to his own ends? Is this a confrontation of old ideologies with the new? If so, for what purpose? Perhaps to best convey his lesson of social chaos versus political order, unrestrained emotions versus restraint.

According to custom, trilogies were presented sequentially, over the span of an entire day—the three plays completing the Playwright's story. The first play began in the earliest hours of pre-dawn, the second at noon, and the third before dusk. We will notice, for example, ceremonial parades together with the use of flares and lit torches at the end of the third play, which would have coincided perfectly with nightfall.

It is noon. For the thrill of theater—in this instance, the thrill of *The Libation Bearers*—central play of Aeschylus' trilogy—spectators of fifth century Greece, BCE, have congregated around a circular space of pounded earth. Here, at the focal point of our concentration, is the burial mound of the murdered king, Agamemnon. All attention is focused on this spot. With ceremonial movement and chanting, Electra and the chorus of slave women draw toward the burial mound; their function? To fertilize Agamemnon's grave with libations of wine (blood) and tears.

ELECTRA
And I will tip libations to the dead.
I call out to my father. Pity me,
Dear Orestes too.
Rekindle the light that saves our house!
Bring up your blessings,
Up into the air [183].

Electra and the women pour libations (and tears) into the earth:

ELECTRA
Father,
You have it now, the earth has drunk your wine [184].

And in a magnificently economical piece of drama, Electra walks in the footsteps of her brother (which are identical to her own) until she is suddenly confronted by the appearance—almost the apparition—of Orestes himself. In the span of just a few stanzas, Electra has poured the libation, sewn the seed and conjured up "a mighty tree" (187), new life from the old. Orestes is the resurrected Agamemnon. According to Jan Kott, he is also the actualized

Electra, for Kott claims that the pre-hero state of Orestes has been dramatically represented here, on stage, as a female. [21] The mature hero, the fully realized hero, is conjured up by Electra and emerges before us fully armed in masculine form. In theatrical terms, Orestes is represented as the self-differentiated Electra. Here, the Greek is the male that has emerged from the chrysalis of the female— his sister.

The entire first part of this play is the goading into action of Electra and Orestes by the chorus. In Macbethian fashion the chorus chants:

CHORUS
"Word for word, curse for curse
Be born now," Justice thunders,
hungry for retribution,
"stroke for bloody stroke be paid.
The one who acts must suffer."
Three generations strong the word resounds [192].

First the chorus goads Electra into calling on the gods for vengeance, then it rouses both Electra and Orestes into a veritable religious ecstasy for vengeance and murder, a holy war:

CHORUS
Now our comrades group underground.
Our masters' wreaking hands are doomed [194].

This vengeance is the justice of the ancient Near East, an eye for an eye. It is the justice of old warlords, founders and destroyers of the house of Atreus. The chorus sings, "What can redeem the blood that wets the soil? (179). At the gravesite, Electra cries out to the spirit of her father:

CHORUS
Your grave receives a girl in prayer
and a man in flight, and we are one,
and the pain is equal, whose is worse?
and who outwrestles death? [193].

For us, this image might evoke the biblical one of Jacob wrestling with the angel (Genesis), for Electra and Orestes are mythically one,

Electra perhaps is the birth of the hero, while Orestes is the "mighty tree," image of resurrection and full manhood. The chorus hails the coming of Orestes with the words:

CHORUS
Look, the light is breaking!
The huge chain that curbed the halls gives way.
Rise up, proud house, long, too long
Your walls lay fallen, strewn along the earth [220].

The central action of *The Libation Bearers* lends credence to William Ridgeway's theory. Greek tragedy, he claimed, emerged initially from pre– Dionysian mimetic dances enacted in order to evoke the protective spirits of dead heroes on the living. [22] Regardless of whether or not we accept this idea, we do believe that tragedies emerged out of earliest religious ceremonies. The burial mound, the ritual pouring of libations and the evocation of the spirit of the dead Agamemnon constitute the core and mainstay of *The Libation Bearers*.

It is essential for the religious, if not the hypnotic appeal of this drama, that the burial mound of the dead king be center stage. For the purpose of this ritual, this spot represents the center of the earth, the mound on which the archetypal hero (Adam, Jesus, Mohammed) is born. At center stage, it represents the hero's voyage to the source of insight, and the actor's journey to his source of imagination.

In Myth of the Eternal Return, Mircea Eliade claims that to the archaic mind every significant human action was a repetition of a divine act. Moreover, it was a repetition of the act of original creation. Eliade claims that in historic times deeds gained mythical significance by virtue of their repetition:
an object or an act becomes real only insofar as it imitates or repeats an archetype. Thus, reality is acquired solely through repetition or participation; everything which lacks an exemplary model is "meaningless," i.e., it lacks reality. [23]

It seems significant that, for the plays in which Aeschylus moves toward law and order, he chooses actions that imitate those of early Greek creation myths: the violent overthrow of the old masculine order for the instigation of the new. The first recording of the Orestes story is found in Homer's, Odyssey, which tells only of the virtuous, vengeful murder of Aegisthus by Orestes for the purpose of his drama.[24] But Aeschylus' trilogy is no longer merely the record of patriarchal takeover, of the son surpassing or defending the father figure—supreme male—in order to gain manhood; rather it is the story of matricide, of the overthrow of the mother goddess. It is possible that Aeschylus is referring to another source for his theater—alluding to the 15th century BCE. For it was then that warriors from Northern Europe conquered the earlier, indigenous Greek tribes. These northern invaders were the first to erect towers and fortified buildings, It was they who instigated a system of rule, law and order—however primitive, and it was they who became fathers of dynasties—dynasties, perhaps, such as the very subject of our plays: the house of Atreus.

Ultimately, this story is an introduction, in dramatic form, to the patriarchal system.

The dramatic innovations of Aeschylus revolutionize the very nature of myth and, as Lévi-Strauss claims, myth is comprised of all its variations. [25]

As we have just noted, Aeschylus is the first known writer to introduce female characters as forces intrinsic to the myth of Orestes. It is Aeschylus who first portrays Clytemnestra as a dramatic figure, indeed as a powerful, crazed, frustrated and wronged woman; and it is he who, for the first time, introduces a second female character—Electra—to become the central figure of his drama. In effect, Aeschylus' "significant action," his "act of creation" (as defined by Eliade) constitutes the act of female rebellion. It dramatizes the revolutionary potential of frustrated and entrapped women. To add to the above, this rebellion is granted mythical status in the eyes of the spectators because it builds on ancient images of chthonic mother goddesses, of fertility and mystery cults still popular in Greece at that time.

It is believed that Aeschylus was playing to a sexually segregated, repressively patriarchal society, yet he was doing so in celebration of Dionysus, mystery god, god of women, of frenzy and of chaotic sexual freedom, a god that epitomized as did none other the greatest threat to the reason-loving Athenian male; a deity that represented the antithesis of Athenian, masculine shrewdness, heroic excellence (arête), public law and social order. Eliade claims that

A sacrifice ... not only exactly reproduces the initial sacrifice revealed by a god *ab origine*, at the beginning of time, it also takes place at that same primordial mythical moment.

He writes that

every sacrifice repeats the initial sacrifice and coincides with it. All sacrifices are performed at the same mythical instant of the beginning; through the paradox of rite, profane time and duration are suspended. And the same holds true for all repetitions, i.e., all imitations of archetypes; through such imitation, man is projected into the mythical epoch in which the archetypes were first revealed.... The abolition of profane time and the individual's projection into mythical time do not occur, of course, except at essential periods—those, that is, when the individual is truly himself: on the occasion of ritual or of important acts. [26]

If we accept Eliade's theory of the relevance of time to the archaic mind, it becomes easier for us to imagine the powerful hold that Aeschylus' theater must have had over his audience. The Oresteia was no isolated work. In the eyes of the spectators it built upon the creation of the world. It was fabricated out of the themes and memories of the earliest deities, creation myths and rites, and the sacrifices that it depicted, both of life and of conscience, became embossed for them as they watched, with the mythical fullness of the sacrifice *ab origine*:

insofar as an act (or an object) acquires a certain reality through repetition of certain paradigmatic gestures, ... there is an implicit abolition of profane time, of duration, of "history"; and he who reproduces the exemplary gesture thus finds himself transported into the mythical epoch in which its revelation took place. [27]

Herbert Blau refers to the meeting of Orestes and Electra over the tomb of their father. He says:

All theory of theater converges there. That's where the real acting takes place. "Are you alive? Where are you living? What is your life?" When we speak of what Stanislavski called Presence in acting, we must also speak of its Absence, the dimensionality of time through the act, the fact that he who is performing can die there in front of your eyes; is in fact doing so. Of all the performing arts, the theater stinks most of mortality. Buber said of Hasidism that it is "the only mysticism in which time is hallowed" somewhere "on the borderland of faith where the soul draws breath between word and word." It is a superb definition of what theater should be. The secret of any craft is mastery of time. [28]

With this in mind, the full significance of the festival of Dionysus and of the Electra plays becomes clearer: Aeschylus' theater is part of time itself. It is neither more nor less than his own chapter—and that of his generation—in an ongoing creation myth; their moment in an eternal reckoning, a self- assessment that is at once religious, social, and political. Aeschylus' questioning was conceived at the dawn of human consciousness by the initial separation of the world parents, heaven and earth, and it will continue until the end of human time. His particular chapter in the framework of creation myths records the leap his generation is making from dependence on irrational forces to reason and self-rule. It is a repetition of the very first sacrifice, a human attempt to be aware, to be in control, to look into the future, and—above all—to be "heroic."

In addition to his understanding of time, Eliade presents the significance of place for the archaic mind. A place becomes a sacred center of the universe, he claims, by means of the significance of the action, of the sacrifice that is enacted there. In such a way, Jerusalem is regarded by many as a reflection of its heavenly counterpart. Many consider Mount Tabor the biblical navel of the earth. A host of other traditions regard acts of creation as having occurred at the center of the world. In such a fashion, Medieval Theater manipulated its cultural promise that chosen man from Adam to Christ rose and fell on the identical spot. It too regarded place as sanctified by its repetition of meaningful action. Consequently, the center of the medieval stage was charged by the accumulated significance of the creation of the world, the births of Adam and Eve, their banishment from Eden, the birth, crucifixion and resurrection of Christ, the final judgment and deliverance of mankind.

Yes. Theater is such a center, and the cyclical repetitions of meaningful actions on this central spot become, themselves, a source of myth, for with each repeated act of creation, with each repeated human sacrifice, the sanctity of the theatrical center is intensified. In such a way, quite apart from the religious connotations of the festival of Dionysus, the act of gathering annually around the circular area becomes a ritual of return. Each return adds mythical depth and heightened meaning for the spectators. The central spot of the stage, at the moment of the performance, at the gathering of the populace, is charged with the sanctity of myth.

In *The Libation Bearers*, Aegisthus assumes the figure of the hero's personal father. His is the voice of reactionism and constraint; as such he stands in the way of Orestes' advancement. On the other hand, the spirit of Agamemnon inside the burial mound has become, over the years of Orestes' absence from Argos, the source and fountainhead of all Orestes' aspirations. Yet, only by eradicating the maternal can Orestes reach his goal. Such is the dragon that this hero has to slay, which might well prove a prototype for all heroic trials.

Simultaneously, in this area, the four thousand Greeks attending this festival are experiencing Orestes' trial. Such is the myth and the ritual enacted in the theater of Aeschylus and the subsequent playwrights in our study.

As the shaman travels imaginatively outward toward his fountain of creativity and returns from there to transform the imagined into the physical on stage, and as the adolescent groping toward manhood journeys outward in his rite of passage from the community to confront his greatest fears and returns as a benefactor of his society, so the Greek tragic actor and the Greek hero draw their creative spirits from a separate space and are inspired into action, ultimately, from the depths of the sacred burial mound.

In such a spirit Orestes is exiled from his immediate community and returns to confront the challenge of his own manhood in the community of gathered Athenians, at the burial mound of his father.

All action emanates from this burial mound. The spectators surround the action physically and emotionally in a gigantic circle creating between them and the players one centrifugal circuit of action and intensity. All are pulled magnetically to the spirit of the dead king; all are held there by the shared, half remembered, half intuited sense of the rite of death and rebirth of Dionysus and by a communal need to evoke the heroic among them.

It is clear that the action in this opening act of The Libation Bearers is no longer merely the evocation of the spirit of the dead king; rather, it is the dramatic transition of one generation for the next and the blessing of the old or the new. More specifically, it is a prayer that Agamemnon condone, from his place under the earth, Orestes' act of revenge and murder,

LEADER
And the ripping cries of triumph mine
To sing when the man is stabbed,
The woman dies—
Why hide what's deep inside me,
Black wings beating, storming the spirit's prow—
Hurricane, slashing hatred! [195].

ELECTRA
Both fists at once
Come down, come down—
Zeus, crush their skulls! Kill! Kill!
Now give the land some faith, I beg you,
From these ancient wrongs bring forth our rights.
Hear me, Earth, and all you lords of death [195].

ORESTES
Father, king, no royal death you died—
Give me the power now to rule our house [198].

ORESTES
O Earth, bring father up to watch me fight [199].

It is believed that when the Theater of Dionysus was rebuilt in stone in the fourth century BC, it accommodated between 14,000 and 17,000 people. Even if there were considerably fewer in the fifth century BC, we might be justified in imagining several thousand spectators roused, at this point, to holy indignation.

Northrop Frye describes the tragic hero as one who becomes increasingly alienated from his community and his chorus, isolated in his solitary heroic vision [29]; yet in Aeschylus' play we not only see the chorus (which, after all, is the only society we have on stage) goad Orestes, Electra and the spectators into a frenzy of revenge; we also see them skillfully veer Orestes from talk to action:

LEADER
And a fine thing it is to lengthen out the dirge;
you adore a grave and fate they never mourned.
But now for action—now you're set on action,
put your stars to proof [200].

Orestes qua hero is acting on behalf of his community. He is performing an act of enfranchisement for himself, the house of Atreus, and the thousands of Athenian males that are congregated here.

As previously mentioned, the story of Orestes and Agamemnon was first recorded in the third book of Homer's *Odyssey*. There, neither morality nor personal compunction was at issue. At issue was simply the duty of a son to avenge wrongs committed against his father. "What a good thing it is that a son should be on the spot when a man is dead." This was the early Homeric heroism that we see even more clearly in the ego, warrior-oriented behavior of *The Iliad*. It was the Greek *arête*: human excellence made manifest by a display of courage—defiance of death and danger for national and personal honor. It constituted manly, heroic action and bore no relationship to orality, conscience, or ethical behavior. Arete was a far cry from our Aeschylean hero who is torn between the masculine, duty-oriented threat of Apollo and the strangulating female ghouls—(*Erinyes, Furies*)—embodiments of his personal conscience.

The essential differences then between Aeschylus' play and its Homeric source are two. For Homer, the fate of Clytemnestra was not even worth mentioning. Homer's emphasis was exclusively on the masculine and the heroic, whereas Aeschylus' is on the human and the moral. Homer's hero "gave a funeral feast to the people over his hateful mother and Aegisthus the coward" [30]; whereas Aeschyus' Orestes is driven insane by the guilt of his matricide, as dramatized by the Erinyes, those hideous projections of the Athenian male's tie with and fear of the female. In addition, in Homer, there was no mention of Orestes' sister or female counterpart, while Aeschylus' account of the emerging hero accords the most prominent position to the female figure of Electra.

Aristotle describes tragedy as a situation play, as the mimesis of action brought about by certain situations. [31] After the evocation of the paternal spirit, the action in *The Libation Bearers* becomes that of Orestes seeking entrance into the house of his mother. Orestes was torn from his mother as an infant. It is his return to her, and the violence that ensues, a violence that is commensurate with the overwhelming emotions he has harbored for his mother since his banishment and which he experiences now at the moment of his reunion with her, that constitutes the main action of this play. At the same time, it is his confrontation with, and murder of his mother that constitutes the hero's (and the growing adolescent's) passage to manhood.

In *The Rise of the Greeks*, Michael Grant describes the precarious relationship that seems to have existed between the sexes in fifth-century Athens. "Of course," he says:

> family affection existed, as anywhere (tombstones bear witness to such feelings), and it would be absurd to deny that women were indispensable in all the obvious domestic ways.[32]

However, for an accurate account of those times, Grant relies on the writings of Hesiod and Semonides:

> A great amount of literature of the Greeks echoes their poisonous hatred of women—or rather reflects a deeply anxious fear of them and of what they might be capable of doing. For in this repressively male-dominated society, marked by a voluminous sexual vocabulary and by exaggerated obscenity at festivals, there existed a curious sort of sexual apartheid. Despite their obvious indispensability for procreation, women seemed a mysterious, dangerous, polluting, "other element, and the Greeks were acutely afraid that they might get out of step, might break out from their appointed and domesticated place.[33]

Later, in Euripides' play Orestes, we will see the hero defend his act of matricide with the following words:

ORESTES
In your defense, no less than in my father's cause'
I killed my mother. For if wives may kill husbands
And not be guilty, you had all best lose no time,
But die today, before your wives make slaves of you,
To vindicate her would be a preposterous act.
As things stand now, the traitress to my father's bed
Has paid for it with her life; but if you now kill me
The law is void; the sooner a man dies the better,
Since wives lack but encouragement, not, enterprise.[34]

Grant says that:

> religion was the one exception to the absence of women from Greek public activities. They were permitted their own rituals, such as the Thesmophoria, in which they played a leading and exclusive part (with

outspoken stress on their role in fertility. For it was recognized that the deities had their wild, savage, untamable side—so sharply opposed to the orderly male culture of the "normal" Greek civilization—and that women seemed well suited to serve this aspect of the divine world, full of disruption and inversion, in which customary rules were in abeyance. After all, that was how Greeks thought of marriage; as the taming of wild, ungovernable, basically irrational womanhood. Thus, many a Greek vase shows a man leading his wife off forcibly by the hand into her wedding, which amounted almost to a symbolic death. [35]

We will recognize the "wild, savage, untamable" female side of the gods when reading the Eumenides—our next and final play in Aeschylus' trilogy.

The misogyny of the young Hippolytus in Euripides' play of that name is no aberration:

HIPPOLYTUS

Zeus! Why did you let women settle in this world of light, a curse and a snare to men? If you wished to propagate the human race you should have arranged it without women. Men might have deposited in your temples gold or iron or a weight of copper to purchase offspring, each to the value of the price he paid, and so lived in free houses relieved of womankind. Here is a proof that woman is a great nuisance. The father who begot her and brought her up pays a great dowry to get her out of his house and be rid of the plague. The man who receives the poisonous weed into his home rejoices and adds beautiful decorations to the useless ornament and tricks her out in gowns—poor fool, frittering away the family property. (He is under constraint: if his in laws are good people he must keep his cheerless bed; if his spouse is agreeable but her relatives useless, the evil he must accept oppresses the good.) Happiest is he who has a cipher for a wife, a useless simpleton to sit at home. A clever woman I hate; may there never be in my house a woman more intellectual than a woman ought to be. Mischief is hatched by Cypris in clever women; the helpless kind is kept from misconduct by the shortness of her wit. No maids should be allowed near a wife; beasts that can bite but cannot talk should be their only company in the house, so that they could neither address anyone nor receive speech in return. As it is, the vile women wear their vile schemes with-in, and the maids carry word outdoors. [36]

Let us look at the way women in this world regard romantic love:

CHORUS

Eros, Eros (god of romantic love) ... may you never show yourself to me to my hurt. May you never come inordinately. Neither the flash of fire nor the bolt of the stars is more deadly than the shafts of Aphrodite which Eros, Zeus' boy, hurls from his hands ... Eros, tyrant over men, chamberlain of the dearest bowers of Aphrodite, the destroyer that brings all manner of calamities on mortals when he attacks. [37]

Grant writes, "In most Greek city states a woman had in law no standing in any question relating to her marriage, any more than she possessed other legal rights. [38]

In his book *The Glory of Hera*, Philip E. Slater describes the extent of the segregation of the sexes in fifth century BCE Athens and the devastating effect that he believes this had on the maturing male of that society. [39] He questions the pathological dependence he believes Athenian males had on their counterparts that could have caused such an artificial separation. Classical Greece was essentially a male dominated society in which women were separated in their own houses. Men came to their wives only to engender children, while for social and sexual pleasure they enjoyed the company of young boys and prostitutes.

In the Greek states, men were required by law to marry. Surely, that must indicate their reluctance to do so. Slater writes that, "many Greek cities punished celibacy as a crime, and at one time, Sparta denied the rights of citizenship to the man who did not marry." [40] It was rare that they married before the age 30 or 35, the limit required by law, for men delayed the obligatory act for as long as possible.

The wives they took were hardly women. Barely pubescent girls in their early teens, these brides would more often than not offer up their dolls to their family goddesses in exchange for their husbands—a less than fair trade. Girls were marriageable commodities to their fathers. They were forced to live a stiflingly cloistered life before marriage—their virginity guarded by their fathers at all costs for economic reasons. Of course, girls did not know their husbands prior to marriage and, for the most part, were married to men fifteen to twenty years older than them. In marriage, girls left the loving care of their mothers and the familiarity of their homes and their family gods to live in the house of a stranger. There are several accounts in Greek mythology of women who find and adopt abandoned babies, leading their husbands to believe that they are the infants' natural fathers. Indeed, one version of the Oedipus myth claims that Merope, or Periboea, told her husband Polybus the same story. Surely such a ruse is feasible only where the husband is estranged from his wife.

Slater maintains that the reason for such segregation of the sexes is the innate ear that Greek males had of the opposite sex. By virtue of their youth, brides bore more resemblance to young boys than to women. Girls were obliged to shave off what pubic hair they had before marriage in order not to repulse their husbands. Such fear, on the part of the male, of female sexuality can be traced back to a primal male fear of the vagina dentate. It is represented by mythical Gorgon heads—gaping, tooth-filled female faces surrounded by snake hair—most familiar to us perhaps in the image of the Medusa.

According to this reading, the Medusa myth itself—which Freud interprets as an embodiment of the male fear of castration, the tooth-filled head being a threatening, female, sexual image, and the snake hair a deliberately misplaced image of pubic hair—is a projection of the Greek mind. [41]

Slater quotes Farenczi as claiming, that "In the analysis of dreams and fancies, I have come repeatedly upon the circumstance that the head of Medusa is the terrible symbol of the female genital region, the details of which are displayed from below upwards. The many serpents surrounding the head ought—in representation of the opposite—to signify the absence of a penis, and the phantom itself, is the frightful impression made on the child by the penis-less (castrated) genital."

He claims that Bettleheim mentions "the frequency with which disturbed boys are concerned about the 'hairy vagina,' and suggests it is related to the 'vagina dentata.'" [42]

Slater believes that Orestes is very much a disturbed boy who has never been able to forgive his mother for having rejected him as an infant. He claims that the hero's boast when challenged by Menelaos in Euripides' Orestes that he "can never have" his fill of "killing whores" is "a sentiment frequently expressed by sex killers. And one which reveals again the significance of maternal seductiveness in generating pathology." Slater regards Orestes' act of matricide as an unsuccessful attempt on his part to rid himself, once and for all, of the excruciating need for maternal affection from which he has always suffered. He maintains that the fiendish presence of the Medusa-like Erinyes in the Eumenides bears witness to the feelings of "longing" and "guilt" that his matricide had failed to assuage. [43] For Slater, the Erinyes are direct projections of the Athenian male's fear of female sexuality, much as witches were associated with women in the Middle Ages: during the persecutions which periodically convulsed Europe between the thirteenth and seventeenth centuries, witches were often shaved in order to uncover the mark of the Devil.

It is worth noting that Slater also quotes Simonides of Amorgos, who compared women to "sows, vixen, bitches, donkeys, weasels and monkeys." [44] Surely, it is no mere coincidence that all these animals have themselves, over time, been described as the Devil.

By virtue of her very being, the Greek woman aggravated the male's already existing fear of castration. The demand, the neediness, the receptiveness of the woman's body and emotional state, combined with the seeming magic with which she engendered and nursed life, threatened the male with a sense of his own inadequacy and a fear of his own extinction. Masculinity was in danger of being devoured, consumed within the body of the female. This reading suggests that the ultimate male desire was to become independent of his female counterpart—a desire that is adequately demonstrated by the male's social independence and by his predilection for those of his own sex.

Unfortunately, the law of nature (as no less the law of the state) demanded communion with women. Several myths illustrate this reading: Myths such as the birth of Athena from the head of Zeus, supposedly without any participation on the part of the female; the birth of Dionysus from the thigh of Zeus; and the all-male birth of Apollo. Are these not projections of the Greek male's deepest need, the need to be self-sufficient?

Consequently, the deserted girl-brides were left only with their children. Daughters were undervalued as were the mothers, so while it is likely that the mother-daughter relationship was of a sympathetic nature—that of a shared fate, the son might well have become the focus of the mother's frustrations. Slater maintains that the Greek mother used her son as "her little man" [45] to fulfill her emotional and sexual needs, and that, in so doing, she terrified the boy with an overwhelming female sexuality he could never hope to satisfy. Such a relationship must have recreated on a personal level the collective male terror of the Medusa. The idea of the son's sense of sexual inadequacy and his terror of rejection on the part of the other is best reflected in the story of Hera who engendered life and gave birth totally unaided to Hephaestus. Hephaestus was lame (which, in Freudian terms means sexually impaired) and ugly. Hera threw him out of heaven in disgust. Clytemnestra's murder of her husband and her extradition of her son accomplish not only Orestes' banishment from heaven, they also constitute a matriarchal rebellion, an all but total eradication of the masculine from her home. (Not for nothing does the chorus complain about Aegisthus. He might be a bully—even a tyrant, but he was not man enough either to fight in the war against Troy, or to murder the king.

The significance of the relative weakness of Aegisthus as a masculine figure and his abstention from the Trojan War, combined with Orestes' surprise when confronted with his mother's genuine expression of love for Aegisthus, become clear. Clytemnestra mourns her paramour when he is murdered because she has never regarded him as a "masculine" antagonist:

CLYTEMNESTRA
Gone, my violent one—Aegisthus, very dear

Aegisthus' violence is expressed—not in risking his own life and limb for a cause, nor in any other act of personal courage—but in his bullying, in temper tantrums, in pitting armed guards against those who annoy him. Clytemnestra's actions, in this Aeschylus' trilogy, have manifested the worst of the Athenian male's nightmares.

ORESTES
You love your man? Then lie in the same grave [216]

Slater maintains that in many instances the Greek male was victim of a frustrated and hysterical mother. He claims that the mother frequently misused her son both as a representative of the male gender and as her husband's natural and political heir. In short, he believes that the Greek woman used her son as a vehicle of her own revenge against her husband. Is this what we are witnessing in Clytemnestra's welcome to Agamemnon on his return from Troy?

CLYTEMNESTRA
Our child is gone, not standing by our side,
the bond of our dearest pledges, mine and yours;
by all rights our child should be here...
Orestes. You seem startled.
... Men, it is their nature,
trampling on the fighter once he's down.
Our child is gone. That is my defense
and it is true [136].

As noted, we recognize the projected wishes and fears of the Greek male in the creation myths of classical Greece. Mythical women bear little or no resemblance to the virginal child-brides that the Greeks married. Neither do the Amazons of Greek theater. Rather, they seem to be embodiments of the male's childhood fears of his mother. For the most part, mythical women are full-blooded, highly-strung, tempestuous and dangerous. Zeus roamed constantly in search of love affairs, as did Theseus and the vast majority of Greek males, seeking (Carl Jung would claim) to find their mother in woman after woman. Yet the king of gods was ultimately cowed and answerable to the insatiable and jealous Hera, and the great King Agamemnon returned victorious from ten bloody years at war to be killed in his home by his queen. Could it be from the mythical goddesses that Carl Jung developed his notion of the mother archetype—magnetic, demanding, devouring, life engendering and murderous?

Gaea, or Ge, original earth mother goddess, engenders and holds in her belly all life; that is, she is the source both of life and death. She is the Greek male's idea of Woman, and Woman in turn is represented in mythology by the equally paradoxical figure of the snake. In a phallic sense, the snake obviously represents the male, yet by means of the snake's ability to devour animals in their entirety, at which time its body bulges with life as does the body of a pregnant woman, it is also a representation of the life-engendering and life devouring female. Bringing together male and female polarities within one symbol represents, it seems to me, an inability of behalf of the male to separate himself from the female and to experience himself as an autonomous being.

We must remember that a child's earliest state is one of complete narcissism in which the child is aware only of its own needs. At this stage, the child is in a total symbiotic fusion with its mother. For both, the oral satisfaction of the infant is the only priority. Mother and child form a single being, one narcissistic entity. Slater presents a fascinating argument to the effect that:

> the serpent represents the oral-narcissistic dilemma because it is the most common symbol of boundary-ambiguity. It appears in connection with the boundary between life and death, consciousness and unconsciousness, male and female.... Thus the sexual organs receive serpentine associations primarily because copulation blurs the boundaries of the organism.

Slater claims that, "the snake represents the insatiable hunger of the child itself—the desire to gobble up the mother and keep her forever inside."[46] Yet, for a man with as damaged a sense of self as the Greek male, this luring of the boundaries must have posed the ultimate threat, that of a repeated and terrifying loss of his masculine independence.

After having spent the first seven to eight years exclusively under the manipulation of his mother, it seems possible that the child's sudden wrench into an all-male world was accomplished before he had relinquished his narcissistic need of his mother. Could it be that the adult male's resistance to the female is commensurate with the intensity with which his childhood self- longed for fusion with her?

What is it that propels The Libation Bearers into action? It is Clytemnestra's dream of the snake, a monster with which Orestes instinctively identifies. The queen dreams of the snake between night and day, which is to say, between a conscious and an unconscious state. It is a dream in which she nurses her infant son, a fantasy world in which her deepest wish and her most dreaded fear are realized: to be bonded with her child. Only in dreams is the image of a snake so charged with significance. It is a dream that brings on the fear of the grave and of retribution and, as such, it lies in the dim region between life and death:

LEADER
She dreamed she bore a snake,...
... she swaddled it like a baby, laid it to rest

ORESTES
And food, what did the little monster want?

LEADER
She gave it her breast to suck—she was dreaming.

ORESTES
And didn't it tear her nipple, the brute inhuman—

LEADER
Blood curdled the milk with each sharp tug

ORESTES
No empty dream. The vision of a man.

LEADER
...And she woke with a scream, appalled,
and rows of torches, burning out of the blind dark,
flared across the halls to soothe the queen
and then she sent the libations for the dead,
an easy cure she hopes will cut the pain.

ORESTES
If the serpent came from the same place as I,
And slept in the bands that swaddled me, and its jaws
Spread wide for the breast that nursed me into life
And clots stained the milk, mother's milk,
And she cried in fear and agony—so be it.
As she bred this sign, this violent prodigy
So she dies by violence. I turn serpent
I kill her. So the vision says [201–2].

For the modern reader, this is a Macbethian nightmare.

"She dreamed she bore a snake": Snake goddess, Minoan, earthenware, 1700–1400 BC, Archeological Museum (photograph by Eric Lessing/Art Resource, New York).

Slater points out that ultimately, Apollo, the much-flaunted patron of Orestes, fails to help him. In addition, Slater claims that the failure of Orestes' matricide to cure him of his maternal longings becomes apparent in his continued dependence on women. At the same time, it is significant that Athena, combination of the male and the female (all male birth, female body,) is the one who restores the much-needed balance to our trilogy. Though Athena still bears the sign of the snake over her robes (relic of her pre–Hellenic status), it is by virtue of her Olympian virginity that she poses no sexual threat to Orestes.

Myth informs us that Gaea, original earth mother, was born of chaos, meaning that Chaos ruled before the Mother, and that the mother is the barrier between chaos and child. It is the mother who prevents the child from regressing to the point which Freud considered humankind's instinctual desire for self-destruction. (It might be worth restating here that the Western European creation myths, from earliest times to our own post Freudian era, has regarded the "child," the "man," "mankind," and the "hero" as male.)

It seems, therefore, that the object of primal man's fascination was the sedentary, nurturing aspect of the mother. The nurturing female represented, in and of herself, the primal order of human experience. She was the barrier between the child and chaos; his protection against the terrifying unknown. We will recall that Gaea gave birth to Uranus (sky) without a mate—again the male's fascination with the females' ability to give birth. Next, we learn that Gaea marries her son Uranus and, through him, gives birth to the Titans, the Cyclopes and the Hundred Handed, giants and monsters of the human psyche. In this way, the first scene of Greek creation demonstrates man's dependence on his mother and his desire through her to gain power and to engender the daemons, which have, throughout human history, represented his innermost fears. By projecting his nightmares into monsters, man could confront them and, perhaps reach some level of control. But it is the mother — primal, ultimate Woman who is regarded, in the male psyche, as the source of such control and, as such, is the primary object of man's desires. According to Freud, all wives, all other female love-objects, are nothing more than displacements of man's primary need for his mother.

Uranus hid his children, the Cyclopes and the Hundred-Handed, inside the body of Gaea, i.e., in the belly of the earth, "causing her great pain." "She resented this tyranny. Making a sickle of flint, she urged her sons to punish her father with it." [47] Do we recognize in this masculine projection of intercourse a desire to destroy the female, together with the male's sense of inadequacy in that he can only "inflict pain"? Here, simultaneously, we see both a fear of the newborn and a sense that the wife uses the fruit of her womb as a weapon against her husband—a weapon with which to replace his own time-limited power.

For we have three generations of male sky gods in the creation myth: Uranus, Cronus, and Zeus; but only one life-engendering, life-devouring, castrating mother-goddess: Gaea. The sky gods, gods of light and of intellect, rise like men to their zenith at the midday of their lives, wane and are replaced by others. In contrast to them, Gaea and her daughters, the Erinyes (earlier, chthonic goddesses indigenous to these Greek isles way before the Doric invasion and only later married into the Olympian system), are of the earth, self-engendering, self-perpetuating, and, thereby, eternal.

All three primary sky gods attempt to devour their offspring. Uranus buries the Cyclopes and the Hundred-Handed within the body of Gaea (for which he is castrated by his son); Cronus is warned that his sons will overthrow him, so he devours them. As for Zeus, Gaea warns him that his first wife Metis will bear him a son who will rule heaven. So, Zeus swallows his wife. Here we see how, with a repetition of the folklore number three, the Greeks relived and reworked the fear of their own mortality and of life-engendering and therefore immortal woman to the point that they could establish Zeus. Zeus, while subject to universal marital strife, was indeed master of his universe.

Surely, it was only when he could establish male supremacy in the heavens and rule by the power of the human spirit that man could see himself as master of his earth.

I suggest then that the basic male anxiety played out in Greek mythology was not caused primarily by his female counterpart but was rather a reflection of his need to work out his own place in the universe. It reflects a longing and an inability, on the part of the male, to accept his own mortality. Again, we can be reminded of Aristotle's claim that meaning is conveyed through action. The action of Orestes re-entering the palace of his mother and confronting her there encapsulates the ambivalence of the male creation myth. Simultaneously, it represents his longing to return home, and his need to separate the world parents—the earth from the sky. It personifies both his desire to regain the paradise of his earliest symbiotic tie with his mother, and his urge to overpower the fecund, repressive female. In addition, it enacts the ultimate male fantasy: to identify exclusively with the masculine and, in so doing, establish himself as spiritual master of a male-dominated world.

As we have said, Homer's heroism was a totally warrior-oriented, masculine concern. For Aeschylus, the issue is more problematic.

For him, heroism and the mature man necessitates a fully integrated personality, the coming together of the Electra and the Orestes as one. Electra is not created as a woman, but specifically as a dramatic figure, as the twin counterpart of the male, a necessary adjunct to an otherwise incomplete hero. Yet her name, A-Lektra, means "the unmated," her story essentially that of a woman who has been separated, and who lives forever, imprisoned and alone. Her character consists only in that of a woman longing for deliverance. In fact, characteristic of Grant's claim that religious ritual or, more specifically perhaps, the practice of religious mysticism, was the one area in which women played an equal role to that of men, Aeschylus brings Electra alive only at the moment of the evocation of her father's spirit. Only then is she at one with her brother. Only then is she recognized as a speaking, feeling being. She serves, in fact, like the women of the chorus, as priestess to the spirit of her father and as a medium for the initiation of her brother into manhood.

Rites of passage for neophytes on the brink of adulthood were common practice among the mystery cults of ancient Greece, among Orphic mysteries, mysteries of Eleusis, of Thrace, of Mithras, Attis, Adonis, Isis and even Dionysus. Though many of the ceremonies of these rituals are lost to us, initiation rites seem to have consisted of the enactment of a symbolic death and rebirth—death to the secular life that the initiates had led up to that point, and rebirth to the sacred and the sexual of their adult lives. In talking of the rites of passage and of ceremonies of death and rebirth, Arnold Van Gennep says:

> Since Attis dies and is reborn, it is thought that the rites of initiation also cause her future worshiper to die and be reborn: (1) through fasting he removes the profane impurity from his body; (2) he eats and drinks from the sacra (a drum and cymbal); (3) he goes down into a pit, and the blood of a sacrificed bull poured over him covers his entire body; then he comes out of the pit, bloody from head to foot; (4) during several days, he is fed only milk, like a newborn child.... (T)he neophyte came out of the pit covered with blood like the newborn child emerging from his mother's body. [48]

We have described Orestes' premature banishment from his mother as a spiritual death; we have described Electra as one of a chorus of women priestesses who walk ceremonially to the burial mound of the dead Agamemnon in order to pour wine (blood) into the grave; and we have suggested that Electra, with her prayers, walks in the very footsteps of her hitherto dead brother and conjures him back into life before the congregated spectators. We have noted that the Greek spectators of that time were familiar with such ceremonies. As with the ancient Egyptian myth of Isis and Osiris, a myth that was still popular in fifth-century BCE. Greece, the hero is here brought back to life by the sister-lover. Everything indicates that *The Libation Bearers* is a play of the hero's initiation and that Aeschylus is deliberately building upon popular and powerful ritual as a basis for his theater.

In all the plays under discussion here, Orestes returns from a symbolic death. At the burial mound of his father, center stage, the hero is brought face-to-face with the challenge of his identity.

Orestes enters the palace and confronts his mother.

CLYTEMNESTRA:
I see murder in your eyes, my child—mother's murder!
...
Watch out—the hounds of a mother's curse will hunt you down

ORESTES:
But how to escape a father's if I fail?

Orestes is indeed caught between a rock and a hard place. Who are the hounds that Clytemnestra evokes? Orestes murders his mother and Aegisthus with the robes they had used to murder Agamemnon and Cassandra, and the chorus erupts in a paean of victory:

CHORUS
Apollo wills it so!—
...
And the pure god came down and healed our ancient wounds,
The heavens come, somehow, to lift our yoke of grief—
Now to praise the heavens' just command

Apollo, son of Zeus, god of sky and reason, it was he, who commanded Orestes to do this deed.

CHORUS
Look, the light is breaking!
The huge chain that curbed the halls gives way.
Rise up, proud house, long, too long
your walls lay fallen, strewn along the earth.

ORESTES
And still, while I still have some self-control'
I say to my friends in public: I killed my mother,
Not with a little justice. She was stained
With father's murder, she was cursed by god.
(It was) the Seer of Delphi (Apollo) who declared,'Go through with this
and you go free of guilt. Fail and—'
I can't repeat the punishment.

Yet, immediately, the furies swarm to the guilty man:

ORESTES
No, no! Women—look—like
Gorgons, Shrouded in black their
heads wreathed, Swarming serpents!
—Cannot stay, I must move on.

Like biblical Cain, Orestes is chased from social contact, his lot: to roam from place to place, from altar to altar, finding no rest, haunted by the Eumenides until he has expiated his sin.

Aeschylus: The Eumenides

Other than for a few short quotations, I will leave my readers to read or re- read this play at their leisure. *The Eumenides* is the last in Aeschylus' trilogy. It opens with the priestess at Delphi, temple of Apollo. After just a few words, she finds Orestes:

I see a man—an abomination to god—
He holds the seat where suppliants sit for purging;
His hands dripping blood, and his sword just drawn,
And he holds a branch (it must have been an olive)
Wreathed with a fine tuft of wool, all piety,
Fleece gleaming white.
…
But there in a ring around the man, an amazing
company—Women, sleeping, nestling against the benches…
Women? No,
Gorgons I'd call them; but then with
Gorgons You'd see the grim, inhuman…

...
   These have no wings,
I looked. Black they are, and so repulsive.
Their heavy, rasping breathing makes me cringe.
... their eyes ooze a discharge, sickening,
...
The tribe that produced that brood I never saw.

For a while now we have heard talk of Gorgons—ugly, foul-smelling, female forms—curse of those who sin against nature. For just as Zeus and his host of sky gods—in this instance, Apollo—represent the male order of reason, light, and level-headed (though, as we have noted, no less cruel) vengeance, so these Eumenides represent the pent-up, primal, female fury of the dead. More: It is believed that the original, most primal gods, and the priests who served them, were female—revered, as previously mentioned, for their magical power of fertility and their as yet unexplained ability to give birth and nurture life. The function of these goddesses and the priestesses who served them was to preserve the most essential order of the universe, i.e., that a son never murder his parent as had happened to Gaia, first of all earth goddesses, and her husband, Zeus. When we talked earlier of women as late as the fifth century BCE serving as priestesses of ancient, mystery cults, it was these beneath-the-earth goddesses that they evoked. Here, in the plays of Aeschylus, they surge up from the bowels of the earth, land of the dead, to hunt down, attack, and destroy Orestes.

Let us listen as Apollo promises to protect Orestes. How does he regard the Eumenides?

APOLLO
No, I will never fail you, through to the end
Your guardian standing by your side or worlds away!
I will show no mercy to your enemies! Now
Look at these—
These obscenities!—I've caught them,
Beaten them down with sleep.
   They disgust me.
These grey, ancient children never touched
By god man or beast—the eternal virgins.
Born for destruction only, the dark pit,
They range the bowels of Earth, the world of death,
Loathed by men and the gods who hold Olympus.

And what do these furies think of Apollo?

FURIES
You—child of Zeus—you, a common thief!
Young god, you have ridden down the powers
proud with age. You worship the suppliant,
    The godless man who tears his parent's heart—
The matricide, you steal him away, and you a god!
—Guilt both ways and who can call it justice?
…I can feel the executioner's lash,
it's searing deeper, sharper, the knives of burning ice—
Such is your triumph, you young gods,
…
Your throne is streaming blood,
Blood at the foot, blood at the crowning head—
—I can see the Navelstone of the Earth,
it's bleeding, bristling corruption, oh, the guilt it has to bear

Nothing can be as antithetical to Apollo, the young, male, Olympian god, as these ancient, foul-smelling, frenzied hags. Yet here, Aeschylus performs an amazing feat of diplomacy. He ushers onto his stage none other than Athena, Olympian goddess, herself a combination of opposites—the male (in that she was never physically born but sprung fully formed from the head of Zeus without the aid of a female) and the female (appearance).

Finally, for the first time in this trilogy, we are presented with the voice of reason. Athena is that voice. She calms the Furies by listening and respecting them (surely a first,) she urges both Orestes and the Furies to state their causes, summons ten citizens of Athens to listen and judge. In short, for the first recorded time and by means of the much-loved, mythical figure of Athena, Aeschylus presents on stage—what was still an experimental concept in Greece of the fifth century BCE—Democracy and self-rule, a court run according to rational thinking, judge and jury. What is more, Aeschylus is offering this during the festival of Dionysus, which was more than any other entity the most hedonistic, orgiastic of celebrations.

This first of all recorded democratic courts was new to Greece, pioneered just a short time before Aeschylus' first presentation of this trilogy. As a respected statesman of Athens who'd fought against tyranny, civil injustice, and in the game-changing Battle of Marathon, Aeschylus was surely an advocate and pioneer of democracy. It is as though our playwright himself has stepped on stage, from some separate space, with a vision for the future, one that will release his nation from its endless chokehold of ignorance, superstition and dependence on the gods, pain, recrimination, and revenge. In so doing, he is endowing humanity with a gift of the new, the civil, and the heroic.

---

13 Erich L. Neumann, The Great Mother (Princeton, N.J.: Princeton University Press, 1974), p. 18.
14 Carol Gilligan, In a Different Voice (Cambridge, Mass.: Harvard University Press, 1982), p. 6.
15 Erich L. Neumann, The Origins and History of Consciousness (Princeton, N.J.: Princeton University Press, 1973), p. 131.
16 Anderson, Myths and Legends of the Polynesians, pp. 367–8, quoted in Neumann, p. 103.
17 Isaiah Tishby, "The Doctrine of Evil and the 'Klipah' in the Lurian Cabala," quoted in Neumann, The Origins and History of Consciousness, pp. 119–20.
18 Barbara G. Walker, The Woman's Encyclopedia of Myths and Secrets (San Francisco: Harper & Row, 1983), p. 1049.
19 Neumann, p. 132.
20 Aeschylus, The Oresteia (New York: Penguin, 1977), p. 161. Hereafter, quotations from this edition will be indicated by page number references in parentheses or brackets.
21 Jan Kott, The Eating of the Gods (Evanston, Ill.: Northwestern University Press, 1987) p. 254.
22 William Ridgeway, The Origin of Tragedy (New York; Benjamin Blom, 1966).
23 Eliade, p.34
24 Homer, The Odyssey: The Story of Odysseus, trans. W.H.D. Rouse (New York: New American Library, 1937), p.36.
25 Lévi-Strauss, p. 217.
26 Eliade, p.35.
27 Eliade, p. 35.
28 Herbert Blau, Take Up the Bodies: Theater at the Vanishing Point (Chicago: University of Illinois Press, 1982), p. 83.
29 Northrop Frye, Anatomy of Criticism: Four Essays (Princeton, N.J.: Princeton University Press, 1973), p. 217.
30 Homer, The Odyssey: The Story of Odysseus, trans. W.H.D. Rousee

(New York: New American Library, 1937), p. 39.

31   Aristotle, Poetics, trans. Gerald Elese (Ann Arbor: University of Michigan Press, 1970), p. 27.

32   Michael Grant, The Rise of the Greeks (New York: Macmillan, 1987), p.

33   Grant, pp. 30–1.

34   Euripides, Orestes and Other Plays (Middlesex, England: Penguin, 1983), p. 333.

35   Grant, p. 31.

36   Euripides, Hippolytus in Ten Plays, trans. John McLean (New York: Bantam, 1985), pp. 80–1.Hereafter cited as Hippolytus.

37   Hippolytus, pp. 78–9.

38   Grant, p. 31.

39   Philip E. Slater, The Glory of Hera (Boston: Beacon, 1968).

40   Slater, p. 25.

41   Slater, p. 103.

42   Slater, pp. 16 and 13.

43   Slater, pp. 186–7 and 187.

44   Slater, pp. 13 and 25.

45   Slater, p. 31.

46   Slater, pp. 91 and 89.

47   Edward Tripp, The Meridian Handbook of Classical Mythology (New York: New American Library, 1970), p. 248.

48   Arnold van Gennep, The Rites of Passage (Chicago: University of Chicago Press, 1960), pp. 92–3.

CHAPTER 2

SOPHOCLES: ELECTRA (409 BCE)

ifty years have elapsed since Aeschylus' presentation of the Oresteia. If we understand classic Greek theater in the way it has been presented so far, it might disturb us to find how great a change has taken place since Aeschylus' trilogy, both in the form and the purpose of theater. In Sophocles' Electra, Agamemnon's burial ground has been removed from its central position on stage. Chrysothemis rushes to her sister from some other, off-stage space to tell her what she has found on their father's grave. Here, on Sophocles' stage, standing erect at the focal point of our attention is Apollo, masculine god of light and reason.

Without Electra, the theme of this play is revenge, plain and simple.

Orestes and his tutor arrive with a mission—and Orestes wastes no time.

The moment the play opens, the moment his feet touch the stones of Argos, Orestes thanks his tutor for having guided him so safely and loyally home, and launches directly into a detailed plan of action:

ORESTES
Listen to what I have decided.... I went to learn from the Pythian oracle how I was to punish my father's murderers...Our plan, then, must be for you to take an opportunity of entering the house; find out what's going on inside, and bring word.... Spin a tale that you're a visitor from Phocis, sent by Pantheus.... Tell them that Orestes is dead—take your oath on it— ... say a fall from his chariot at the Pythian games.... Meanwhile, Pylades and I will go and visit my father's grave—for the god ordered this

… and deceive them with the comfortable assurance that my body has
been burned to ashes and is no more.

In this play, Orestes' tactics are the personification of the Greek
term *Dolos*—deceitful, wily means to a just end. His behavior is
directed by *erga*—facts, actions, and tangibles.

But Orestes' actions are drowned out by the mourning lyricism
and emotionalism of Electra. Electra represents the agons—
dialectics and sufferings of a more ancient, primal, female order; a
belief system which Thomas Woodard calls "high melodrama" and
which violently opposes the tactics of Orestes and his tutor. Both
Orestes and his tutor are taciturn, purposeful, noble, successful,
action and goal oriented. As such, they represent idealized Athenian
masculinity.

Sophocles' Electra is the victim of the actions of others. She
emerges from the palace depressed, disheveled, and dressed like a
slave. Woodard maintains that she personifies the interior of the
woman's house which is present as a backdrop throughout the action
and which serves throughout as a reminder both of Electra's royal
birth, and of her eventual degradation.

Woodard claims that despite her efforts to goad Chrysothemis
into action, Electra herself remains all talk, all tears. For most of the
action, she stands center stage, a dramatic embodiment of suffering
for her father's murder and her own loss, and a stark, theatrical
contrast to the unobtrusive yet determined manner of Orestes and
his companion. As we have noted, Orestes' manner is pragmatic.
He is practical. His stance is essentially un- theatrical, which might
be why most interpreters translate the original Greek poetry of his
speeches into prose:

ORESTES
I am trying to find the place where Aegisthus lives….
Which of you I wonder, would be so good as to tell them within
that a long- expected visitor is here? [Watling, p. 102].

In contrast, Electra's attitude and speech is lyrical and poetic:

ELECTRA
I know,

How well I know,
Through every month of the year

ELECTRA
O the sad day! Is this the confirmation of the news
that we have just heard?
...
His dust lies there ...
please give it to me sir.
I want to hold it in my hands and weep,
Weep of this dust, and remember with tears
All my sorrow and the sorrow of my house
[Watling, pp. 102–3].

Woodard maintains that Electra represents logos—conviction, imagination...inwardness. She is physis. She has the repetitiveness of nature. She has nature's faithful adherence to blood-ties and nature's inability to accept compromise. Woodard claims that Electra's truth, like that of nature, goes beyond appearances, beyond the surface truth of erga apprehended by the senses or sensible intelligence.

Here, in Sophocles' play, the female figure of Electra no longer represents the premature state of the masculine hero. As we have said, Orestes and his tutor open the play with their cunning plan of action, yet they remain silent and unseen after the matricide. Electra, on the other hand, languishes in despair and spiritual death at the opening of the play,

ELECTRA
Alas, alas!
... Sweet light, clean air,
As wide as earth!
Each night that dies with dawn
I bring my sad songs here
And tear my breast until it bleeds [Watling, p. 71].

Yet at the end she is larger than life—seething with vigor over the death and demise of her mother. The images Electra uses are those associated with death, for indeed, as a dramatic character in this play, Electra belongs to the principle of death.

Though Electra is not as symbiotically close to her brother in this play as she was in the play by Aeschylus, the moment they recognize each other the two are drawn together in a close emotional bond. It is part of Orestes' scheme (*dolos*) to bring the urn of his own purported ashes onstage.

With overwhelming grief, Electra embraces the urn she believes holds her brother—and for that one moment, for her expression of the deepest form of human pain, the urn assumes, on stage, the prominence of a dramatic character.

More significantly, for that moment of mourning, the urn assumes the stature of the central burial mound that we had noted in Aeschylus' *Libation Bearers*. As such, the urn is a theatrical device that has grown out of the sacrificial altar, and even beyond—out of the center of death and fertility of the great mother.

As the embodiment of physis-nature, Electra clutches the ashes to her in an attempt to draw death into herself:

ELECTRA
You were never your mother's, always mine,
Of all in the house I alone was your nurse, …
I dread in you, you vanished into death
………………………………………………………………
… a-aa- a pitiful body a—aa—a!
you came a hard road, my love, it was my death,
a hard road, my love, my brother.
And now you must receive me under your roof.
[Force, pp. 79–80].

Electra had nursed her brother in time of death, and in death she now draws him to her. In these words, we recognize the dread gravity of the earth mother.

Overwhelmed by his sister's grief, Orestes reveals his true identity:

ORESTES
A-a! What to say? Among the helpless words,
Which to choose? But I can no longer keep from
words [Force, p. 80].

Woodard claims that here Orestes steps beyond his erga and reaches out to the logos, the physis of his earthbound sister. She in turn is so moved my Orestes that she transcends her own nature and adopts his more action- oriented ideology.

Thus, in an astoundingly modern sense, Orestes and Electra represent two opposing sides of a single personality: Orestes, the rational, political man of action and cunning so valued by the Classical Greek male; and Electra, the more primal, instinctual and volatile female so threatening to the Greek male.

Let us retrace our steps, for a moment, and observe Clytemnestra. As previously noted, the statue of Apollo stands center stage for the duration of this play. It is he who demands our attention, and it is to him that Clytemnestra offers her sacrifice and her self-serving prayer:

CLYTEMNESTRA
I speak as I must; hear thou as I would be heard.
O lord Lycean,
If it was for my good,
That dream of double meaning that I saw this night
Let its fulfillment come; but if for ill,
Then let it fall on those that wish me ill.
If there be any plotting in secret
Against my present welfare, hinder them;
And grant that I may long live safe from harm,
Queen of this life and country,
Living in happiness with those who love me As I live now...
....
Lycean Apollo, graciously hear me,
And grant to us all our desires.
The rest, thou surely knowest, though I be silent.[49]

H.D.F. Kitto directs our attention to Sophocles' use of irony in bringing the tutor on stage, immediately after Clytemnestra's offering, with the false news of Orestes' death. By positioning his scenes in this sequence, the reported death of Orestes seems almost a response to the queen's supplication. In fact, the deception inherent in this news stands in direct correlation to the corruption of Clytemnestra's prayer. Aeschylus' Electra had descended to the spirit of her dead father and there had conjured up Orestes, the hero, to avenge the wrong perpetrated against her household. Here, in sharp contrast to the primitive purity of that earlier play, Sophocles has Clytemnestra offering a hollow prayer—much like that offered two thousand years later in a similar situation by Shakespeare's (Hamlet's) Claudius—and receiving an immediate, dramatic—and ingenuous—response.

Despite the central position, on Sophocles' stage, of Apollo's statue, the onus in this work is on the human players rather than the gods. Aeschylus' gravesite, as sanctuary and as medium for the balance of nature, has gone, replaced by the statue of a rational and cunning god not unlike the Orestes of this play. Like the hero, the god is scheming, yet he has remained the avenging arm of justice. Could Sophocles be asking why?

Electra does not vanish from view at the point of murder, as did Aeschylus' heroine; rather here, the son murders out of sight while the daughter rages on stage, goading her brother into action. Clytemnestra, Electra's mother, cries for mercy from within the palace, "child, child, pity your mother!" while Electra rails in full view of her audience: "But you did not pity him, nor pity his father," and to Orestes, she calls "Strike, if you can, again" (Force, pp. 85–6). After the murder of her mother, to complete the act, Electra orders Aegisthus, "Go in at once. The struggle is not in words/But for your life" (Force, p. 88).

The heroic action of Orestes has liberated Electra from her regressive, repetitive, earthly nature to the action-oriented personality of the sister- helpmate. Death and the central burial ground, which we first saw in Aeschylus' *Libation Bearers*, and which are represented on center stage here by the faux urn of Orestes, are transformed, in Sophocles' play, into the theme of death and resurrection. They are nothing less than the revitalization and the power of Electra herself. Once again, we are witnessing the ancient theme, noted in the previous chapter, of the mythic, dark, chthonic vortex of death and rebirth; yet this time it is not the death and rebirth of the hero, but of Electra, the imprisoned sister helpmate.

What we need to examine now is the nature of Electra's newfound power. What is the dramatic purpose of the heroine's rebirth? What is the nature of the heroine? What is Sophocles' dramatic intention in ending his play with Orestes, the murderer, off-stage, silent and unseen; and with Electra ranting uncontrollably over the corpse of her murdered mother?

Orestes' long absence from his home and his return at the opening of the play still, no doubt, represent, the separation of the adolescent from maternal society and his return and rebirth as hero, yet what kind of hero does he become at the end of this tragedy?

We have seen him presented here as the idealized Hellenic male, as a man of arete—heroic action, of skill and craftiness who, like the heroes of Homer's *Iliad*, is intrepid and unflinching in his desire for revenge and the restitution of family honor. If this is the case, why does he not appear to us at the end of the action, crowned with the laurel of victory?

In a sense, there is no denouement here, for we are given neither pangs of remorse on the part of the murderers nor any sense from the protagonists that the fallen house of Atreus has been reestablished—only the silence of Orestes and the savagery of Electra. Order might have been restored as far as the community (chorus) is concerned, but what has happened to the agents of that order? Matricide, the most primal and awful of deeds, has been perpetrated here.

The play ends with the chilling sight of Electra, un-lyrical and unloving; metamorphosed, in fact, more into the murderous figure of her mother than to any image of liberation. She looms large at center stage over the blood- drenched corpse of Clytemnestra as the chorus chants, perhaps even dances their paean of liberation:

CHORUS
Now for the House of Atreus
Freedom is won
From all her suffering,
And this day's work well done [Watling, p. 117].

"This day's work." What of tomorrow's?

Again, vengeance and murder have risen out of death and despair, bringing in their wake justice against the living. Sophocles' theater has made it painfully and dramatically clear that those who suffer most from such acts of retribution are not the victims, but the victors who are still conscious, who remain with the sword and the blood on their hands. As for the spectators, they have surely been so horrified by the spectacle that they are jolted into their own private, and perhaps separate, reexaminations of the entire issue of vengeance and justice. For, there is no doubt that the spectators have been confronted head-on here by the enormity of murder (no matter what its justification,) and by the moral and psychological price it exacts.

Perhaps, then, it is here (who knows?) for the very first time, that Sophocles has separated justice from morality. For a short moment, the two opposing elements, the male and the female, fuse for action— only to fall forever apart, after their horrendous deed, in what today's post Jacobean audience might recognize as the most Macbethian of manners. This is no Aeschylean ritual by means of which the community of spectators is purged of contradictions. Here, for the first time, the spectators leave the theater at odds with the characters and the action they have just witnessed. It is this contradiction that forces spectators to assess the real purpose of the playwright, and to recognize that in theater the playwright might well be at odds with the very action he (or she) is bringing to life on stage.

Another theatrical theme that begins to emerge in Sophocles' Electra, which we will see later in a much more developed form in the theater of Euripides, is that in which sanity is represented as the voice of the political establishment (the Sophoclean hero is the projection of the Athenian ideal) while madness is represented as the irrepressible expression of the individual conscience—a moral, essentially female voice that is ultimately independent of and even dangerous to publicly sanctioned law and order. In describing the Greek peoples, Kitto writes:

As Attic sculpture and architecture combined Dorian austerity with Ionian grace ... so for a short time Athenian life was able to combine Ionian liberty and individual brilliance with a Dorian sense of discipline and cohesion. [50]

By means of these dualities, Sophocles' art has moved completely from ritual to theater and, as theater, it has become not the centering, religious, ritualistic experience of Aeschylus, but rather its opposite, for it brings to life on stage the destructive force within the soul of the Western human being. It has become the dramatic record of people as de-centered, fragmented beings. In my view, Western theater from this point on becomes a quest for wholeness, an attempt to regain the psychological integrity that had been reached and maintained earlier by means of religious ritual.

As we have seen, the traditional hero is masculine because he is the projection of an all -male fear and an all-male hunger. Perhaps with time, as we move toward a more heterogeneous society, we will be able to reunite the divorced parities of the human being—the male and the female, the passionate and the rational. In a society which recognized the essential interdependence of the male and the female within each individual, we might yet see the hero change, his need for violence and revolution might be mitigated, or—who knows—we might be witness to the disappearance of the hero himself.

Until that time, only the strident, hysterical, female voice of Electra calling on her brother to strike again, to kill their mother without mercy, together with the unspeakable horror of her subsequent silence, is left to reverberate in the minds of the spectators as they leave the theatrical arena, and the "hero" remains speechless throughout his act of vengeance. For him, as Jan Kott points out, as for Hamlet centuries later, the unfathomably painful "silence" of human despair "is all."[51] Until then, the dramatic figure and the human "hero" are as fixed as a Pirandello-like character, condemned to play and replay for all eternity their dramatic roles, to question for all times notions of revenge, jihad (holy war), an eye for an eye, loyalty, personal humanity and morality.

Orestes has emerged as the archetypal hero, as the challenger of the morals of an earlier generation and the herald of those of the next. He embodies the theatrical "raising of issues" which Herbert Blau suggests is the essence of theater, for he is the son reaching maturity, coming into his own vision of life at the moment of his confrontation with the death of his father, and he comes, each time, equipped with the challenge of a new and unwanted moral perspective:

> Side by side in history with the idea of progress is a natural instinct for thinking of advance as an act of recovery. Our most telling compulsion is a loss ... it's also what moves us in theater. [52,53]

---

49 Sophocles, *Electra*, in *Electra and Other Plays*, trans. E.F. Watling (New York: Penguin, 1978), pp. 87–8. Hereafter, quotations from this edition will be indicated by "Watling," and a page number reference, in parentheses or brackets.
50 Thomas Woodard, "The Electra of Sophocles," in *Orestes and Electra*, ed. William M. Force (Boston: Houghton Mifflin, 1968), p. 281.

Hereafter, quotations from this edition will be indicated by "Force," and a page number reference, in parentheses or brackets.

51   H.D.F. Kitto, The Greeks (New York: Penguin, 1986), p. 89.

52   Kott, p. 267.

53   Blau, p. 4.

CHAPTER 3

EURIPIDES: ELECTRA (CA. 400 BCE)

Although younger, Euripides was a contemporary of Sophocles, yet there is a radical difference between the elder poet's treatment of the Electra myth and that of Euripides. The sense of royalty, of ritual and of the avenging dead is absent from the latter. Here we have no palace, and neither altar nor tomb anywhere on stage. The only thing here is the humble shack of a peasant because the subject of this play is not the aristocracy, but the poverty of both society and spirit.

The play opens with the traditional prologue as introduction to the action, but it is delivered, not by a prince and his tutor, a royal messenger, or a chorus (representing the community) but by a single peasant in tattered clothes, owner of the shack, whom the spectators soon learn, no doubt much to their concern, is the husband of princess Electra. Here, for the first time in Western tragedy, aristocracy is wedded to poverty. What is more, this peasant husband demonstrates a personality far more stable and honorable than that of the fallen aristocrat: Though humble, the peasant is generous, levelheaded and loyal. He has natural dignity and compassion. This innovation of Euripides provokes the spectators, to question the nature of nobility itself.

Euripides adds other innovations to the traditional myth. In this play, Aegisthus is aggressively dominant over Clytemnestra. He has placed a price on Orestes' head for his own personal safety, and he has married Electra into penury—not for her wellbeing, but for his own.

For her part, Clytemnestra is a more human, more fully developed version of her Sophoclean counterpart, perpetually tormented by her memories of Iphigenia and by the brutality of Iphigenia's sacrifice at the hands of Agamemnon.

CLYTEMNESTRA
My father Tyndareus gave me to your tender care, Not to kill me, not to kill what I love and loved.
And yet he tempted my daughter, slyly whispering
Of marriage with Achilles, took her from home to Aulis Where the ships were stuck, stretched her high above the fire And, like pale field grass, slashed Iphigenia's throat. [54]

G.M.A. Grube notes that, while Electra appreciates her husband's gentleness and the honorable way in which he has respected her superior status, she is obsessed by self-pity and her desire for revenge. So obsessed, that she turns every facet of life, even something as insignificant as drawing water from the nearby spring, into the issue of Aegisthus, Clytemnestra, and the wrongs they have perpetrated against her. [55]

Electra is portrayed with skilled psychological insight. Her mother has spent her life mourning Iphigenia to the total rejection of her; consequently, the venom of the daughter is directed squarely against the mother. Grube points out that Electra considers her mother the murderer of her father and Aegisthus merely her helpmate; while, for Orestes, Aegisthus is the villain and Clytemnestra an added horror too awful for him to even contemplate. It is for this reason that we see Orestes hesitate before he mentions her. "The condition to which / Aegisthus has reduced me, murdering my father— / He and my fiendish-hearted mother." It is made quite clear, in this version of the myth, in contrast to the plays of Aeschylus and Sophocles, not only that Aegisthus and Clytemnestra were equal partners in crime, but that, since that time, Clytemnestra's paramour has assumed the position of dominant, repressive, masculine authority and has taken full command over her and her entire household. In this play, Clytemnestra is reduced to a pathetic picture of uncertainty and remorse.

Euripides skillfully guides his spectators to the source of their social and moral sickness. He presents the female onstage at her most neurotic and impoverished state, and as the dramatic personification of the deepest and most repressed fears of the Athenian male. Again, in this way, theater has become the physical embodiment of underlying social and psychological problems. Euripides' Electra is neurotic, unbalanced, and self-pitying. She exaggerates her degradation to the point that she seems to revel in her poverty and her troubles. In fact, she has the arrested development of one who has been caught in a cataclysmic disaster. Her husband begs her not to draw water from the well, but she insists. Yet later she tells the guest, whom she doesn't recognize as her brother, that she was forced to draw water. In like manner, she refuses to accompany the chorus of supportive young women to the festival of Hera, preferring to cling to her own misery, only to complain to the stranger that she is barred from any revelry or festivities. Grube claims that the reasons Electra gives for wanting to murder her mother, and the order in which she gives them, betray her self-interest and her confused sense of priorities, for first she complains about her own misery, then she compares her wretchedness with the wealth and glory of her mother, and only finally does she mention the desecrated condition of her father's grave.

Orestes sees the unsuspecting Electra returning from the spring and hears her lament out-loud about her parentage and her stolen heritage. Besides the obvious dramatic convenience of this scene in terms of providing information for Orestes, it reveals the perverse, self-interested nature of the heroine. In addition, Grube draws our attention to the fact that when Electra first senses the presence of strangers, she is thrown into a complete frenzy of fear, hysterically calling to the chorus to run for their lives, although there doesn't seem to be any other indication of danger, and the other women on stage are perfectly calm. Later, after the murder of Aegisthus, without listening to reason, Electra is again seized by panic—this time almost to the point of suicide. For sure, this protagonist is unreliable and emotionally unbalanced. When asked by the stranger what Orestes should do, Electra reveals herself as a veritable virago, eager and ready to murder her mother herself:

When I have shed
her blood to requite this, then I shall die content [102].

Euripides' play is a starkly realistic portrayal of a loveless and deranged woman. She is manic—even fiendish, yet pathetic in her manipulation of Orestes and Clytemnestra. The fact that Electra's mother had saved her life by persuading Aegisthus to marry her to a peasant means nothing to her.

Similarly, though she knows Clytemnestra cares enough to come to her should she give birth, Electra cruelly toys with her mother's efforts to make peace. Sadistically, she lures her mother into her hut for the ultimate sacrifice.

ELECTRA
Please come in,
to our poor house. Take care this smoky wall does not dirty your dress.
Now you shall offer to the gods the sacrifice that is due. [56]

Hungry for vengeance to the last, this Electra directs her brother's reluctant sword, and drives it home.

Reader: Imagine this case brought before today's Western, twenty-first century court of law. Would Electra get the death penalty? Would Orestes? How about Clytemnestra?

As we've seen, Euripides' Electra is a far cry from that of Aeschylus or Sophocles. No longer is she the fledgling hero, nor is she the female spirit of remembrance. Rather, she is the tortured, twisted, misshapen image of a female principle gone awry—repressed, in fact, into the very image of death and destruction. Hers is the insanity of one who is given over entirely to vengeance. Only the most extreme act of violence can exorcise the hatred by which this Electra is possessed.

Indeed, after the murder, her venom is abated:

ELECTRA
Tears, my brother, let tears be endless.
I am guilty
I was burning with desperate rage against her [126]

Do the purging and the tears bring promise of new life, or do they emphasize the pathos of this now wasted shell of humanity? The end of tragedy is independent of happiness or grief. If at all, it consists, as Northrop Frye maintains, in the correction of an imbalance of nature:

CHORUS
Your mind has returned to itself.
And blows now with the wind of truth [126].

Only now, Electra is released from the stranglehold of hatred, able to recognize, too late, way too late, what love and normal life has to offer.

ELECTRA:
Oh, what shall I do?
Where shall I go?
What happy company will welcome me?
To a dance or a wedding? [126].

The denouement of this play brings us back to the words of Joseph Campbell when talking of the nature of myths, and the manner with which people cling to them:

preferring even to make life a hell for themselves and their neighbors in the name of some violent god, to accepting gracefully the bounty the world affords? [57]

For Orestes, matricide has brought about recognition and reversal.

ORESTES
O, Phoebus, in the command of your oracle justice was hidden from me.;
but in its fulfillment
you have made torment clear [126].

Tragedy is born out of a world that is off-kilter; that has lost its bearings. It works its way through suffering, death and destruction, to a point of awareness, reversal, and a world that regains its balance.

Do Orestes' words reflect such a reckoning, balance, the regaining of a lost center? It would seem, from the quote just cited, that matricide has made "torment clear," nothing more; that, having fulfilled the will of Apollo with no understanding whatsoever of how vengeance was connected to justice, his present kinship to evil is all too clear. They are his burden, his torment from here on out.

Perhaps our emphasis should not be on "torment," but on "clear." Can our hero see the futility and the evil—the very nature—of murder clearly now that the deed is done? Has he gained an understanding of evil and its claim on him that he would never have had without having done the deed? Is this in fact the "wisdom" Aeschylus' chorus had referred to when he'd claimed that wisdom is gained through suffering? Clearly, nothing could have prevented Orestes from murdering his mother once the idea was set in motion. Is wisdom, for Orestes, found in the awful clarity of what he has just done; in the torment of having to look evil in the face for all eternity and claim it as his own; in living day in, day out, with the atrocity he has committed?

How genuine, how modern and recognizable is this?

The gods (with a small "g") are forces of irrational violence and instruments of torture. Only through suffering does the hero gain insight and a measure of wisdom. The will of the gods, not the wellbeing of mankind, is carried out in tragedy.

I am writing this work as Isis fighters swarm across the Middle East, torturing and beheading, wreaking havoc, leaving death, devastation, widows and orphans in their wake—fighting, they claim, in the name of Allah, against the moral corruption of the Infidel. What furies hold these men—boys mostly—hostage to the extent that they cannot be appeased until they've wrought murder and mayhem in the hundreds and thousands; until they've pillaged vast terrains, left devastation, rubble and nothingness in their wake?

What force could have shifted the worlds of lone killers so off kilter that only murder (including their own) will set them free? Which furies are these that squat in the brains of empty-eyed boys and grizzly old men in the countries of the West, that only carnage and their own death will release them?

If not for the excessive repression of the more lyrical, spontaneous aspects within the soul of the Greek male of the Classical period, a repression dramatized so explosively in Euripides' play, the Bacchae; if not for the repression of those aspects, dramatically characterized as "female," there might have been little or no need for the downfall of the ancient Greek world. Female characters, in the plays we have studied so far, are dramatic representations of a flaw, recognized by these playwrights, as the result of an uncompromisingly male society. The female spirit of survival, the need for revenge on the part of the rejected female world of fifth-century Athens, BCE, as represented by Electra, is the protagonist's *hamartia*. It is the violently repressed female that threatens the Greek male with destruction. The chorus which, at the beginning, had been so supportive of Electra, now recognizes the enormous danger to society that she epitomized:

CHORUS
Dear Electra, you did a dreadful wrong to your brother,
Forcing him against his will [216–7].

As for the Euripidean hero, the act of matricide has propelled him into an altered state of consciousness. For the individually maturing adolescent, as for the dawn of civilization, the destruction of the maternal represents the beginning of reality, the birth of tragic experience. Orestes says, "Avenging him I am pure; but killing her, condemned." The paradoxical nature of the human conscience, one that experiences simultaneously two contradictory needs and which we see emerging for the first time in this play, is the nature of the hero. More: Orestes' actions afford him consciousness—awareness that he stands apart and estranged from the world of matter by which he is surrounded, and that he is guilty.

The aspect of Euripides' theater that is brought home most forcefully, is the change of heart experienced by the perpetrator of violence. It is as though the poet were trying to dramatize for his spectators, the aftermath of their wars and the mourning they will have to endure. Euripides' play ends with the keening of both protagonists and chorus over their wasted lives and their denied humanity.

CHORUS
Wretched, miserable woman! How could you bear
To see with your own eyes
Your mother gasping out her life?

ORESTES
I held my cloak over my eyes, while with my sword I performed
Sacrifice, driving the blade into my mother's throat.

ELECTRA
And I urged you on,
And held the sword, my hand beside yours

CHORUS
Could any act be more dreadful? [127].

Orestes, the gentle hero, forced against his natural inclinations into the most brutal form of murder is now exiled, separated from his newfound sister/partner:

ORESTES
And now the love that I need from you
Is taken away.
I love you, and you love me [130].

Like Cain in Genesis, the conscious, guilty hero is banished. Only Pylades, his mute and constant companion, shadow of his spirit and his will, remains behind to marry Electra. Here, in a supreme act of poetic fantasy, the freed captive merges with the unexpressed loyalty and love of the hero. Orestes' inner, spiritual life is imaginatively fused and balanced with his earthly, feminine counterpart. To my mind, this romantic union represents Euripides' hope for the future of his city-states. It is what Carl Jung called the *hieros gamos*, the sacred marriage of opposites, the one union guaranteed to produce perfect offspring. To the modern audience, it is reminiscent of Faust's or even Goethe's own imaginative evocation of Helen and Paris as the perfect union, representative of the highest feats of Goethe's creative creativity. Ironically, the Romantic poet himself was incapable of maintaining an image of such perfection. It was the male flaw, the grasping intrusion of Goethe's own ego that had (for him) destroyed any promise of such and ideal. Euripides? He does not intrude onto his vision. He merely proposes it as a utopian cure for the ills of his generation while maintaining throughout a clear-eyed assessment of reality.

Euripides: Orestes (408 BCE)

Again, let us remember how, in Aeschylus' plays, the mound of the dead hero had been center-stage, altar-like, the central focus of everyone's attention. Here, however—as in Euripides' Electra—the gravesite is conspicuously absent, for the central focus is not the spirit of the dead hero, but the suffering man.

In this play, the Orestean figure is essentially moral man torn by conflicting ideologies, by irreconcilable moral codes, by the discrepancy between the personal and the public good, and by his loyalties to both the male and the female within the social structure. Here Orestes enjoys the full support of the loving sister-helpmate. Ultimately however, the action is his, and he is a victim of the gods.

ORESTES
You, I know, consented
In word, but it was I who shed our mother's blood.
I blame Apollo; he urged me to this hideous act,
Encouraged me with promises—and did nothing.
I believe my father, had I asked him face to face
Whether I ought to kill her, would have gripped my hand
And begged, implored me not to lift my hand against
My mother, since that could not bring him back to life,
While it doomed me to the agonies I now endure.[58]

The Euripidean hero wishes to do the right thing but is misdirected by the gods, by forces propelled more by an amoral impulse akin to that of physis— nature, than by any consideration of the human being. It is experience that drags the hero into disaster. Insight is not granted him until after the fact, until after his irrevocable act of violence.

ORESTES
The gods have not spared me; I sink in agonies.

MENELAOS
What agonies? What is the disease that ravages you?

ORESTES
Conscience. I recognize the horror of what I did [313].

The Euripidean hero learns his lesson too late. It will be interesting to compare this hero with that of Shakespeare when we reach the Jacobean period, for there we shall see how progress, achieved by the man of a more modern consciousness than his forebears, exists in the fact that the Jacobean hero is granted insight before the deed; that he is, in fact, ravaged by pangs of conscience even as he begins to contemplate the horrors he has to face:

GHOST (of Hamlet's father)
But, howsoever thou pursuest this act,
Taint not thy mind, nor let thy soul contrive
Against thy mother aught. Leave her to heaven,
And to those thorns that in her bosom lodge
To prick and sting her. [59]

In Euripides' Orestes, the hero's feeble state is dramatized by means of his sickbed and, in a manner not unlike Clove's stage position in Beckett's Endgame, the ailing Orestes is propped up at the center of his stage and his world:

ELECTRA
There is not fate so terrifying to describe,
No bodily pain or heaven-sent cruelty so sharp,
Which human flesh may not be destined to endure [301].

If there is the suggestion of a panacea for human suffering, it is in humanism, in the role of the friend, and it is surely for this reason that, at this point, for the first time, Pylades assumes an active, verbal part in his play. If there is a character in this play of heroic stature, it is surely Pylades who lives and is willing to die for his friend. In contrast, Menelaos' treachery consists of his unwillingness to commit himself to a cause. As Orestes tells him:

ORESTES
Friends who in times of trouble are no longer friends
Mock the true force of friendship with an empty name [316].

The Greek city-states were famous for their self-government and for the lengthy legal debates in which all male factions of society were encouraged to participate and in which all sides of an argument were granted equal exposure. Euripides seems to be deliberately manipulating both the Athenian passion for justice and its love of debate for his own dramatic purpose:

MESSENGER
Well, now, I saw a stream.
Of people going to take their place on that hill, where
They say, Danaus first called a council of citizens
When brought to trial by Egyptus. So, seeing this
crowd I asked someone, "What news in Argos? What has
put the city of Danaus in a flutter? Is there a war?"
"Look," said he, "Don't you see Orestes there, coming
to stand trial for his life?"
When the full roll of citizens was present, a herald
Stood up and said, "Who wishes to address the court?
To say whether or not Orestes ought to die
For matricide?" At this, Talthybius rose, who was
Your father's colleague in the victory over Troy. ...
Next there stood up a man with a mouth like a
running spring ... an enrolled citizen, yes, yet
No Argive;
...
... His words seemed sensible
To honest judges; and there were no more speeches.
Then,
Your brother rose
In your defense, no less than in my father's cause,
I killed my mother, for if wives may kill husbands
And not be guilty, you had all best lose no time,
But lie today, before your wives
make slaves of you [331–3].

By now, we are familiar with Orestes' misogynist argument, yet here it no longer represents the unanimous view of the people. Euripides is appealing to the reason-loving, democratic Athenians, for whom reality implies a great deal more complexity than the comfort of a narrow, bigoted perspective. To my mind, the point of the play is that there is no single argument, no right or wrong. Human experience is multi-faceted and the social being is caught in a web of ambiguities. We are presented with the arguments of all the disputants because this play is a trial, and the audience has become both judge and jury.

In a similar manner, the characters of Euripides are neither innocent nor evil. Rather, they assume the contradictory perspectives of opposing ideologies. Let us look at the way Orestes' messenger describes the following scene:

MESSENGER
Pylades and Orestes walking side by side
Your brother's head bowed, his frame shattered by disease Pylades
like a brother
sharing all his pain,
Tending his sickness, guiding and supporting him [331].

And now at the very different way Helen's Phrygian slave describes the same two friends:

PHRYGIAN SLAVE
The twin Hellenic lions,
One was the son of the famous general;
The other was a bad-hearted man,
The son of Strophius, A man like Odysseus,
who deceives you and says nothing,
A bold fighter, loyal to his friends,
A shrewd soldier and a bloodthirsty monster.
Curse him for his smooth treachery—
He was up to no good! [349–50].

And Menelaos from yet another perspective:

MENELAOS
They tell me frightful news of violence perpetrated
By those two strange animals—I won't call them men (355).

Heroism to one is treachery; to another, it is honorable. From the point of view of Pylades, Helen's murder is justified,

PYLADES
Helen's death
Brings satisfaction to all Helas—to everyone
Whose son, or father, she destroyed, and every wife
She made a widow [340].

while from the perspective of her husband and daughter, it is the most despicable of deeds. Influenced by the contradictory but equally persuasive perspectives of both sides, our own views vacillate together with those of the chorus. The chorus consists of women who are first indoctrinated by the dominant male ideology:

CHORUS
The daughter of tyndareos who has disgraced her sex, deserves the
loathing of women everywhere [352].

yet are then so easily swayed by the horrifying report of the
Phrygian slave.

CHORUS
What of the other Phrygians in the palace?
Could they not help? Where were they? [352].

No emotion is constant. The impressive and no-doubt authentic
display of honor that Orestes exhibits in the face of death,

ORESTES
Come, sister, let the manner of our dying show
That we are royal and worthy of Agamemnon's line.
I'll show all Argos what nobility is, driving
My sword home to the heart; with equal courage
You must do the same. Be umpire of our rival deaths,
Pylades, and wrap our dead bodies decently;
And take us both and bury us in our father's grave
Goodbye. I'm going now to do what must be done [337].

disintegrates all too quickly into a mean-spirited cunning:

PYLADES
Let's kill Helen—and send Menelaos raving mad.

ORESTES
How can we do it? I'm ready, if the plan will work [339].

The manner with which these friends scheme the deception,
capture, and murder of Helen and Hermione—both in this instance
defenseless, trusting women—is a far cry from the masculine cunning
that was so idealized in Sophocles' play. Here nothing is absolute.
The ideal takes on different connotations in different circumstances
while heroism shifts into expediency.

This play seems to be Euripides' reaction to a failed heroic world,
to a world in which civilization, torn between absolutes, between
contradictory idealized behavior patterns, becomes self-destructive:

ORESTES
I know I am a polluted man—

I killed my mother. But that is not the sole truth
I avenged my father; and for that act I am pure [319].

The world of the Greek Arete hero believed in the unflinching pursuit of absolutes: honor that must be avenged, and murder that must be punished. Ironically, it was also a world that thrust the hero into a realm of experience totally alien to that of the ideal; that bound him on a rack of moral ambivalence from which there was no release. Aristotle condemned Euripides' Orestes for its lack of heroic consistency and for its escapist, deus ex machina ending. Yet to me it seems that this ending is a deliberate, ironic demonstration of the poet's practical realism, of his belief that only the impossible intrusion of the gods into men's lives can mitigate the self- imposed polarities of a failed heroic ideal.

As in Aeschylus' *Libation Bearers* the protagonists pray to the spirit of their dead father before embarking on their act of violence. Yet, by means of the democratic judicial system that has characterized the game so far, the spectators in this latter play are separated from the emotional and moral stance of the characters. Is the grave of the father on stage calling into the empty air? Are the actors? An altar to the gods is no doubt present here, but we have already pointed out the possible ironic implications of Apollo's last- minute intervention. Unlike the earlier play, these characters undertake the ancient liturgy without the undivided support of the community of spectators. In fact, this supplication, together with Orestes' later attempted murder of Helen and his attack on Hermione, seems to be an indication of the moral depravity into which the hero's initial experience of violence has plunged him. Orestes' prayer is glaringly modern in its manipulation of the gods and of the "noble cause" for the justification of violence:

ORESTES
My father, swelling in the shadowy halls of night,
Your son Orestes calls on you. We need your help;
Come now and save us! For your sake I am condemned
Unjustly. Though my act was righteous. I am deserted
By Menelaos; now I intend to take his wife
And kill her. Be our helper in this enterprise!

ELECTRA
Father, your children call on you. If, from your grave
You hear us, come! We die for our loyalty to you.

ORESTES
I killed my mother—

ELECTRA
Father, your children call on you. If from your grave
You hear us, come! We die for our loyalty to you.

ORESTES
I killed my mother—

ELECTRA
My hand too was on the sword

ORESTES
For offerings, receive my tears—

ELECTRA
My cries of grief.

PYLADES
Cease now; let's to the work at once. If prayers can thrust, Like javelins, through the deep earth, Agamemnon hears —Grant, Zeus, our ancestor, and holy Justice, grant To Orestes, and his sister, and to me, success! [343].

Throughout the act, the opposing arguments of the play have mounted to the point of extreme dramatic opposition: purity of action versus purity of heart. Euripides utilizes the ancient tragic form of stichomythia to create theatrical dialectics of the honor system.

MENELAOS
You would perform the sacred cleansing—?

ORESTES
And why not?

MENELAOS
Sacrifice victims before battle?

ORESTES
And would you be worthier?

MENELAOS
Yes; my hands are clean.

ORESTES
Your heart's corrupt [357].

The above is an opposition that counteracts, once and for all, the effectiveness of community ritual.

In addition, Euripides manipulates the ritualistic form of stichomythia for his own highly ritualistic, dramatic purpose—to demonstrate the mounting anxiety of Electra and her chorus of women—at the moment of murder:

ELECTRA
I am afraid that someone standing to watch the palace Might discover this murder,
And make disaster even more disastrous.

SEMI-CHORUS I
Come on, let's be quick;
I'll go here and watch the highway
Looking towards the sunrise.

SEMI-CHORUS II
And I'll watch seaward, along this path.

ELECTRA
Turn your eyes this way and that.

SEMI-CHORUS I
We are looking from left to right,
Then behind us, as you ask.

SEMI-CHORUS II
Who is that on the road? Look hard; who is it?
Some countryman prowling round your palace.

ELECTRA
Friends, this will destroy us!
At any moment he will betray us to our enemies!

SEMI-CHORUS II
Don't be afraid; you were mistaken, the road is empty.

ELECTRA
What of your side? Is all safe still?
Give us a welcome report
If all's safe over there, facing the courtyard

SEMI CHORUS I
All's clear on our side; keep a watch on yourself

ELECTRA
Wait, now—I am going to listen at the door.
You in the house there!
Why do you take so long?...
When will you blood the sacrifice?
—They aren't listening. O gods, what misery! [344].

The drama, the dramatic technique quoted here, cannot but whip spectators into a frenzy of anxiety.

Again, in this play, an imbalance has come about in what should have been a natural harmony between the feminine and the masculine. The feminine life principle we had recognized in Electra's nurturing of her brother is again being sacrificed to the "masculine" principle of violence and cunning. Thus, when she reveals her blood-curdling scheme to Orestes and Pylades, Electra is greeted with the accolade:

ORESTES
Oh, what a manly spirit and resolve shines out
From your weak woman's body! You deserve to live, Not die! Pylades,
this is the wife you'll die to lose,
Or live to win as a rich blessing on your house [342].

If it were not for the forced, artificial wedding of victim and victimizer that takes place here under the unlikely instigation of the gods, the lives of both Electra and Orestes would be irrevocably consecrated to death and destruction. The pathetic attempt of the protagonists to unite on the brink of their own deaths is their attempt to simulate a wholeness of life attained only by means of union of the feminine with the masculine, the union of the nurturing and the loving with action. Electra's infusion of love into Orestes robs him of what he has identified as his "manly" capacity for violence:

ELECTRA
My dearest! Oh, my darling brother! How I love

To call you my own brother! Our two hearts are one.

ORESTES
Oh, you will melt my firmness. Yes. I must hold you
In my most loving arms—come! Why should I feel shame?
Body to body—thus, let us be close in love.
Say 'brother,' sister! These dear words can take the place Of children,
marriage— to console our misery.

ELECTRA
...I wish one sword might kill us,
one carved in cedar wood receive us both. [60]

In the first chapter of this book, we had identified the bark of the tree or the coffin as a prehistoric Egyptian symbol of death and rebirth. Here, by means of their union in death, our divided protagonists aspire to rebirth as one integrated being. For it is only when the masculine and the feminine principles are united—when they are not divorced from each other by means of their blind dedication to violence—that they can hope for normalcy. Only the fusion of the masculine and the feminine can bring about the birth of a nation dedicated to life.

---

54 Euripides, Electra, in David Greene and Richmond Lattimore,
    Euripides V (Chicago: University of Chicago Press, 1959), p. 53.
55 Force, p. 96.
56 Force, p. 124.
57 Joseph Campbell, Primitive Mythology: The Masks of God
    (New York: Penguin, 1987), p. 4.
58 Euripides' Orestes, pp. 310 and 313.
59 William Shakespeare, Hamlet, ed. Louis B. Wright
    (New York: Washington Square Press, 1958), p. 29.
60 Euripides' Orestes, p. 337.

CHAPTER 4

SHAKESPEARE: HAMLET (1601)

At the beginning of this study, we suggested that the origins of the Electra myth lay in ancient fertility rites and, by means of the symbolic expression of those rites, in the murder of the male by the matriarch and the incorporation of his body into the mother earth for the purpose of fertility.

We suggested that, in patriarchal times, the focus of the murder was transformed primarily into that of the female (mother) by the avenging male (son), itself the story of what many believe was the patriarchal takeover of earlier matriarchal, mystic religions. Finally, the story became that of the repressed female (Electra) as emblem of the stifled emotional life of a people and its desperate attempt to be liberated and incorporated into some vision of the future. At times, it almost seems as though Sophocles and Euripides were warning their generations of violence that ensues as a result of the artificial separation of the male and female principles within both the individual Athenian male and the state.

Ancient Athens experienced enormous military, political, and social expansion. It is believed that, prior to the Dorian invasions the Ionian people had enjoyed an autochthonic identity; a sense of individual, rural freedom that found expression in artistic forms and in mystical practice. Between the end of the Mycenaean and the beginning of the Hellenic era lay vast, unrecorded, "dark" ages. In this study, history started as Athens became the center of the maritime league of nation states, Hellenic ruler of the known world, and institutor of organized, national religion. It was a Greece in which Protagoras could proudly proclaim the human as the measure of all things, yet which, in many ways, still clung to old, half intuited, half-forgotten superstitions and forms of mystical expression. Though empire building was antithetical to the Greek concept of self- government, by fifth-century BCE, Athens had become an empire in spirit, size and stature if not in political reality. Conquest, foreign rule, expansion and constant warfare forced the fiercely independent nation states of soldier- statesmen to resort to the hiring of mercenary soldiers and paid military officials. As Athenian power expanded it became increasingly difficult for its citizen-statesmen to maintain a balance between the polarities of their existence: urban versus rural living; political, military and social action versus personal reflection; ambition and self-confidence versus faith in supernatural forces. Contradictions such as these, which lay at the very core of the Athenian personality, reflect the oppositions that existed between the more emotional, mystical and lyrical nature of the indigenous Ionians, and the reason and order loving Hellenes. Indeed, these same polarities were recognizable in the figures of Apollo, male god of reason and order, versus Dionysus (Bacchus) god of wine, sensuality and emotion. Then again, the male-female opposition was repeated over and over in the characters of Greek theater.

A necessary balance between the two was essential for the spiritual and psychological well-being of the ancient Greeks, but that had disintegrated as they moved from a god-centered to a man-centered world.

In a period of a hundred years, as evidenced by works such as Aeschylus' *Oresteia*, Sophocles' *Oedipus*, and Euripides' *Hippolytus*, Greece progressed from a rural people that had placed implicit trust in the supremacy and omnipotence of the gods, to a nation of at least semi-urban humanists, sophists, and philosophers. All entertained grave doubts about the omniscience of their deities and even graver doubts about the nature, power and position of humans within their universe. It may be correct to assume that, by the end of the fifth-century BCE, foreign rule, expansion and constant wars had plunged the Athenian hero into a state of self-doubt, despair and existential confusion.

It might well be argued that to read Shakespeare's Hamlet (the source of which can be traced to a thirteenth-century Latin history of the Danes) as a play that conforms to the deep-structure of the Electra myth, is to invite endless such free associations. This might well be. However, I wish to propose that, indeed, Hamlet's structure, together with the sociological background that fostered it, teased an Orestes/Electra constellation into theatrical reality.

L.C. Knight describes Renaissance society:

> Social organization was marked by three general characteristics; the close connection of the whole population to the soil, the large corporate or cooperative element in the life of the people; and the extent to which the whole structure rested upon custom not upon either established law or written contract. [61]

He describes the Renaissance social structure as one of different self- supporting, self-sufficient village communities, which were ruled not by edict, but by social reciprocity and mutual caring. Knight claims, for example, that village guilds cared for the needs of those members who had fallen on hard times and that villagers would raise funds for burials, for the marriages of young girls or for their confinement into convents. The peasants, he maintains, had a reciprocal, universally accepted, stable and mutual—if grossly unbalanced—relationship with their feudal lords. Knight claims that citizens had not yet developed a sense of national concern, that attention was focused still on village and on small town life. This does not mean, of course, that life was idyllic. England was subject to bouts of plague, high infant mortality, feudal strife, superstition, and religious persecutions. Despite these horrors, the peasants shared a common understanding of God and knew their place and purpose in their world.

Like Athens of the fifth century, BCE, England enjoyed enormous prosperity, expansion, and a booming trade during Elizabeth's reign. America was discovered, and American gold was introduced into Europe. England plundered exotic riches—spices and jewels from the Indies and the Orient. Drake undertook his first expedition in

1573 and from it he brought back enough wealth that England was able to free herself from her many overseas creditors and invest as much as 42,000 English pounds in what was to become famous as the East Indies Company. With increased wealth came increased expansion and the need for further conquests and discoveries; with increased expansion, in turn, came increased spending. England was involved in more foreign wars during the reigns of Elizabeth and King James that at any previous time in her history and, as she hired mercenary soldiers, she had an ever-increasing need for funds. Money-lending syndicates emerged and were the cause of the first growth of capitalism in England. With wealth and prosperity came a new class of moneymakers, a blurring of class distinctions and a sense of loss and social confusion on the part of the peasants and the aristocracy alike. With capitalism came gross materialism, questionable ethics, and subjective morality.

Like Greece at her height of power, Renaissance confidence was built on the knowledge that "man" stood securely at the center of his universe and that the earth turned at the center of the cosmic hierarchy (in the case of the Renaissance—with woman at his side, God and the angels above, animals, then vegetation beneath.) Copernicus' contradiction shattered the very foundation of human faith and left people floundering in disorder. To this confusion, Machiavelli added his own profoundly disturbing influence. Not only did he instantly propel humankind into modernity with his objective, scientific approach to the field of politics, but, by separating each aspect of reality from the collective whole and subjecting it to its own independent criteria and moral code, he also demonstrated the subjectivity and the fragmentation of all knowledge. By means of his theory of political expediency, Machiavelli destroyed all sense of global harmony and objective meaning. In short, his contribution to society, his "enlightenment," lay in his demonstration that unity in human experience is an allusion. It simply does not exist. From Machiavelli to our own time, Reality is fragmented into myriad, independent areas of experience. It is the fragmentation of knowledge itself.

No facet of reality was exempt from disintegration. Universal belief in the Church as guardian of the mysteries of Hell and Eternity and as the medium for the salvation of the soul was itself under attack by Martin Luther's theory of personal redemption. Morality, until then an objective matter of right and wrong, was now reduced to a personal, invisible struggle in the privacy of each human's very questionable soul. The subjection of religion to the political arena of the Reformation with its incumbent cruelties and persecutions, and the need for the Roman Church to defend itself by means of the Council of Trent, all combined to bring about the disintegration of the Renaissance spirit.

As with Greek theater, the art of the late Elizabethan and Jacobean periods reflects a restlessness of the human soul, a sense that the world and the individual are inextricably intertwined, and an impression that the individual is constantly confronted by oppositions within the human spirit. Protagonists of Shakespeare's "dark" plays—Lear, Macbeth, Hamlet and Othello—are riddled with such oppositions, with the conflict between their public and their private selves, and with the need to satisfy their immediate desires while transcending the smallness of their natures. As with the Greek playwrights, Shakespeare provides a mirror of people perpetually struggling against the dualities and complexities inherent to their inner selves.

Like Classical Greece, England in the Renaissance and Jacobean periods was essentially a male-dominated society with relatively rigid ideas regarding the appropriate status and demeanor of women. Linda Woodbridge supplies us with the following quotes together with her own commentary:

(As a man should) showe a certain manliness full and steadye, so doeth it well in a woman to have a tenderness, soft and milde, with a kinde of womanlie sweetnes in everye gusture—that in goyng, standinge and speakinge … may always make her appeere a woman without anye liknes of man. It is not comlye for a woman to practise feates of armes, ridinge, playinge at tenise, wrastling, and manye other thynges that belonge to men.

Yet, though men might want to keep their womenfolk gentle and soft- spoken, underlying many of the writings of the time was the fear that, in actuality, their true nature was sexual, wild and untamable:

Emonge them of olde time the maner was that women wrastled naked with men, but we have lost this good custome. [62]

Of the author of this quote, Woodbridge writes:

Aretino is an early practitioner of a tactic familiar in our own day— the insinuation that women who interest themselves in masculine pursuits are mainly desirous of gang rape.

Men of the Elizabethan period seemed fairly confident that:

Generallye everye woman wisheth she were a man, by a certain provocation of nature, that teacheth her to wishe for her perfection. [63]

Yet there are also those who defended woman, believing that if she did wish to be like a man, it was so

,,,that she might be free from the filthinesse whiche men did force her to ... like as ye little chicke being caught by the kyte, would wish with all his heart hee were a kite, and yet the kind of kites is not to be thought better then of the chicken. [64]

The following question from Tasso bears an uncanny resemblance to the misogynistic writings of the ancient Greeks:

If thou marry one that is faire, she will grow to be common: If one that is fowle, she will waxe loathsome. If (she) should chaunce to be good ... must I loose her.... If shee should be badde, I must beare with her perforce ... and if shee be faire, I must keep a watch and guard ouer her. [35]

and with the following quotation from Tasso we arrive full circle back to the mentality of the Classical Athenian male and recognize that the need of Renaissance man to confine his female counterpart to social niceties was not much more than the expression of his overwhelming fear of female otherness:

an unworthy and contemptible thing is a woman ... not framed for any other respect or use, then for a Receptacle of some of our Ex-cremental humors; standing vs in the same steed, as the Bladder, the Gaull, and such other uncleanly members of our bodie.

Woman, argues Tasso,

...is under the moon's pernicious influence, as evidence by disgusting physical attributes—menstration, thick phlegm, "driuling spettle," "smoking vapors coming from the stomach." [66]

Among the characteristics of the art of this period that resembles the art of Classical Greece, is the sense of enormous human vitality, of explosive passion and human will so volatile, it threatens to burst the seams of reality. And so, once more, in a society in which women are lauded for their pliability, their discretion, their devotion to their husbands, their humility, piety and chastity, we have a theater of Amazons, of sexually rapacious women, and women as passionate, strong and centered as The Duchess of Malfi who, in the midst of sexual and political perversion, violence and madness, staunchly clings to her sanity and sense of self; of women as ruthless and deceptive as Beatrice in Middleton's *The Changeling*; as corruptible as Bianca, in Middleton's *Women Beware Women*; as ruthless as Vittoria, in Webster's *The White Devil*; and as sensuously gullible as Mistress Frankford in Thomas Heywood's *A Woman Killed with Kindness*.

With humanism and the disintegration of the Renaissance spirit, theater returns to the tragic form, for tragedy is the expression of a society that has lost its religious optimism, its belief that ultimately God will save. Madness, as common a feature in Jacobean tragedy as in the ancient Greek form, is the result of a failed idealism; as such it becomes the one remaining vehicle of expression for Hamlet.

The Greek Orestes was told by Apollo to avenge the murder of his father and, despite the torment he later underwent, he found no reason to doubt the nature and authority of his god. Indeed, in Aeschylus' play, the spirit of the father entered into the son propelling him into the heroic and tragic action, and setting him, from that moment and for all time, as a figurehead by which to measure revenge, honor, justice and public versus private conscience. But while Hamlet has no qualms about the absolute quality of evil and knows beyond all doubt that regicide and murder must be avenged, his seventeenth- century god is silent and the ghost of his father questionable. Because by the time of the well Christianized society of the seventeenth century, the forces of good and evil that had comprised the dual nature of the Greek gods have been split into God and the Devil and need to be assessed for their validity. The Aeschylean ghost, granted so prominent a place at the center of the ancient Greek stage, and conjured with skill and deliberation until it took possession of the prime mourner, forces itself on to the outermost perimeter of the Shakespearean stage, at the "very witching time of night," [67] when the spirit of the unconscious and of human conscience tug at the innermost recesses of the mind.

Hamlet is much like the Orestean-serpent of Clytemnestra's dream, filled with ambiguity and with the ambivalence of the mother- or father-son relationship. Uncertainty is like a growth surfacing in the corner of an "enlightened" mind, threatening it with eclipse.

Hamlet's ghost is not only a phenomenon of the otherness of the spirit, but a manifestation of anxiety that has characterized modern man since the seventeenth century.

HAMLET

Be thou a spirit of health or a goblin damned,
Bring with thee airs from heaven or blasts from hell,
Be thy intents wicked or charitable,
Thou com'st in such a questionable shape [1.4.44–47].

The ghost appears on stage shrouded in the mist of the confused and questioning mind.

Here there is no central burial mound, no circular arena. Actors and spectators are not possessed by their dead; rather, their dead need to be tested. There is, in fact, a conspicuous absence of a mourning space and of ritual in the court of Claudius, the secular king. The ghost is always off-center, on the parapet of the castle or in the bedroom, forcing itself into the mind, into the world of dream or fantasy, because the spiritual and the abstract are not accorded space in this society. The ghost is at once desired and pitied, yet he is also the source of the most profound fears. He has many of the dangerous complexities of the ancient Greek gods and ancestors, yet the seventeenth century mind needs to assess it, to apply reason and define it.

HAMLET
Let me not burst in ignorance, but tell
Why thy canonized bones, hearsed in death,
Have burst their cerements, why the sepulchre
Wherein we see you quietly interred
Has oped his ponderous and marble jaws
To cast thee up again. What may this mean
That thou, dread corse, again in complete steel
Revisits thus the glimpses of the moon,
Making night hideous, and we fools of nature
So horribly to shake our disposition
With thoughts beyond the reaches of our souls?
Say why is this? Wherefore?
What should we do? [1.4. 50—51].

Protestant England, and the Anglican Church which served
Elizabeth the Protestant queen, regarded ghosts as devils that surface
periodically from hell in order to wreak harm and destruction on
the dreamer. Purgatory was part of the Catholic belief system.
It was a waiting room in which souls could be cleansed on their
way to heaven. As an aspect of the Catholic church, Purgatory
was repugnant to, and forbidden on pain of death by the Anglican
court. Shakespeare could have been sent to the Tower of London
and possibly executed if Hamlet had regarded his father's ghost as
a benign spirit. Consequently, Hamlet features as a contrast to the
Greek Orestes who had conjured up the spirit of the dead, in such a
guilt-free manner, by means of ritual. Earlier, we observed the ease
with which the ancient Greeks had recognized the separateness of
the gods and the imperative and objective nature of their orders.
Now we find Hamlet tormented by doubts, unable to distinguish
whether his ghost is a product of the Devil, or the demons inside his
own imagination.

HAMLET
I am myself indifferent honest but yet I could accuse me of such Things that
it were better my mother had not borne me; I am very Proud, revengeful,
ambitious, with more offenses at my back, than I Have thoughts to put
them in, imagination to give them shape, or Time to act them in. What
should such fellows as I do crawling be
—
Earth and heaven? [3.1. 132–139].
Observe my uncle. If his occulted guilt
Do not itself unkennel in one speech,

It is a damned ghost that we have seen,
And my imaginations are as foul
As Vulcan's stithy [3.2.81–85].

Here, the spirit of Hamlet's father is not the masculine, Apollonian voice of male retribution so necessary for the hierarchical order and wellbeing of the patriarchal state; it is the spirit of the Orestean dilemma itself. The Homeric Arete hero had avenged wrongs perpetrated against him free of moral compunctions; the moral world of the later Greek poets questioned and struggled with the paradox of heroic Greek action versus personal conscience; but the humanist of the post Judeo-Christian tradition is rendered impotent, frozen in his tracks with the confusion and self-doubt of Western culture. Hamlet is the Orestes who can see the moral implications and psychological torment implicit in the act of revenge before crime is committed. Can this prince assume leadership of his country without "tainting" his "mind, without becoming a Claudius with his court of flatterers? The spirit of his father-king warns Hamlet to "revenge his foul and most unnatural murder."

GHOST
But howsoever thou pursuest this act,
Taint not thy mind, nor let thy soul contrive
Against thy mother aught. Leave her to heaven,
And to those thorns that in her bosom lodge
To prick and sting her [1.5. 91–95].

Hamlet's aim is to maintain a mind that is free of guilt and to inflict his mother not with death, but with the daemons in her own conscience. The modern hero knows that the worst punishment is not physical death but human awareness. This Jacobean Orestes is not interested in restoring the fallen house of his father on a political level; rather, he wants to cure its sickness of soul. Part of his mind has been conditioned by the military and action-oriented ideals of his society; it is the other part: his inner, moral voice so essential to his nature, that bids him restraint, watchfulness, and instruction.

Susan Letzler Cole points out that Hamlet's intention is not to act but to speak. [68] Unlike the Greek Orestes, this hero's weapon is not the axe, but the spoken word:

HAMLET
Soft, ... now to my mother
Oh heart, lose not thy nature, let not ever
The soul of Nero enter this firm bosom.
Let me be cruel, not unnatural;
I will speak daggers to her; but use none.
My tongue and soul in this be hypocrites.
How in my words somever she be shent,
To give them seals never, my soul, consent! [3.2.399–406].

In fact, his closet speech to his mother has the desired effect:

GERTRUDE
Oh Hamlet, speak no more
Thou turn'st my eyes into my very soul,
And there I see such black and grained spots
As will not leave their tinct [3.4. 99–102; emphasis added].

Hamlet's doubts about the nature of his universe and his questioning of the spirit pull the audience emotionally onto his stage because the anxieties that are embodied onstage are the unspoken fears of all present. It is that shared skepticism that makes Hamlet, and all the thinkers of his day, antiheroes, fathers of the whole tribe of antiheroes that populate modern theater. Peter Brooke claims that:

All religions assert that the visible is visible all the time. But here's the crunch. Religious teaching ... asserts that this invisible-visible cannot be seen automatically—it can only be seen given certain conditions. The conditions can relate to certain states or to a certain understanding. In any event, to comprehend the visibility of the invisible is a life's work. Holy art is an aid to this, and so we arrive at a definition of a holy theater. A holy theater not only presents the invisible but also offers conditions that make its perception possible. [69]

Is it fair to claim that theater has assumed the place and function of ancient ritual?

In a myopic, secular world such as that which characterized the close of the Elizabethan and the early Jacobean, did the theater of Shakespeare create the "holy"? Did it bring to life, onstage, the buried uncertainties and horrors, the invisible Titans and Cyclopes inherent to the soul of the modern person?

The world of Claudius' court, while spiritually stifling, would be centered were it not for Hamlet. Hamlet is the hero in the sense that he forces into the complacency of this secular world his own revolutionary moral stance. And his revolutionary moral stance begins with the romantic embodiment of a ghost (a devil, or a nightmare) that has to be reckoned with in the space of daily life. In his need for a space in which to mourn, Hamlet journeys outward to the realm of the spirit (ghost) and returns to force that spirit into the space of the court and on to the Jacobean stage. Whereas it was the priestesses, Electra and her chorus of slave women, who had conducted the Aeschylean hero to his source of inspiration within the burial mound; here, in the predominantly male world of the Danish court, it is Hamlet, the male heir, so rudely separated from his mother and from the object of his romantic affections, who functions as the priest for his own community of Elizabethan spectators. The Greek hero had evoked the spirit of his father in an accepted manner, as a member of a community. The hero of the Jacobean world does so as a rebel, in the silence and loneliness of his memory. Hamlet is still the shaman, the actor, the adolescent emerging into manhood, and the Orestean hero, for like them, he voyages imaginatively outward into a symbolic death, and returns to materialize the abstract on stage.

Hamlet's philosophical bent and training grants him an outlook that is foreign to that of the world around him. Claudius keeps an anxious eye on his nephew and stepson because he expects him—as no doubt others do in the Danish state—to react physically, if not militarily, to Claudius' usurpation of the throne. However, Hamlet does not think in terms of material action. His aim is to regain supremacy by means of spiritual maturity. For this he needs not merely to enter the palace of his mother as Sophocles' Orestes had done, but to reach and adopt as his own the royal spirit of his father-king. While making a different point, Letzler-Cole points out that, "In his dialogue with his mother, Hamlet's very use of stichomythia, the ancient mode of communication between the living and the dead, reveals the degree to which he has usurped the role of his deceased father." Letzler Cole writes:

The Ghost's final command is "Remember me," and Hamlet "remembers" his father by assuming an antic disposition. His immediate reaction to the Ghost's revelation of regicide, fratricide, and adultery has been thought puzzling, especially in its emphasis on memory rather than on revenge:

> O all you host of heaven! O earth! What else?
> And shall I couple hell? O Hie! Hold, hold, my heart,
> And you, my sinews, grow not instant old,
> But bear me stiffly up. Remember thee?
> Yea, from the table of my memory
> I'll wipe away all trivial fond records,
> All saws of books, all forms, all pressures past
> That youth and observation copied there,
> And thy commandment all alone shall live
> Within the book and volume of my brain,
> Unmixed with baser matter. Yes, by heaven!
> O most pernicious woman!
> O villain, villain, smiling, damned villain!
> Now to my word:
> It is "Adieu, adieu, remember me."
> I have sworn it. [1.5. 99–119].

Hamlet is to make his liminal journey in his mind. The act of recollection is the act of allowing himself to become haunted by what he wishes to recollect. Dying to his former self, "all forms, all pressures past," Hamlet is taking on the disposition of the deceased with a vengeance.... In Claudius' court, memory is a kind of revenge. Hamlet's "antic disposition" will eventually turn the court into the mourners thy refuse to be, will provoke the response that his father's dead body could not. [70]

Letzler-Cole maintains that, "the experience of death, though it may be universal, is inevitably solitary." [71] Indeed, perhaps the discrepancy between the extreme sense of isolation that the mourner experiences and the public and ceremonial expression of that mourning is what constitutes the pathos of the Electra figure. Perhaps this discrepancy is the cause of modern society's alienation from and ambivalence with ritual, and perhaps this discrepancy between the personal and the public constitutes the starting point for all the plays that fall within the Oresteian pattern:

GERTRUDE
Though know'st 'tis common. All that lives must die,
Passing through nature to eternity.

HAMLET
Ay, madam, 'tis common.

GERTRUDE
...If it be,
Why seems it so particular with thee?

HAMLET
But I have within which passeth show—
These but the trappings and the suits of
woe [1.2. 76–91; emphasis added].

The audience is asked to journey imaginatively from the general form of ritual, "the trappings and the suits of woe," to the particular and personal suffering of the protagonist.

Only when I lost my own father was I hit by what I now consider the full import of these lines. Of course, "'tis common, all that lives must die". With such equanimity, we all accept the passing of others. But when it is our own loved one, our own mourning; when the death is "particular" to ourselves, then and only then are we catapulted into an experience of pain and loss so harsh it defies the boundaries dividing this world from the next. If we could but feel that anguish at the passing of the stranger and at the passing of the loved ones of the stranger, if the deaths of others could be experienced with that same "particular" feeling as the death of the personal and loved father, we would forbid the shedding of a single drop of blood. Surely, if we could feel such pain for others, wars would be abolished. Is this not the suggestion made by Lady Macbeth when, referring to the planned murder of Duncan, she says, "Had he not resembled/ My father as he slept, I had don't"? (Macbeth: Act 11. Scene 2, lines 12–13).

The quest of the hero is the human being's struggle with his or her conscience, and the purpose of heroic theater is to embody that struggle, in its most naked and aching form, on stage. Such theater is the perpetual struggle of the hero with death and the father. Letzler-Cole maintains that:

The central shareable experience of death is the enactment of mourning. In suggesting that this profound communal experience resides at the heart of tragedy, I am clearly drawing on the power of mourning as an archetype even in cultures which, like our own, do not encourage fully released ex-pressions of grieving for the dead. As Geoffrey Gorer has cautioned, "a society which denies mourning and gives no ritual support to mourners is thereby producing maladaptive and neurotic responses in a number of its citizens." [12]

Yet, for the court to which Hamlet has returned specifically to mourn his father, mourning constitutes insurrection, "a course/ Of impious stubbornness (and...) unmanly grief" (1.2.99–100). Hamlet's mask of madness is a neurotic reaction, but in the context of this court it is the only way he has of assuaging his feelings of sorrow and resentment. Ophelia, imprisoned like Electra in a loveless, sexless, youth-less world in which she can neither woo nor mourn, is forced beyond neurosis into the abyss of that madness which Hamlet merely assumes.

It might be fair to suggest that Ophelia drowns in, or because of, an all- male world. Unlike the Sophoclean Electra, who had lived in an all-women's house; whose very being (as expressed through her language) was that of Physis—the undammable force of Nature; unlike Electra, who had burst the confines of her prison with a velocity measured only by the extent of her repression, Ophelia is delicate and sensitive. She is buffeted clumsily by the grasping materialism of her father and her brother. Still, as a theatrical figure, Ophelia is an extension of the Electra who'd been rejected by her mother. The Greek Electra had turned her back on female sensuality as a characteristic of her hated mother. Jan Kott writes:

Electra is a king's daughter, deprived of all the privileges of her birth and station. In Sophocles she has been made to remain a spinster....Electra has been placed in an enforced situation, having to make the fundamental choice between total acceptance and total refusal; acceptance of her fate, or refusal to accept it; acceptance of a world in which her mother has murdered her father, or rejection of that world with all the consequences of such a decision. In Electra's argument with her sister Chrysothemis, just as in Antigone's argument with her sister Ismene, all the great oppositions are presented: loyalty to the dead and loyalty to the living; revolt against authority and obedience to those in power; renunciation and compromise. Electra is asked to forget, but she is the one who remembers. Electra's memory is the presence of the past and the foretelling of vengeance.

"Loyalty to the dead," "revolt against authority," "renunciation," and, above all, "memory" and "vengeance" are characteristic of the Electra (and the Antigone) figures because they have become mythically and theatrically indistinguishable from the female principle. Referring to both the Antigone and the Electra figures, Jan Kott states that, "those who rebel against authority, against kings, who oppose their loyalty for the dead to their duties to the living, who refuse to accept the world, are mad." [73]

In fact, madness in the context of our theater has become associated with all the above-mentioned characteristics of the "female," as with femininity itself. In the Christian world this female principle has become subsumed within the ego-restraint of the rational, morality-oriented male. The female "mad" principle separates Hamlet from his society and thrusts him back into the liminal regions of memory and the spirit of his beloved father, much as Orpheus, in that beautiful Greek legend, managed to recapture the beloved essence of Euridice by means of the lyrical power of his muse. But "loyalty to the living," "obedience to those in power," "compromise," and "forgetfulness" are masculine attributes and it becomes essential for the hero to eradicate the female within him in order to buoy himself for action and for life.

In Hamlet, the ambivalent situation that Electra had entertained vis-à-vis those of her own sex is accelerated even further. Not only does Ophelia have no mother to recognize and encourage the beauty of budding sexuality and the twinges of first love, she does not have, in her immediate world, any model of femininity. There are only two women in this play, both of whom are subservient to the male power system; and the chorus of courtiers consists entirely of male opportunists. There is no indication in the text that Claudius, or any other of the men in this court, are affected by Gertrude's obvious sensuality, because their attentions are focused more on political power than romance. Rather, it is Hamlet, the Orestean adolescent, whom we have already recognized as having an alien sense of values to the men of this court, who is troubled by—and in need of mastering—his attraction for his mother. Ophelia stands timidly at the threshold of womanhood but all her first hopes, her first twinges of desire, are cruelly nipped in the bud by her male guardians. Essentially, the Ophelia/Electra character is reduced to an asexual tool of the male political system.

In the Greek plays, we have already recognized Electra as the repressed female principle within the Athenian male. To my mind, Ophelia serves the identical role in Hamlet. We have already noticed that Hamlet's social self desperately wants to be convinced by the revenge ideology of his day:

HAMLET
Witness this army of such mass and charge,
Led by a delicate and tender prince,
Whose spirit, with divine ambition puffed,
Makes mouths at the invisible event,
Exposing what is mortal and unsure
To all that fortune, death and danger dare,
Even for an eggshell. Rightly to be great
Is not to stir without great argument,
But greatly to find quarrel in a straw
When honor's at stake [4.4.49–58].

Yet despite these momentary patriotic bursts of enthusiasm, the enormous discrepancy between our hero's sensitive, reflective soul and the act of cold- blooded murder he is called upon to exact, constitutes the dialectics of the play. In order to harden himself to the act of revenge, it becomes essential for Hamlet to snuff out the more lyrical, feminine life-force within him. In this light, the devastating verbal cruelty which Hamlet inflicts on Ophelia (and which merely confirms for her the worldly cynicism with which she had been bombarded by her father and her brother at the beginning of the play) begins to be understood, for by destroying Ophelia, the feminine, he is emptying his soul of the gentle; of moral compunctions, in much the same manner as Agamemnon had sacrificed his virgin daughter, Iphigenia, to the all-male spirit of war.

HAMLET
I did love you once.

OPHELIA
Indeed, my lord, you made me believe so.

HAMLET
You should not have believed me, for virtue cannot so inoculate our old stock but we shall relish of it. I loved you not.

OPHELIA
I was the more deceived.

HAMLET
Get thee to a nunnery!...
We are errant knaves all; believe none of us. Go thy ways to a nunnery. Where is you father?

OPHELIA
At home, my lord.

HAMLET
Let the doors be shut upon him, that he may play the fool nowhere but in's own home. Farewell.
If thou dost marry, I'll give thee this plague for thy dowry: be thou as chaste as ice, as pure as snow, thou shalt not escape calumny. Get thee to a nunnery. Go, farewell. Or if thou wilt needs marry, marry a fool, for wise men know well enough what monsters you make of them.... To a nunnery, go, and quickly too. Farewell [3.1. 131–150].

Shakespeare seems as aware as the ancient Greek playwrights were of the devastating effect that the repression of the female has on society, for Ophelia, denied the maturing influence of a lover and the nurture of female council, sinks pathetically into the whirlpool of her imprisoned mind.

In Hamlet, the murdered lover assumes the energizing office held in the time of the Greeks by the ancient dead heroes. Ophelia as gentle virgin falls prey to a harsh, male reality; but Ophelia as female archetype reemerges in the image of her open grave. Ophelia's burial site, like the Greek burial mound, forces itself onto this seventeenth century stage. In so doing, it grants the hero the experience of mourning, denied him at his father's death, and provides him with the necessary transition to adulthood: the death and rebirth of Hamlet as hero. Only when he physically immerses himself in the Great Mother, as represented by the open grave of Ophelia, does

Hamlet become part of the ancient chain of ritual mourners, part of the cycle of death and rebirth which we'd observed in ancient mythology. In the open grave of his denied love, Hamlet dies and is reborn as hero. In such a way the Hamlet- hero grows, like the Aeschylean, out of the chrysalis of the feminine Ophelia- Electra. Jan Kott writes:

> From the end of the first scene of Act V, Hamlet is in the situation of Orestes, while through the first four acts he was in the situation of Electra—deprived of his rights, dependent on his father's murderer, threatened, like Electra, with exile or death.

In addition, Kott claims that

> One can exactly define the point at which the real action of Orestes begins in Shakespeare's Hamlet. It is at the end of the first scene of Act V, when Hamlet jumps into Ophelia's grave. [74]

Kott points out that from this point on the structure of the play changes. It observes the unities and assumes the structure of the classical tragedy. Viewed in this light, the Shakespearean protagonist becomes a hero—not when he destroys the feminine within him (as the male-hero of Western culture seems to believe) but, on the contrary—when he reconciles himself to the very same feminine principle that, in his zeal for focus, clarity and action, he had so cruelly destroyed.

Earlier, we had suggested that Shakespeare was writing during England's adolescence. Could it be that he, as well as the playwrights of Classical Greece, foresaw the demise of an empire capable of sacrificing loyalty, remembrance and introspection for action, power, and political expediency?

But Shakespeare's idea of heroism is very different from that to which the "sane," the conscious, and the socially processed aspects of Hamlet aspire: heroism that characterizes the demonstrative bravery and mindless action of Fortinbras (Fort-en-bras—strong in arms) and Laertes. In this sense Shakespeare, as artist, follows in the path of the Greek poets, and again the spectators are forced to recognize a discrepancy between the ideology of the hero and that of the playwright. For Shakespeare, like Sophocles before him, recognizes that the underlying threat of Western civilization lies as much in the human soul as in the social structure. Cole quotes Ionesco:

> Drama is one of the oldest of the arts. And I can't help thinking we cannot do without it.... To bring phantoms to life and give them flesh and blood is a prodigious adventure, so unique that I myself was absolutely amazed, during the rehearsals of my first play, when I suddenly saw, moving on the stage of the Noctambules, characters who owed their life to me. It was a terrifying experience. What right had I to a thing like that? Was it allowed? It was almost diabolical. [75]

Is it because modern man has separated his deities into God and the Devil that the "holy" evocation of the imagined has become so charged with ambivalence?

---

61   L.C. Knight, Drama and Society in the Age of Jonson (London: Chatto and Windus, 1977).

62   Woodbridge, p. 55.

63   Woodbridge, p. 56.

64   Woodbridge, p. 61.

65   Woodbridge, p. 67.

66   Woodbridge, p. 68.

67   William Shakespeare, Hamlet (New York: Washington Square Press, 1958), p. 82. There are numerous editions of Shakespeare. This edition was convenient for the author. However, for the convenience of the reader, quotations are accompanied by act, scene and line indications.

68   Susan Lettzler Cole, The Absent One (University Park: Pennsylvania University Press, 1985), p. 51.

69   Peter Brook, The Empty Space (New York: Atheneum, 1984), p. 56.

70   Cole, pp. 46–7.

71   Cole, pp. 51, 46–7.

72   Cole, p. 5.

73   Kott, pp. 252–3 and 257–8.

74   Kott, pp. 254 and 253.

75   Cole, p. 11.

CHAPTER 5

ELECTRA: PLAY OF
AMBIVALENCE

Ambivalence, irony, alienation, and the disjunction between surface and subtext have become the hallmarks of modern theater and, as such, are themselves appropriate subject matter for the Electra myth: the confrontation of the fragmented modern mind with the relative certainty of a more classical worldview as the meeting and assessment of the old and the new.

In *Madness in Literature*, Lilian Feder [76] traces madness, itself a recurring theme in the Electra myth, to its earliest known literary form, to the ancient Dionysian ritual that we find enacted in Euripedes' The Bacchae. The fifth century BCE experience of Dionysian rites, she maintains, was not so much an expression of the ecstatic, as of the already fully realized conflict between Apollonian (rational, masculine) restraints and the human being's instinctual gravitation toward the Dionysian (frenzied, orgiastic) life-force. The rites of Dionysus, Feder maintains, reach back at least as far as the thirteenth century BCE, to a period when the primordial person could not yet differentiate between him or herself and objective reality. According to Feder, human existence at that time was comprised solely of the ecstatic and the instinctual, a time when the pleasure principle was not yet impeded by ego control.

According to this theory, the birth of civilization occurred when the human being began to separate from his or her physical surroundings and to regard him or herself as an independent entity. It was at that point that the human began to feel the need for stability and self-regulation. Primordial rites and totem ritual became attempts on the part of this newly enlightened creature to incorporate in itself some of the principles that regulate the outer world. They became a way of imbibing into human life the strength and the surviving spirit of nature. From a modern perspective, this effort of man and woman to literally fill themselves with outer reality might well testify to an existential need, even at that early period, an attempt to physically incorporate a sense of being into an otherwise devastatingly aching void.

In this way, from the very birth of civilization the rational human has struggled with his or her chaotic, frenzied nature; the conflict itself producing its own madness: the madness of conflict superimposed over the madness of the untrammeled instinct.

Nietzsche idealized the Dionysian person. For Nietzsche, as for Carl Jung, it was Socrates who inflicted the curse of reason on humankind, reason that over the ages has alienated men and women from their true natures. Reason, according to Nietzsche, is not intrinsic to the human; rather it is an arbitrary concept, a sort of Pirandellian mask superimposed over and stifling one's basic life force. In the following chapter, we'll see that in Salomé, whose title character was an immensely popular figure among the artists at the turn of the twentieth century, Oscar Wilde brought into direct confrontation the two extremes: the untamable pleasure principle which, since the time of the Greeks, has been depicted as the archetypical female, and the "masculine" principle of order so deadly in its distance from the vital life-juices of human nature. It is a confrontation that obliterates the last vestiges of civilization.

Nietzsche acknowledged the fact that the human person would never have survived, would have long fallen victim to his or her orgiastic frenzies, had the Apollonian factor not existed in some form or other since earliest times. It is only in recognition of this that Nietzsche reconciled himself to the necessity of human development within the Apollonian factor.

Freud recognized the essential interdependence of the pleasure principle with the human being's instinctive death-wish. According to him, the instinct for destruction is intrinsically bound to that of survival. One destroys in order to devour, to imbibe, to be nourished and to live (a pattern that might again remind us of the ancient Earth Mother or Mother Goddess). These contradictions have characterized the human person since his or her earliest attempts to incorporate the rhythms of winter-spring and death-and-rebirth manifest in external reality. We will encounter them again in Wilde's Salome. (I am conscious, as I write, that by according women their grammatical place in this text, I am granting them a place in history, imagining a voice that has been heard rarely if ever, in the recorded history of humans.)

Men and women swing eternally on their pendulum of reason and madness, life and death. Nietzsche recognizes human redemption only in the cruel frenzy of the unadulterated life force, in the human being's regression to a pre–Oedipal state in which neither he nor she is subject to any superimposed governing body. According to Nietzsche, the Socratic rule, reason, and the Apollonian factor all represent the splintering of ourselves from our true natures to a distanced vantage point from which we attempt to administer control. Ironically, it is from this distance that we recognize the incompatibility of "masculine" control with the more nurturing, "feminine" aspects of human nature. It is from the vantage point of critical reasoning that we are forced to recognize the frailty and the pathos inherent in the human condition, and it is from this distancing of ourselves from our true natures, from the double vision we have now created, that the grotesque emerges. As for irony, now so common an aspect of modern theater, it is the irony of the mirror, the irony of the artist who sees—from a third vantage point—that human nature is equally enslaved to passions and dedicated to control.

Here we have recognized several layers of madness: the destructive, orgiastic frenzy of our instincts (pre–Hellenic, pre–Hebraic chaos; the chaos of early Genesis, perhaps); the madness created by the tension of opposites— life and death, instinct and reason, survival and destruction, love and hate; and, perhaps the ultimate madness, that of the "objective" vision, of being able, by means of reason, to observe the pathos of our human condition and the arbitrary nature of those qualities we hold as absolutes: Heroism,

Vengeance, and Honor. All of these constitute the subject matter of our modern Electra plays.

But the theme of madness extends even further, for it becomes emblematic of the splintered, alienating theater of the twentieth century, a theater which reflects the shattered, subjective reality that Kant portrays in his Critique of Pure Reason. Since Kant there is no Truth, no Reality, no shared experience. Reality is at best a momentary, shifting subjective matter, the awareness of which thrusts the individual even further into the loneliness and the separateness of his or her personal vision. Perhaps even that would not be so painful were it not that men and women suffer both from the hope that they are members of a community, and from the recognition that their hope is a delusion:

> I could be bounded in a nutshell, and count myself a king of infinite space, were it not that I have bad dreams [*Hamlet*: 2.2. 270–272].

The latter half of nineteenth-century Austria might, perhaps, still be regarded as a focal point of contemporary reality. Cultural life blossomed. Art, music, theater, and especially opera flourished. The Conservative Party tried to preserve its elegant lifestyle for the upper classes and protect it from the contamination of the ambitious and threatening bourgeoisie, while the latter, consisting of merchants, Jews, and intellectuals, placed their faith in the Liberal Party, believing that Vienna could be enjoyed by all. The peasants and the lower classes, on the other hand, whom the Liberals had hoped to attract, identified more with the reactionary Catholic orthodoxy of the Conservatives. The National Socialist Party of Vienna headed by Karl Lueger was overtly anti–Semitic. Its assumption of political power in 1895 spelled the doom of the Liberal Party and saw the beginning of the moral, social, and political disintegration of Austria, and the horrors of Europe as a whole. [22]

It is this moral disintegration and the effect it had on society that concerns the playwrights and the artists of the twentieth century. The turn of that century saw the beginning of what was to become an overt and mass disregard for human life, yet it was, at the same time, the age of Sigmund Freud, who devoted his life to the most minute and intricate workings of the individual human mind. Carl Schorske, in his book Fin-de-Siecle Vienna, questions how two such disparate conceptions of human life could form within the same time and place.

It is relevant to mention Freud in this study because, by means of his research on human psychology, he irreversibly changed our human perception of reality, because his life is an excellent reflection of the intellectual mood and conflicts of his time, and because he both constitutes in his own life the prototypical Orestean experience and provides a model by means of which modern artists can challenge the creative form of their fathers.

Freud lived from 1856 to 1939. He was raised in a liberal Viennese Jewish family from which he watched the political development of his day. He identified strongly with the Dreyfus case in France and regarded Emile Zola as his political hero because Zola had championed the Dreyfus cause. As a schoolboy, he had idealized Napoleon as conqueror and champion of a backward Central Europe. He admired England and the historical advances of Oliver Cromwell and he despised the aristocracy. Freud's father and friends set their hopes for an emancipated Austria on the Liberal Party. The young Sigmund himself had entertained hopes throughout his high school years of growing up to be a politician and of realizing his father's hopes for the future, in the Liberal Party. In 1895, however, the Nationalist Socialist Party came into power, thereby crushing the hopes of the liberals and reinstating an era of racial prejudice and social discord. The effects of anti–Semitism were widespread Freud himself was squeezed out of a well-earned position in the respected upper-class intellectuals of his day into the more urbane middle- class of Jewish medical practitioners. He even joined the *B'nai B'rith*, an international Jewish fraternity at this point, out of a need for social comfort and personal acceptance.

When Freud was ten or twelve years old, his father told him of an act of anti– Semitism which he had experienced as a boy. Sigmund was humiliated that his father had not responded, in any way, to such an attack on human dignity. He felt that his father had behaved un-heroically and had failed to live up to the principles of the Liberal Party, which he had espoused. Years later, in an interesting transmutation of this incident, Freud recorded in his *Interpretation of Dreams* a dream in which Hannibal, the classical Roman conqueror, forced his son to swear before the altar that he would avenge the insults that his father had received at the hands of the Romans. It would seem that the increase of anti–Semitism during his lifetime had forced Freud, by means of the pattern of classical heroism, to avenge the humiliation of his father.

Sigmund's father died in 1896. Sigmund wrote that such a tragedy is "the most important event, the most poignant loss, of a man's life." He was painfully aware that his father had never realized his political aspirations. Schorske writes:

> To lay his father's ghost, Freud had either, like Hamlet, to affirm the primacy of politics by removing what was rotten in the state of Denmark (civil task) or to neutralize politics by reducing it to psychological categories (an intellectual task). [78]

Here we have the origins, perhaps, of Freud's revolutionary descent into the human mind. Schorske suggests that Europe's mass disregard for human life and the individual may be the very cause of Freud's scholarship into the most minute and intricate workings of the individual psyche.

For a time, the National Socialist Party in Austria was led by an Austrian aristocrat by the name of Count Thun, who had become a controversial figure due to his constant struggle to unite two factions—the Hungarian and the Italian parties—both threatening to disband. Schorske narrates that once, while waiting at a railway station, Freud witnessed an incident he no doubt considered typical of aristocratic arrogance. Count Thun had brushed aside the stationmaster, refused to purchase a ticket, and established himself in a first-class carriage, merely by virtue of his political prominence. At this, Freud's egalitarian instincts rose to the fore. "He found himself whistling a subversive air from Mozart's *Marriage of Figaro*: "If the count wants to dance, I'll call the tune." [79]

Schorske writes that, on the train, Freud slept, and dreamt that he challenged Count Thun's arrogance and elitist political views. He dreamt that he was his father straddling two chairs, thereby physically connecting the two opposing parties, the Hungarians and the Italians with whom the Count was having such difficulties. In this manner, Freud was performing the task of Hannibal's son: he was avenging the wrongs perpetrated on his father while restoring him to a position of political power.

Schorske writes, "In the dream, he had discharged by his defiance of the Count, the commitment of his youth to anti-authoritarian political activism, which was also his unpaid debt to his father."

The third section of Freud's "revolutionary dream," as related by Schorske, shows Freud's aging father at the railway station. Freud is holding a urinal so that his father can relieve himself. Analyzing this dream, Freud remembers two childhood instances in which his father had chided him for urinating in public. One of those times, his father had been so angry, he'd yelled at Freud's mother that their son would never be successful in life. In his dream, Sigmund is simultaneously reestablishing his father in a position of power and getting even with him for his childhood insult. Here, in his dream, after his father's death, Sigmund is demonstrating his mastery over him: "From political encounter, through flight into academia, to the conquest of the father who has replaced Count Thun, patricide replaces regicide; psychoanalysis overcomes history. Politics is neutralized by a counter-political psychology."

For Freud, victory over one's father signifies victory over politics. He writes,

"The whole rebellious content of the dream, with its lese majeste and its derision of the higher authorities, went back to rebellion against my father. A prince is known as father of his country; the father is the oldest, and, for children, the only authority, and from his autocratic power the other social authorities have developed in the history of human civilization."

Schorske claims that Freud's Oedipal quest (which might be as easily recognized as the Orestean quest) was "a moral and intellectual one: to escape a fate and acquire self-knowledge. He writes, "By reducing his own political past and present to an epiphenomenal status in relation to the primal status between father and son, Freud gave his fellow liberals an historical theory of man and society that could make bearable a political world spun out of orbit and beyond control." [80]

This, it seems to me, is the function of the Orestean hero. Equally important to our understanding of modern theater is Nietzsche. Nietzsche wrote in the tradition of Schopenhauer. He recognized that Europe at the end of the nineteenth century was falling apart; its institutions and its customs no longer relevant. He witnessed the dissolution of the ruling upper middle class. New ideas were taking hold: a-historicity, the idea that men and women should make a clean break from the past, from the patterns of patriarchal society, and that there should be a movement away from government and the family structure. The entire patriarchal structure was in question. If a truth existed beyond history, it was art. Nietzsche believed that, in this newly psychologized world, art was the one way of reaching a truth that existed beyond the accepted social structure, beyond logic, reason, and even the linear use of language.

Nietzsche, Freud, Ibsen and Pirandello entertained similar ideas though they worked in different disciplines and did not know one another. All four advocated the dissolution of power politics and called into question the social mores of their time. Nietzsche foresaw that the twentieth century would be a battleground of simultaneous but disparate and conflicting ideologies. Indeed, it became a very real and tortuous battleground due to Nazi and Fascist ideologies. At the close of the twentieth century, people manifested the same need for reassessment as they had at the end of the nineteenth, and the same issues were at stake. A cyclical nature to certain social issues seems to exist, one that is fundamental to western culture: birth control, women's rights, the need to redefine the respective roles of the male and the female, and equitable treatment for minority groups and the indigent. Our own twenty-first century world is no better than the twentieth: we are still sending our children and loved ones off to fight, our world is still at war, we are still battling with conflicting absolutist ideologies. Our world is still a stomping ground for insane, drug-imbibing murderers, this time bearing the flag of ISIS.

Nietzsche questioned the nature and existence of Truth. He looked for a new reality to replace the outmoded historical perspective. He questioned the nature of existence. What is the human condition? What does it mean to be alive? What is the nature and purpose of human reality? Nietzsche preached, as Hagel had seventy-five years earlier, that God is dead. He believed that the general public was clinging to an obsolete concept, that people were living "in the shadows of the dead god." He believed that people everywhere should get over their dependence on a paternalistic culture because it no longer represented reality.

Oscar Wilde: Salome (1905)

Oscar Wilde belonged to the Aesthetic Movement at the turn of the 20th century, believing that the function of art was not to recreate reality, but to create art for art's sake. Wilde was not interested in linear progression, in cause and effect. Rather, he concentrated all aspects of his theater on one point in time, on one focal point of heightened dramatic tension. Above all else, his theater was sensual. For Wilde, an exploration and a revolution of the senses provided the necessary access to reality. To this end, perfume was sprayed liberally throughout the house during the performances of his play. By means of his repetitive, hypnotic use of language, his poetry, his use of alliteration and his symbolism, his concentration on the decadent, on the mystical and the macabre, Wilde, the ultimate symbolist, created a world of fantasy and the subconscious. As such, the Orestean figure of Oscar Wilde confronted the old theater of linear form and rational meaning with the inner, dream-like sensuality of a new generation.

Again, the explosion of the inner sensuality and life-force is presented in the irrepressible female form. Salome is chaste, cold and deadly as the moon. Like the moon, she is hypnotic. Like the moon, she brings madness, passion and death:

PAGE OF HERODIAS
Look at the moon! How strange the moon seems!
She is like a woman rising from a tomb.
She is like a dead woman. You would fancy she

112

was looking for dead things. [81]

THE YOUNG SYRIAN
She has a strange look.
She is like a little princess who wears a yellow
Veil, and whose feet are of silver.
She is like a princess who has little
White doves for feet...

PAGE OF HERODIAS
She is like a woman who is dead.
She moves very slowly. (319)

Salome is erotic love. She is the Id, willful and irresponsible. In the single shaft of the moon shining on the stage Salome is crushed between the shields of the soldiers. It takes the congregated army of the king to extinguish the threat of her sexuality.

The play luxuriates in the sensuousness of death, decay and eroticism. It is the sensuousness of Electra, this time—a Judean princess, young, mysterious and distant as the virginal moon. Again, we see her as a projection of the male fantasy.

Wilde's play is filled with the complexity, the heightened sounds and colors of the Orient, and with the suggestion of danger lurking in the shadows:

SALOME
...barbarians who drink and drink, and spill their wine on the pavement and Greeks from Smyrna with painted eyes and painted cheeks, and frizzed hair curled in twisted coils, and silent, subtle Egyptians, with long nails of jade and russet cloaks, and Romans Brutal and coarse, with their uncouth jargon [322].

It is filled with the sensuality of the Song of Songs, a sensuality that constitutes the subtext of the Book of Prophets, for this play is a deliberate attempt, on the part of the poet, to reach beyond Christianity, and to strip the Bible of the Puritan straight-jacket that was thrust upon it by scholars of a post-biblical era.

SALOME
Jokanaan, I am amorous of thy body! Thy body is white like the lilies of a field that the mower hath never mowed. Thy body is white like the snows that lie on the mountains, like the snows that lie on the mountains of Judaea and come down into the valleys. The roses in the garden of the

Queen of Arabia are not so white as thy body. Neither the roses in garden of the Queen of Arabia, the perfumed garden of spices of the Queen of Arabia, not the feet of the dawn when they light on the leaves, not the breast of the moon when she lies on the breast of the sea.... There is nothing in the world so white as thy body. Let me touch thy body.

...

...It is of thy hair that I am enamored, Jokanaan. Thy hair is like clusters of grapes, like the clusters of black grapes that hang from the vine trees of Edom in the land of the Edomites. Thy hair is like the cedars of Lebanon, like the great cedars of Lebanon that give their shade to the lions and to the robbers who would hide themselves by day. The long black nights, when the moon hides her face, when the stars are afraid, are not so black [327].

In this play the image of the moon stands in opposition to that of the people. Wilde deliberately creates the dialectics of pagan versus Christianity to mirror that of the Dionysian versus the Apollonian (which we had discussed in the first chapters of this work). Like the theme of the virgin– Electra that we have noted thus far, the fascination of Jokanaan lies in his inaccessibility.

Note the hypnotic rhythm even in the severity of this prophet:

JOKANAAN
Daughter of Sodom, come not near me! But cover thy face with a veil,
And scatter
ashes upon thine head, and get thee to the desert and seek Out the Son of Man.

SALOME
Who is he, the Son of Man?
Is he as beautiful as thou art, Jokanaan?

JOKANAAN
Get thee behind me!
I hear in the palace the beatings of the wings
Of the angel of death.
...
Back! Daughter of Babylon!
By woman came evil into the world. Speak not to me.
I will not listen to thee.
I listen but to the voice of The Lord God [327].

From a post–Puritan perspective, Woman is synonymous with the Devil. Jokanaan (John the Baptist) on the other hand, is the prophet of the loving figure of Jesus, yet he is represented as totally antithetical to him in nature— as rigid and vindictive. Does Wilde depict him in this way to demonstrate society's misunderstanding of Christianity? Is he saying that the denial of the senses, which is the purpose of both Christian and Apollonian austerity, necessitates the abolition of love? All the poets in our study recognize a necessary relationship between sensual freedom and the love of the heart. In this play, Wilde claims that puritan Christianity does not.

Simultaneously, on the same stage, we are presented with Jokanaan and his rejection of the sensual, and with the savage paganism of the Nubian gods, deities that rip men to shreds and revel in their destruction:

THE NUBIAN
The gods of my country are very fond of blood.
Twice a year we Sacrifice to them young men and maidens;
fifty young men and a Hundred maidens.
But it seems we never give them quite enough for
They are very harsh to us [320].

In her deadly dance of the seven veils, Electra reveals to its fullest the beauty and violence of pagan sensuality.

This Judaean princess is the indomitable Electra who subverts the law for her own gratification, yet who is held against her will beneath the lecherous gaze of her uncle-stepfather. Jokanaan is the Orestes, raised up out of the bowels of the earth by his sister-lover. What is dramatized here is the attraction of opposites and the human fascination for the forbidden fruit— again an ironic blend of Christian and pagan themes. Salome is tied to Jokanaan dramatically by means of color. The moon is silver. Salome's hands and feet are white like a dove's and the body of Jokanaan assumes an ivory tinge as he emerges from the pit in which he has been held (itself an image of death and rebirth that is ironic in its similarity to the ancient rites of passage described earlier in this work.) Both these opposites are bound also by the redness of roses and pomegranates associated with The Song of Songs and the land of Judea, by the redness of blood and violence, of Salome's lips and the tongue of Jokanaan:

SALOME
It is thy mouth that I desire, Jokanaan. Thy mouth is like a band of scarlet on a tower of ivory. It is like a pomegranate cut with a knife of ivory. The pomegranate- flowers that blossom in the gardens of Tyre, and are redder than roses, are not so red. The red blasts of trumpets that herald the approach of kings, and make afraid the enemy, are not so red. Thy mouth is redder than the feet of those who tread the wine in the wine-press. Thy mouth is redder than the feet of the doves who haunt the temples and are fed by the priests. It is redder than the feet of him who cometh from a forest where he hath slain a lion and seen gilded tigers. Thy mouth is like a branch of coral that fishers have found in the twilight of the sea, the coral that they keep for the kings!.... It is like the vermilion that the Moabites find in the mines of Moab, the vermilion that the kings take from them.... There is nothing in the world so red as thy mouth.... Let me kiss thy mouth [328]. [82]

The language that binds them is filled with exotic riches of the earth and with the violence and rapaciousness of kings. It is, at once, biblical, savage, and erotic.

Herod Antipas is the tetrarch of Judea. Like Claudius in Hamlet, Herod has murdered his brother, in this case, in order to take for himself the queen of Judea. He is the representation of Roman, secular law, and his function is to subjugate the disparate factions of Judea under the canopy of the Roman Empire. As such he is recognizable to us as the repressive and myopic Aegisthus. Jokanaan represents divine law, the law of the spiritual fathers. He is called from the pit (as in Aeschylus' play, read earlier) by the figure of Salome (Electra). It is the combined word (spirit) of Jokanaan and the action (dance) of Salome that constitute defiance, and that bring about the downfall of Herod and Herodias (just as the combined actions of Electra and Orestes had brought about the immediate, if short-lived, liberation of the House of Atreus).

The religious law represented by Jokanaan is overruled by the civil law of the Roman tetrarch, yet ultimately secular power is also overthrown because of the tetrarch's fidelity to his word:

HEROD
Ah! Wherefore did I give my oath? Kings ought never to pledge their word. If they keep it not, it is terrible, and if they keep it, it is terrible also.

Ultimately, the overwhelming law of the play is neither politics nor religion, but sensuality/sexuality. In a manner uncannily reminiscent of Macbeth, the tetrarch attempts to extinguish the fires of conscience and sexuality and hide beneath the canopy of power and possession:

HEROD
Put out the torches! Hide the moon! Hide the stars! Let us hide ourselves in our palace, Herodias. I begin to feel afraid [347].

With the bombardment of the senses that we have witnessed in this play, Wilde has dealt with sexuality as the aesthetes of the nineteenth century had dealt with art. On this stage, sexuality is no longer the subtext of theater, rather, to put it as bluntly as he does, "sex for sex sake." By these means Wilde forces his spectators to confront all the credos by which they live: their sexuality, their humanitarianism, and the function and purpose of their faith.

Hugo von Hofmannsthal: Electra (1903)

Hofmannsthal says of Friedrich Hebbel's poetry that it

penetrates in such a way that the secret ... inner depths stir in us and the actually demonic, the natural in us, sounds in dark intoxicating sympathetic vibration. [83]

While attempting to describe the creative dilemmas of the aristocratic and liberal aesthetes and artists of fin-de-siècle Vienna, Schorske writes that "the instinctual element in man ... provided the power whereby one could escape from the prison of aestheticism, from the paralysis of narcissistic sensibility. [84] Hofmannsthal felt that engagement in life

demands the capacity to resolve, to will. This capacity implies commitment to the irrational, in which alone resolution and will are grounded.

And so, affirmation of the instinctual reopened for the aesthete the door to the life of action and society.

To this, Hofmannsthal added: The nature of our epoch is multiplicity and interdependency. It can rest only on "das Gleitende" (the moving, the slipping, the sliding), and is aware that what other generations believed to be firm is in fact "das Gleitende." [85]

Hofmannsthal was not unaware of Freud and his controversial theories about sexual, emotional, and political repression. He was only too aware of the dynamics of repressed emotions in his own society, and recognized within these dynamics, as did many artists of that period, an untapped form of artistic expression, one that had not already been worn threadbare by traditional use and which he grasped for himself as the one means by which to combat both the insipid and inertia-bound aestheticism of the aristocracy, and the stifling hold that religious morés and ethics wielded over the middle and lower classes. Of Hofmannsthal's *Der Turm*, Schorske writes, "Where law ignores instinct, instinct rebels and subverts order. Politics is here psychologized, psychology politicized." [86] The old vanguard of Catholic aristocracy in Vienna was no longer able to withstand the threat of the Liberal Party at the turn of the twentieth century. Both constituencies were in constant competition from the Social Democrats and the Pan Germans for their moment of political power. Hofmannsthal, an intellectual of his day, was the grandson of a member of the Jewish bourgeoisie who had been granted membership by the Emperor into the much-coveted aristocracy. He was only too aware of the dangerous anti–Semitic agitation of such social and political climbers as Georg Von Schonerer and Karl Luerger, precursors and ideologues of no less dangers than Adolph Hitler and Nazi Europe.

Like the Renaissance and Jacobean societies, fin-de-siècle Vienna was a quicksand of class disintegration and social instability and, in this case, it fostered the most insidious and volatile forms of political insurrection.

From this pattern, the figure of Electra emerges, again as a force of violence commensurate with the degree to which she has been repressed. The emphasis in this play is not on Orestes, the heroic-masculine instrument of right and retribution. On the contrary, Orestes appears here as little more than a boy trembling in a lonely, godless world at the act he is about to commit:

ELECTRA
I've never seen the gods, and yet I'm certain
That they will be here for you, they will help you.

ORESTES
I do not know the gods, but I know this:
They have laid this deed upon my conscience,
And they will scorn me if I tremble at it. [87]

He is an innocent, forced into action by the living horror of his sister and the act of violence that has possessed her since childhood:

ORESTES
Does your mother look like you in any way?

ELECTRA
Like me? No. I will not have you look her in the face.
When she is dead, then we together will look her in the face. O my brother, she threw a white shirt upon our father, and then she struck away at that which stood before her, helpless, sightless, which could not turn its face to hers, whose arms could not work free—are you listening to me? She struck down at this with her axe held high above him [110–1].

The masculine principle here is little more than a child, product of Electra's need. In a society of such despotism and repressed violence as that of nineteenth-century fin-de-siècle Europe, there can be no masculine heroism, only an Electra—the volcanic eruption of a long over repressed female principle.

Here, the heroine serves as the agent of liberation in an essentially amoral world, one that does not rotate on a scale of right or wrong, but of repression and liberation. This is not an aesthetically self-reflective world, but one that explodes from imprisonment to violent action. In this play, then, in stark reaction to that of Sophocles on which it is patterned, Electra is not merely the female pattern of lyricism, remembrance and inertia, but the embodiment of the "deed" of enfranchisement. She is the driving, underlying force of demonic energy that propels the play into action. The "deed," the act of revenge, constitutes her very raison d'être.

ELECTRA
Happy the man who does! Who dares to do!
A deed is like a bed on which the soul can rest,
a bed of balsam where the soul that is a wound,
a blight, a running sore, a wound that flames like fire! ...
... when I was steeped in hatred
I kept nothing but silence. Hatred is nothing,
it consumes itself, and love is still less than hatred,

it grasps out at everything,
but fastens onto nothing, its hands are like flames that cannot grasp; and
thought, too, is nothing, and all that comes from our mouths is feeble air;
that man alone is happy who comes to do!
And happy who dares to touch him and who digs
His axe from the earth, who holds his torch for him,
Who opens the door, who listens there [111].

Here, Electra is the demon who infests all the other characters with her spirit and provokes them into action. When Chrysothemis tells her sister of the terrible dream their mother had, Electra cries out:

ELECTRA
I! I!
I sent it to her, I sent her this dream from my own breast! I lie in bed and hear the footsteps of the specter haunting her.
I hear him make his way from room to room and lift the curtain from her bed: screaming she leaps from the bed, but he is always there, close behind her on the stairs, the chase continues from one vault to another and another. It is far darker now than any night, far darker and quieter than the grave, she gasps and staggers in darkness, but he is there: he swings the torch to right and left of the axe. And I, like a hunting-hound am at her heels: should she hide in a hollow, I spring after sideways, upon her trail, and drive her on till a wall ends her flight, and there in darkness, there, in deepest darkness—I see him still, his shadow, and his limbs, the light of his eyes— there sits our father, who neither sees nor hears, and yet, it must happen; we drive her to his feet, and the axe falls! [93–4].

Electra is the demon that weaves a "sinister dance" around Aegisthus as she herds him into his death-chamber, and, at the end of her play, when Chrysothemis runs joyously to her sister with news of their liberation: "and rejoice; / a thousand torches are lighted. Don't you hear it?" Electra, the demonic spirit, responds with:

ELECTRA
Don't I hear it? Hear the music?
That music comes from me. Those thousands and thousands with torches, they who with boundless, myriad footsteps make hollow rumbling round the earth, all these, these, wait upon me: I know that they all, all, wait upon me to lead the dance [113].

Electra is witch-like, maniacal. Her insanity is the stuff of revolution and theater; it explodes from the inside out and refuses to recognize any authority. She is nothing less than the tumultuous, volcanic force of the repressed female. She burns herself out in a frenzy of insanity, yet it is her insane, essentially theatrical magic that produces the hero. Electra dies for the birth of Chrysothemis. Her dance becomes the web of the black mother-spider herself. It is the relentlessly historical dance of death and rebirth which holds both actors and spectators in a single magnetic center. Modern dramatists have directed their attention to the question of the bourgeois audience and its lack of intrinsic relationship to the theatrical act; yet here, in this play, there is no need to stimulate the audience, in an Artaudian fashion, with momentary, emotional stimuli. Nor is there any need to alienate the spectators into political reflection or separate thought patterns. This vortex of hatred and expiated passion constitutes, in and of itself, the theatrical event as defined by David Cole: "Theater does not serve purposes; it has a purpose: to bring us the presence of imaginative events … 'interpretation'—is ultimately a refusal of the theatrical event itself." [88]

There is need of the irrational frenzy of violence in the context of freedom and theater, and with this—the protagonist's long-awaited dance of life and liberation—Electra spins herself out.

ELECTRA
Be silent and dance. All must come!
All must join with me! I bear the burden
Of joy, and I dance here before you all.
One thing alone remains for him who is happy:
To be silent and dance! [114].

Despite the protagonist's desperate efforts, human experience cannot be fathomed by means of the logic-oriented harness of verbal expression. Ultimately, it is the irrational world of instincts that propels human behavior. The joy of liberation and the pain of the sacrifice it demands can be realized only in movement—and silence.

In a manner reminiscent of Shakespeare's Ophelia, or of Goethe's Faust (the hero who so desperately sought to reconcile himself with the female), Electra, female figure of loyalty and remembrance, drowns in the waters of the feminine principle.

It might be worth observing here how nineteenth-century scholars questioned the authorship of certain Shakespearean plays, believing that the written texts (which was all they had to work with) were lacking in a number of sections; inadequate for the emotion required. Indeed, the lacking element was not written text, but something else, something capable of expressing the silence of the spheres, the collusion of stars and of celestial bodies i.e., the meeting of souls in love. These scenes, often the most beautiful and moving, could not be served by words, they demanded music—and dance. Here too, the most powerful emotions are expressed through dance.

ELECTRA
...The ocean, the monstrous ocean,
the manifold ocean weighs me down with its burden
in every limb; I cannot lift myself [114]. [89]

Ultimately, for Electra as for Hamlet, "silence is all."

In previous chapters, we noted an evolution from the world of ritual, characterized by the grave-centered work of Aeschylus' Libation Bearers, to that of the more formal religion as noted in Sophocles' Electra, in which Clytemnestra had prayed to Apollo, the masculine god of light and reason. In the present play, we are propelled into the twentieth century, a man-centered world, characterized more by anxiety and superstition than by dependence on any outer force. In this world, there are no determining forces. Calamities happen by chance. Even the murder of Agamemnon is presented more as an error in timing than a deliberate act of treachery:

ELECTRA
There are customs. Yes,
There must be customs, usages for all things.
How one articulates a word or sentence can make much
Difference. Even the hour it's spoken.
And whether one's fed or fasting. Many a man
Has perished for entering too soon into his bath [96].

In this world, the gods are deaf and blind and people clutch desperately at any straw for an answer to their ignorance. Here, it is not Apollo but the demented Electra who stands center-stage and to whom Clytemnestra prays:

CLYTEMNESTRA

I do not know them who play this game with me, whether they are at home above and below, but when I see you standing there before me as now you are, I cannot but believe
that you are in league with them. Who are you really? Why can't you speak, now, when I would hear you? [97].

Religion is closed to the modern consciousness. In its place are desperate, blind attempts at the occult:

ELECTRA

Are you thinking of my father?

CLYTEMNESTRA

That is why
I am so behung with jewels, in every one
Exists a certain power. One must but know
How to use them [96].

In her confusion, Clyemnestra, the mother, reels pathetically from dependence to despotism. In the absence of a god, Clytemnestra, the queen, prays to her enslaved daughter whose very power lies in the force of her enmity:

CLYTEMNESTRA

...If it were your pleasure,
I know that you could tell me how to use them.

ELECTRA

I, mother, I?

CLYTEMNESTRA

Yes, you! For you are wise.
Your mind is sound. You talk of old things
As if they happened yesterday. But I
Decay. I think, but all things are confused.
And when I start to speak, Aegisthus cries,
And what he cries out is hateful to me,
And then I would rise up and would be stronger
Than all his words, but I find nothing, nothing! [96].

There are no absolutes in the world of this play. Nothing is secure. The gods are arbitrary and unrecognizable. Human—even family—relations are suspect, and Aegisthus is reduced from the status of lover to that of a weak and hated bedfellow. Reality, like quicksand, is Gleitende.

The elegant theatergoers of fin-de-siècle Vienna attended the performance of this play no doubt to be entertained, to watch comfortably as the players acted on stage. Yet the reality of the performance proved, as do most realities, to be far different from the expected. Instead of entertainment, the spectators were bombarded by pre-expressionistic images of sound and light. The stage was filled with symbols of blood; of overripe, wasted sexuality; of death and physical decay. Pitiful cries of slave women wailed, jackal-like into the night air; furtive, sadistic sounds of whips were heard lashing over bent bodies; shuffling of reluctant feet, of women and beasts being dragged off to sacrifice; the constant play of light and darkness; of hope and despair; uncertainty; mystery and fear. All combined to crack the veneer of complacency with which the spectators had entered the theater, and overwhelm them with the un-verbalized, demonic world of instincts pulsating beneath the veneer of elegant reality.

Clytemnestra appears on stage in the mummified guise of the eternal despot, a wasted figure dredged of life, purpose and desire. Her life-blood has been drained from her complexion to the outer trappings of her garb—gaudy baubles, symbols of royalty and decadence. The director is told,

> The figure of Clytemnestra appears in the wide window. Her sallow, bloated face, in the light thrown from the glaring torches, appears even more pale above her scarlet dress. She supports herself upon one of her women, dressed in dark violet, and upon an ivory staff embellished with precious jewels. Her train is carried by a yellow figure, whose black hair is combed back like an Egyptian, and whose sleek face resembles a poised snake. The queen is almost completely covered with precious stones and talismans. Her arms are full of bracelets, her fingers almost rigid with rings. The lids of her eyes seem excessively large, and it appears to be a great effort for her to hold open [94].

She is, in fact, none other than the prehistoric Egyptian mother goddess. The snake that we had seen in Aeschylus' play as symbol of the mother's ambivalence toward her son and as a projection onto him of her innermost fears, has here become the emblem and the staff of the queen herself; its venom is as deadly to her own person as it is to her children. Here, she is a personification of the horror and the decadence of end-of-the 19th century Europe. With his sumptuous repetition and contrast of colors, gems, and textures (the red-blue hues of blood and the Queen's gown as they are mirrored in her jewels) and with his wax-like, ghostly interplay of the yellow tinge of the lighted torches and candles as they reflect onto the ivory staff and the face of Clytemnestra's serpentine manservant, Hofmannsthal seems to be borrowing the gorgeously erotic art of the popular and controversial artist Gustav Klimt, and subverting it into grotesque images of horror, death- within-life, and human waste.

Again, we might cast our minds back to the language and imagery of the biblical Song of Songs and recognize our fall from the ecstatic and the beautiful to the grotesque. Suzanne Bales describes how, in a manner reminiscent of the Ghost of Hamlet, Max Reinhardt (for whom this play was written) manipulated the colors and the light and shadow in such a way as to create the presence of Agamemnon on stage. [90]

It is the erotic principal that constitutes the underlying energy and determines the relationships in this play. Hofmannsthal was specific in his directions for his stage: a sprawling fig-tree overhanging the women's house of imprisonment laden with overripe fruit, fermenting figs strewn over the stage floor, and the stage itself, bathed in pools of blood and overripe, wasting sexuality. Because she has, in fact, become transformed into the very figure of Hatred, she is unable to realize her feminine, reproductive identity, the principal of life. In this sense, she is again Electra the unmated. Electra's reunion with her brother has erotic undertones. With him, the first loving male to enter her world, she is reminded of her ruined femininity and the audience is granted a glimpse of the way life could have been, even for Electra, had she not been traumatized by a sick and loveless world:

ELECTRA
Who am I
that you should cast such loving looks
at me? See, I am nothing. All I was
I had to sacrifice: even that modesty,

that sweetest thing of all, which, like the silvery, milky haze of the moon, hovers about a woman and protects her and her soul from all things horrible! My modesty was sacrificed as though I'd fallen among thieves who stripped my last garment from me! I have known the wedding-night, as no other virgins, have known the pangs of women who bear children, but have brought nothing into the world, nothing; I have become a perpetual prophetess, and have brought nothing forth from my body except eternal curses and despair [110].

Electra, who has aged and hardened before her time, stands in sharp, dramatic contrast to the fullness and gentleness of her sister Chrysothemis, principle of life, love and fruition. Electra sacrifices life, for she is the conscience and the watchman of her generation. In an uncanny way, she foreshadows both the violence that was soon to rip apart Hofmannsthal's Europe, and people like Simon Wiesenthal and Ellie Wiesel, those watchmen of remembrance who devoted their lives in the twentieth century to perpetuating the lessons of the European holocaust and to hunting down its perpetrators.

We might recall Hamlet's vow that he would remember the ghost of his father:

ELECTRA
Forget? Forget?
Am I a beast then that I should forget? The beast will sleep with its half-eaten prey hanging from its jaws; the beast forgets itself and starts to chew, the while death sits on him. Strangling out life; the beast forgets what crept from its own body, and with its own young allays its hunger—I am no beast. I cannot forget!

Electra is the epitome of the tragic hero in her relentless singleness of purpose:

ELECTRA
At night I never slept, but made my bed high in the tower and cried down to the court and whimpered with the dogs. I have hated. I have seen everything; have had to see everything just like the watchman on the tower, and day is night and night becomes day again, and I have found no joy in sun or stars, for all things, for his sake, were nothing to me, all things were but signs, and every day a marker on the road [110].

Memory, in this sense, is synonymous with the principle of death. In a world in which the gods are indifferent to human suffering, the relentless vigil of the tragic heroine becomes, Antigone-like, the only way to exorcise evil:

ELECTRA

...this time is given you to know the fear that shipwrecked men must know when their vain cry gnaws at the dark clouds and the blackness of death; this time is give you to envy those chained to prison walls, those who cry out from the bottom of a well for death as though for deliverance; for you, you lie so prisoned up within yourself as though in the glowing body of a beast of bronze and, just as now, you cannot cry out! And I stand there beside you, and your eyes Can never leave me, for you hope in vain to read that word upon my silent face; you roll your eyes, you'd grasp at any thought, you'd have the gods smile down at you from the clouds; but the gods the gods are at supper, just as when you slew our father, they're sitting there at supper and are just as deaf now to any death-rattle! Only a half-mad god, the god of laughter, staggers in; he thinks it's a game, a love-game that you're playing with Aegisthus, but when he sees his error, he laughs at once, loud and shrill, and vanishes like that [100].

Electra and Chrysothemis are mirror images of the same personality. They merge and split asunder, impelling the action toward the final climactic sacrifice and demise of Electra, and the emancipation of Chrysothemis and her fellow prisoners:

ELECTRA

...and here I stand and see you
die at last! You will dream no longer then, and
I will dream no more, and who lives after,
let him rejoice and be happy in his life! [101].

Electra represents the death wish, Physis, the destructive aspect of nature, vengeance and remembrance—all attributes that we have thus far characterized as "feminine." She perhaps best exemplifies Freud's theory of history as a force that is propelled by an endless chain of violent eruptions, for she personifies the natural, and sometimes cyclical, movement toward violence and release. Such a force forms the basis of theater as well as historical action. In the plays that we have observed so far, Electra is the personification of hatred who spins itself into self-destruction. Hers is the tragic death and precursor of life and, in this play, she has become a terrifying prophecy of European history.

Chrysothemis, on the other hand, represents the benign, regenerative and, by definition, un-heroic life principle.

CHYSOTHEMIS
Before I die
I want to know what life is! I want children
before my body withers, and even though
they marry me with a peasant, I will bear him
children and will warm them with my body
through cold nights when storms beat at our hut! [91].

Claude Lévi-Strauss claims that tragedy is the result of relationships that are either strangulating in their proximity, or that suffer from too great an alienation. He writes:

The overrating of blood relations is to the underrating of blood relations as the attempt to escape autochthony is to the impossibility to succeed in it. [21]

It is interesting to note that Hofmannsthal constructs his play by means of a series of such strained, parasitical dualities. Electra and Orestes are siblings whose kinship is laced with unnaturally erotic undertones. Electra is the violent force of repressed anger while her brother, conjured by her in an Aeschylean fashion, is merely the instrument and expression of her will. Aegisthus is described by Electra as "the other woman," who is "too narrow around the chest"(95) to wear her father's clothes. Clytemnestra, whom we have already recognized as a grotesque mask of political power, decayed female sexuality, and pathetic vulnerability is, in this way, paired with an image of emasculation, no more than a woman in man's clothing. Yet Aegisthus seems to be draining her of her own life-force. The absence of any positive masculine ideal is conspicuous throughout this play. Electra and Chrysothemis, on the other hand, are chained together as mirror images of the same being.

CHRYSOTHEMIS
It's you who have bound me here with hoops of iron.
Were it not for you, they would not keep us here.
Were it not for your hate, for your unsleeping
and excessive temper, which makes me tremble,
they would not keep us locked and
chained here in this prison, sister! [191].

They are as symbiotically intertwined as life and death. Electra, the principle of vengeance, robbed of her last hope of deliverance, coils herself physically around the body of her sister in her effort to impregnate her with her hatred. With utmost desperation, Electra pledges herself as midwife to Chrysothemis' unborn children in return for her help in the necessary act of revenge. Viktor Auburtin described this moment in the Max Reinhardt production in the following way:

> the most beautiful moment in the piece is when Electra kneels before her sister and begs her with gently, sweet, ingratiating words to help kill her own mother. [92]

Here again, Eros is the demon that motivates the action, and here again, as in Sophocles' play, Electra has become Clytemnestra. In this case, she is the snake that entwines herself around those she would love in her attempt to infest them with her venom. As with Aeschylus, the snake here represents the "boundary ambiguity" which "appears in connection with the boundary between life and death, consciousness and unconsciousness, male and female", [93] Suzanne Bales points out that Electra's attack against her sister is an illustration of the enormous sexual frustration from which she is suffering. As we saw earlier, "the sexual organs receive serpentine associations primarily because copulation blurs the boundaries of the organism." [94]

ELECTRA
I'll hold you! With my wretched withered arms
I'll wind about your body, and if you resist
The knot is pulled tighter; I'll twist myself
Like tendrils round your body, sink my roots
Deep inside you and engraft my will
Into your blood! [104].

With uncanny insight Hofmannsthal recognizes and pinpoints the turning point between memory as the province of one's moral conscience, and that kind of often pseudo-nationalist poisonous hatred, borne of despair and supreme frustration, that threatens to destroy life itself.

ELECTRA
I will not let you go.
We two must grow like one, so that the knife
That severs both our bodies will bring death

...at once, for we are alone now in this world. Out of your chase strong mouth a
terrible cry Must come, a cry as terrible as that Of the Death goddess [104].

And in an action that parallels and is directly antithetical to the act of creation, Electra breathes death into the body of her sister:

ELECTRA
I'll hold you here
Till you have sworn to me, mouth upon mouth,
That you will help me [104].

Ultimately, the generative life—principle is antithetical to the principle of death and Electra is unable to hold on to her sister. Like Aeschylus' heroine, even like Hamlet, Electra must move into a liminal space, a space beyond life, in order to bring the spirit of the past into the present. Like Aeschylus' heroine, and like Hamlet (when he jumps into the grave of Ophelia), Electra claws at the earth (the most primal symbol of life and fertility) with her bare hands. From this she resurrects the spirit of her father in the form of Orestes. For Hofmannsthal, as for Aeschylus and Shakespeare, dynamic action is the direct result of the protagonist's contact with the past.

Richard Strauss: Elektra (1909)

Strauss was inspired to adapt *Electra* to his own operatic score by the Max Reinhardt production of Hofmannsthal's play, particularly by Reinhardt's musicality and superb sense of rhythm. To that end, much of the written text has been forfeited in favor of the composer's musical language. Naturally, Strauss introduces musical motifs to indicate atmosphere, time periods, characters and conflicts. Mostly, music evokes mood, emotions—yearning, regrets, fear, tenderness, lost love—all essential for really "getting," *Elektra*, for understanding it, not with words nor with the mind, but by reaching with our own hearts into the inner recesses of Elektra's, Clytemnestra's, Orestes' and even Agamemnon's. So it is that here, the verbal struggles, the guilt, the conflicts, the longing and the mutual incriminations of the original text are pulled, not by words, but by music, from the deepest recesses of our own hearts—we, the audience. So that, when we understand Clytemnestra, Elektra and Agamemnon—and we do understand them; when we forgive them, and we do forgive them— it is by means of our common humanity. Music strikes a chord in us so deep, so raw and defenseless, it resonates with others in pain, in joy, and in love. In this presentation of the myth, Clytemnestra seems to be responding with an aching nostalgia to Elektra's prompting. She is perhaps reaching back into her past with a longing that almost bridges the gap between the mother and the daughter, and which illustrates a deep, unspoken need that each has for the other, a need that has been, in large part overlooked in the various written texts. Yet, how can mutually longing between mother and daughter have been glossed over, if not entirely missed, in the various written versions? How essential and obvious? How could we even approach the subject without taking the mother/daughter longing into account? Surely it underlies all other considerations? Was it because we were busy talking, because we were preoccupied by ideas?

Suzanne Bales points out that the motif associated with Agamemnon is introduced at the very moment the queen reaches hungrily backward — perhaps to her former self, perhaps to that forgotten innocent girl, a girl obliterated by time and experience, who had existed way back before loss, before grief and her own heinous act of murder. The motif associated with Agamemnon is introduced in a beguiling and excruciatingly painful manner, suggesting perhaps that Clytemnestra is unable to reach her daughter without first re-encountering war, her husband's betrayal, and his murder of Iphigenia. Memories evoke both the good and the bad; Clytemnestra's effort to regain her former innocence necessitates her confrontation with her worst nightmare, that which she is struggling against with all her might: ten long years of mourning and bitterness toward her husband; ten long years to plot and scheme her revenge, and then her own ghastly act of retribution. As mentioned earlier in this work, music, not words, is the language of emotions. There is more here to be dredged up by music, than words ever dreamed of. Here, music has taken the place of the spoken word for the expression of the irrational, of those powerful emotions that underlie reality, and which Hofmannsthal suggested are the cause of rebellion and violence.

Here again the action takes place in an all-female world, one in which heroism, in the figure of the murdered king, is a painful memory which must be avoided. Orestes appears again, only at the end of the action, as a timid, waiting youth, as the pre-hero, as one who is conjured up again by Elektra, the priestess, and goaded into the painful action that manhood, in such a world, exacts. Here again the stage represents the outer court of the women's prison. It is an area of violence, of darkness, of suspicion and of lurking shadows. It becomes the passage through which beasts of burden and human slaves pass on their way to the sacrificial altar. As such, it suggests the endless chain of violence and murder that characterizes human behavior today, and since time immemorial. It is the haunting-ground of Elektra, perpetual mourner of the dead.

It is in this space that the chorus of slave women and female overseers open the action of the play. The difference between this chorus and those of Aeschylus and Sophocles is that the slaves of the earlier plays agitated for liberation, while these women are agents of despotism, and work to repress any expression of freedom. As such, they appear in much more sinister form than the slave women of ancient Greece. They gossip about Elektra with vindictive malice while at the same time providing us with a vivid account of the protagonist's own fiery temperament and hostility toward them— the slave women who represent the establishment and the world of this play. This Elektra is the perfect example of Northrop Frye's definition of the tragic hero as one who is essentially estranged from society. [25] Within a few lines it becomes obvious that our protagonist is an outcast, alienated in a world of savagery in which even the slave that defends her thinks only in terms of hatred and cruelty. Elektra's madness is the madness of political and moral isolation. The sadism of the chorus provides a grotesque mirror image of the protagonist's madness, and also of the insanity of a decadent body politic.

Elektra enters alone, for she is quintessentially alone in this hostile world, and the reason she has clasped so tenaciously and so long to the memory of her beloved father immediately becomes obvious. Agamemnon is the one being she can turn to, if only within the recesses of her own tortured memory. He belongs to her if for no other reason than by virtue of her loyalty and need of him. Strauss has here psychologized the Greek theme of revenge and remembrance. Here, the daughter clings to the memory of her beloved father, as does any lonely child in an oppressive and hostile environment. The spirit of the dead king is not confined to any single area of the stage. Unlike the Ghost of Hamlet who had been banished from his own court, Agamemnon lies here in an undefined grave somewhere, and consequently everywhere, beneath the flagstones of this outer courtyard. This opera works along the psychological principles of repression: it is because Agamemnon and his murder are so utterly denied by the queen and the world of her servants that the dead king becomes the most forceful and all-pervasive in the play. The musical motif associated with Agamemnon therefore represents an untamable force in a repressed subconscious that threatens to overthrow both the individual and the state.

The tragic heroine enters at dusk, the hour at which her father had been murdered so many years earlier. She laments his murder and calls to him, as to her only ally, not to leave her languishing in this hostile world but to appear to her as he had done the previous night, by means of his shadow passing along the wall. In this sense, the ghost of her dead father constitutes Elektra's very life force. She lives for him alone. Here, in place of the red light that Reinhardt had used to indicate the ghostly presence of Agamemnon, Strauss has introduced a musical "Agamemnon" motif, one that together with the shadows, the desperate call of Elektra and the sense that this entire stage is in some way the burial-ground of Agamemnon, introduces the presence of the murdered king and father as one that will be pervasive throughout. Elektra is the only one to mention Agamemnon. It is she who keeps the spirit of her father alive and palpable in the courtyard in which he was buried. It is because of Elektra, the daughter, that the presence of the father permeates the play and propels the characters into action.

Elektra is the guardian of the grave and spirit of her father. When, in the recognition scene, Orestes asks if she is "related in blood to them who died," Elektra proudly declares: "Related? I? / I am that blood!" [26] and, as such, she is the priestess of the dead.

Elektra, the unmated, has dedicated her life to the spirit of her father in a way that a Christian nun dedicates herself to Christ. She is the virgin-priestess that we had met in Aeschylus' play and, as such, she is endowed with powers from the invisible gods. It is surely in recognition of this—Elektra's particular role—that Clytemnestra approaches her daughter across the barrier of their mutual animosity as a suppliant for a cure against her nightmares.

Bales points out that in Strauss' opera, Clytemnestra and her two daughters are victims of their own arrested psychological development. Chrysothemis comes to warn her sister that Aegisthus and the queen are planning to remove her forever from the light of day should she not curb her anger against them (a punishment that Chrysothemis herself, who so longs for life, could never tolerate), but Elektra considers her sister a collaborator, the "daughter of your mother." [27] She greets Chrysothemis with the petulance of the adolescent, ordering her to deliver her message and remove herself from her sight. However, it is not Elektra's poisonous memories and vindictive nature that destroy the single half-moment Clytemnestra and Elektra share, but Elektra's being confronted again by her mother's infantile savagery. This queen is blinded by her egocentricity, by her childlike horror of her dreams, and by her need to rid herself of them regardless of the suffering it might cause others. Bales claims that ultimately it is the queen's cruelly selfish cry

> And must I let blood each beast that creeps and flies! And rise each day and sleep each night in the steam Of their blood, like the race that lives in farthest Thule In blood-red mist: I will not dream again.

that thrusts Elektra from her once again in hostility and rebuttal:

> Your dreams will end when the right blood sacrifice falls beneath the axe. [28]

Elektra represents the moral conscience of a world that cruelly resembles Europe at the end of the nineteenth century. She is symbiotically tied to her sister, Chrysothemis, the principle of life, and, like a dead husk, she, the old order, is shed at the end of the action in order to grant life to the new.

Despite the psychological interpretation that Strauss gives his opera and despite the expressionistic style that Reinhardt used, both artists remain true to the classic Greek form of the play. Are they illustrating, by means of this classic form in modern garb, that the passage of time is no guarantee of human progress? Are they dramatizing Freud's theory that violence is an integral part of man and of Western civilization; that, for the sake of civilization, it must be repressed—yet which by force of nature, is bound, periodically, to erupt? [22] Were these artists recognizing, in Elektra's dance of death, the inevitability of war and devastation in Europe?

What has happened to ritual in this world in which there is no longer any shared view and where spectators arrive for the performance with a contradictory approach to life and theater than that of the performers? The emotional threat that this dramatization of wild, imprisoned women must have had on its audience, the savage outburst of instinctual violence that it depicts as an underlying force threatening to erupt and destroy the orderly world of 1909 Berlin, must have been devastating. The screams, the colors of blood and of violence, the ghostly musical reminder of an older, better age together with the threat of revolution that bombarded the audience behind the doors of the Berlin theater—all these must have bonded the audience as fellow travelers in a hijacked airplane or co-participants in any other civil or natural disaster. For the duration of the performance all are ensnared in the same traumatic eruption of the intellect and the senses, all are jolted out of their protective cloak of complacence, and all are forced to reevaluate their previous understanding of reality. This, I believe, is the ritual of today's theater. It is the drawing together of strangers in an enclosed space in such a way as to change their awareness. The values that are dramatized here with such force are not those of the general society. Sanity, heroism, and the act of theater itself are foreign in this space from the way they seem in the familiar, outer world. And we cling to the elements of violence in the theater as one does to the carriage of the fairground rollercoaster with the fervent prayer that we will not crash.

Eugene O'Neill: **Mourning Becomes Electra (1931)**

Freud transformed human experience to the extent that it has become difficult, since the publication of his theories, to perceive reality in pre– Freudian terms. The change of focus that he created, from the effect that the many have over the individual to that which the individual, with his myriad emotions and complex psychic structure, has over his society, very much influenced American art forms during the 1920s and '30s. Thus, in O'Neill's play, the repression of the Electra figure, which even in Greek times had physical, sexual and emotional connotations, has become an exposé of arrested sexual and emotional growth. The myth of death and rebirth has moved from the universal to the personal. Here the theme has morbidly turned in upon a totally solipsistic Lavinia/Orin personality, one that is unable to move beyond the point of its own stifled development. In sharp contrast to early Greek society, which had encouraged the process of death and rebirth by means of ritual, this society, like this household, becomes itself the instrument of a death that can allow for no rebirth:

MANNON
Nothing was clear except that there'd always been some barrier between us—a wall hiding us from each other! [100]

The individual is the mirror of his society, which we get to see in the caricature-like chorus of gossips and islanders. In a tight-lipped New England town such as this, characterized more by its closed doors and shuttered windows than by manhood or the heroic, there can be no growth, no journey toward manhood and the heroic, and consequently, no future; only an excruciating longing that is always there and that can never be appeased:

BECKWITH
Oh, Shenandoah, I long to hear
you A-way, my rolling river
Oh, Shenandoah, I can't get near you
Way-ay, I'm bound away
Across the wide Missouri [688].

The play moves from the exterior to the interior of the house and outward on to the water, as the dramatic concentration moves from objective reality to the internal, psychological motivations of the individual and, finally, to the diseased, unconscious regions of the mind. In this way, the structure and separate spaces of the play create the theme. The life-defying alienation that exists between the characters on stage, and between the actors and audience, is theatrically created in the structure and separate spaces of the play.

Mourning Becomes Electra is the expression of a stagnant society. The house which, in Giroudoux' play (as we shall see later), is torn between tears and laughter, is here a house of doom. The curse of the House of Atreus here becomes the repressively Puritanical outlook of the Mannon family:

MANNON
That's always been the Mannon's way of thinking.
They went to the White meeting-house on Sabbaths and meditated on death.
Life was A dying. Being born was starting to die. Death was being born [738].

We are told that white pillars from its pagan façade cast dark, prison-like shadows across the Puritan front of this house. Despite their denial, these people are ultimately prisoners of their passions. The face of the house with its shuttered windows forms a mask of death, as do the faces of Clytemnestra, Electra, and Orestes, and is a theatrical representation of the repression of emotions, a "putting on a front" for the outdoor world while, at the same time, it represents a diminution of the exterior in order to explore the emotions seething within.

Here the theme of incest is a theatrical imaging of a family and of individuals who are turned in on themselves in a way that can only presage death. Orin is an abomination, a victim of the oppressive and, consequently, dead aspect of what we had identified in the Greek world as the Great Mother. He has been reduced from hero to impotent child, not by his society as much as by the psychological forces in his own family structure. In this way, "fate," that had played so powerful a part in the Classical world, has become the inescapably intertwined forces of hereditary factors and family relationships. The interior of the house, with its massive furniture and its family portraits on the wall, personifies on stage the enormous ancestral burden that these characters bear. They cower Ibsen-like beneath the portraits of their ancestors. In this way, the ghosts of their fathers are tangible at all times and, like the Aeschylean ghost, they directly influence the fate of their household. True to the traditional portrayal of the myth, Mannon has survived the death and destruction of civil war only to be overcome by the fate of his own family.

Since Sophocles, Electra's insanity has represented the vigor of the antirational, and opposition to the establishment. Here, it resurfaces in Lavinia's insistence on maintaining, at all costs, a façade of normalcy over a consciousness of increasingly violent and volcanic behavior. It is also the disintegration of a boy who is incestuously attached to his mother and who will therefore never experience the "heroic" break from the maternal, so necessary for his journey toward manhood. Insanity is no longer an affront to the body politic. Here it is the cause of chaos and devastation in the individual human being. Fate has moved from the realm of the gods to the insurmountable forces inside the human soul, and is represented as such in images on stage.

In this play, as in *The Prodigal* (which we will see later in this study), water symbolizes what Peter Brook has termed the "empty space" and Herbert Blau "the conscious state." It is the space, which constitutes the beginning—the silent moment, the drawing in—of any theatrical event, and here it is specifically the meeting-place of the unconscious mind around which the performers and the audience are congregated. It is Aeschylus' burial mound, the sacred center of the ritual, which draws actors and audience magnetically together in a common focus of concentration. It is the space to which the growing adolescent withdraws before taking upon himself the heroic return and subsequent heroic action. It is the spiritual center that was covered over in Hamlet but which forced itself onto the periphery of the Shakespearian mind and stage. But here, in *Mourning Becomes Electra*, everything has become a quagmire of hatred and repressed sexual desire from which the protagonist can never escape. Water is the unconscious, the place of seething passions, memory, fear, violence and murder. It is an element of the human makeup that we most try to avoid, yet which, on this stage, we are forced to witness and directly assess.

The stagnant, Puritan society of this small New England town has so alienated its members from one another that the Mannon household has become totally turned in on itself. It is knotted and gnarled by incestuous introversion until, like some horrendous, sick beast, it attacks and devours its own flesh. In Greek terms, it is the epitome of the destructive Earth Mother.

Hatred has become the only vehicle of expression. Lavinia has always been as we see her here, with her frigid exterior desperately controlling an illicit sexuality. Her tragic fall occurred before her birth with her grandfather's construction of this house of hatred and vengeance. Her mordant cry for revenge is her desperate appeal for love in a house that disdains the simple expression of emotional needs. Christine has evolved from the Terrible Earth Mother of pagan times, who had sacrificed her drone-like husband for the fertility of nature, to a product of the Christian domestic tradition who just "wants out," and plunges tragically from one human trap to another. For, in this deadly locked society there is no new blood, no hope for new life, only the ghostly repetition of the same name and the same house and the same situation over and over.

Orin is the last of this sick chain of being, and the end of the Orestean line. As such, he is the weakest link. We see him entrenched in his preconscious stage, incestuously tied to the figure of his mother/sister:

ORIN
If I had been he I would have done what he did!
I would have loved her as he loved her—
killed father too—for her sake [803].

For him, there is no heroic voyage for there is no hope for manhood. The demise of the mother necessitates the death of the undifferentiated son:

ORIN
Do you remember me telling you how the faces
of the men I killed
Came back and changed to Father's face and finally became my
own?... maybe I've committed suicide! [198].

Jean Giraudoux: Electra (1937)

In a world without absolutes, the ironic takes the place of the tragic, and the tragic hero becomes the un-hero. The justice that Electra anticipates as the culmination of her aspirations becomes a grotesque mirror of violence. Orestes, the avenging arm of his sister and, as such, the youth seeking that heroism which we have recognized so far as manhood, perpetrates the deed out of mindless indifference. Manhood, heroism and justice are re-examined in this play and are found wanting.

It is perhaps a sign of their innocence that the Greeks had experienced guilt only as the aftermath of evil. The modern world is not so fortunate. Jean Giraudoux' *Electra* is a satirical parody of the tragic mode. Here the Eumenides do not appear after Orestes' murder of Clytemnestra and Aegisthus. Rather, they walk in with him as he first appears, suggesting, in an almost Jacobean way, that they are accompanying him onto the stage of life. In this play, the Eumenides are grotesque, nasty little girls who swell visibly as Orestes experiences the reality of his myth. This is an anti-heroic play in an age of anti-heroes. Human beings are pursued throughout life by guilt, and by grotesque, ugly, irksome questions.

The Eumenides form the chorus of the play. They introduce the characters and the action. More than anything, they infuse a sense of foreboding, an atmosphere of alienation and discomfort. They are the furies of the modern stage, and of modern life.

The setting is the palace of Argos. Never has Orestes seen such a sensitive building. The right side of the building is built:

GARDENER
of stones from Gaul and sweats at certain seasons that the people say
the palace is weeping. The left side is built of marble from Argos which is
flooded by sunlight even at night. [101]

The palace laughs and cries at the same time. It is a house as neurotic and divided against itself as the lives of those it shelters, and as the opposing forces of a divided Europe. Giraudoux develops his characters along Euripidean lines. Clytemnestra is not totally evil, rather she is a confused, middle-aged, unloved woman who appeals desperately to her daughter for understanding. She wants to be accepted as a woman, but Electra sees her only as a mother.

As a daughter, Electra can neither understand nor forgive Clytemnestra's repugnance for Agamemnon; neither can she understand or accept her mother's need or right or to be loved. Giraudoux' Electra, like her Euripidean counterpart, is dangerously unbalanced. Her need for revenge against her mother has been smoldering for seven years. Ironically, unlike the Electra character of ancient Greece, this Electra does not know the real reason for her hatred. She persuades herself that it is because her mother had allowed Orestes to fall, as a baby—the fall symbolic, perhaps, of his fall from royalty to anonymity in exile, yet it is dealt with on a personal level.

Clytemnestra claims that she dropped Orestes while holding him at arms' length to prevent him from being pricked by a sharp pin she was wearing. We will remember the sting by now, the adder in the maternal breast of Greek mythology, symbol of the ambivalence that the mother has for her son, and of the son's desire to grow closer to his mother.

For her part, Clytemnestra accuses Electra both of pushing Orestes away from her out of hatred, and of attempting to clutch him to her in an incestuous embrace. No doubt, all these conflicting emotions were authentic, and all, no doubt reflected the feelings that Giraudoux, the French diplomat, experienced in prewar Germany.

The theme of incest between brother and sister is developed here, not to demonstrate the emergence of the hero, and not as any enactment of our theme of fertility—of death and resurrection of the hero in nature as it had in the original, Aeschelean version—but as a powerfully satiric devaluation of the "heroic." Despite the neurotic ambivalence of Electra, the heroic in this play is not masculine action. Here, men live by means of compromise and political expediency, not by commitment to truth. Heroism is presented, rather, in the guise of female integrity, memory, and the insistence on abstract ideals—an insistence that is both insane, and impossible to live with. Again, the female is the uncompromising figure of Electra. Again, the female is associated with madness and truth.

PRESIDENT
If criminals don't forget their sins, if the conquered don't forget their defeats. If there are curses, quarrels, hatreds, the fault is not with humanity's conscience, which always tends toward compromise and forgetfulness, it lies with ten or fifteen women who cause trouble.

STRANGER
I agree with you. Those ten or fifteen women save the world from egoism.

PRESIDENT
They save it from happiness. I know Electra. Let's agree that she is what you say—justice, generosity, duty. But it is by justice, generosity, duty, and not by egoism and easy-going ways, that the state, individuals, and the best families are ruined.

PRESIDENT
…Happiness is never the lot of implacable people. A happy family makes a surrender. A happy epoch demands unanimous capitulation [143].

Giraudoux regarded pre-war France as a nation which, for the sake of happiness, was making a "unanimous capitulation"; as one that was rapidly losing its moral fiber; whose innate sense of justice, loyalty and patriotism was being forfeited for economic security and modernism. Moral values were corroding; institutions were disintegrating. In short, Giraudoux believed that his country was selling out to Prussianism, mechanization, power and money, and that, ultimately, despite the enormous inconvenience, only France's involvement in World War II would be able to set it back on a course of courage and moral stability. In 1940 he wrote, "This war, the worst of evils, must be made to serve a purpose: to act as the sluicegates between a bygone era and a new age." [102]

As in the Greek plays on the same theme, Electra longs for Orestes. He alone is capable of arousing in her embittered soul, any feeling of love. He reveals himself, and she clasps him to her in the archetypal embrace of sister- lover. She was the captive. He will be her redeemer.

As an extension of the Euripidean suggestion, Electra and Orestes sleep in total mutual symbiosis. This sleep is again the Hieros gamos—the sacred marriage and the longed-for fusion of the oppositions in a hitherto fragmented mind, as in a divided Europe. The *Hieros gamos* is the perfect coming together and should give birth to the ideal human being, the ideal action—or, perhaps, the ideal nation. Yet, Electra will settle for nothing short of Justice as her ideal. Ironically, justice is achieved, but wears the mask of evil. The ideal action might be the restoration of justice, but to what extent was one able, in the twentieth century, to perpetrate such a horrendous act and maintain one's humanity? To what extent are we of the twenty-first century able to maintain our humanity? The perfect union represents the self- fulfillment that the hero wins after his greatest struggle. As mentioned, it brings to mind the sacred marriage of Faustus' Helen and Paris (Goethe) which, had it not been disrupted, would have produced the purest alchemical ideal—a golden child. Giraudoux' scene, however, is played backward. The sacred marriage takes place before his Orestes murders his mother and, instead of giving birth to a golden child, it produces, in Electra, a knowledge and memory of her mother's crime against her father: an image of horror, an image of the *imperfect*. So, with extreme irony, it is Electra's uncompromising insistence on justice that gives way to the horrors of war.

As with Euripides, Giraudoux's Agamemnon wanted to marry Electra to a commoner (the gardener) because, as the beggar realizes, he fears that "one day she will become Electra," that "she will begin to bite, to turn the city upside-down, to push up the price of butter, start a war" (150).

Electra becomes Electra, that is, she grows from the neurotically hateful girl to an avenging fury during that one night of sacred union with her newfound brother/deliverer. Instead of producing hope for the future, this union has teased monsters from the past.

Electra stands for the absolute. She has the potential for light and clarity but she is, by nature, violent and uncompromising. It is

as though she has been channeled through the deeds of her mother (earth and remembrance) to explode with ruthless clarity over mankind. Aegisthus recognizes the seer in Electra:
I knew I'd find her looking toward me, her statuesque head, her eyes Which see only when the lids are closed, deaf to human speech [186].
The world that Electra inhabits is one of compromise. In this play, Electra is an anachronism. In an age of humanitarianism, she is the visionary who cannot see humanity. If there is a Chrysothemis character in this play, we might find her in the less likeable Agatha, the mindless, childlike bride of the President of the Council, a woman who marries for status and protection and loves for the satisfaction of her sexual appetites. In Giraudoux' play, all the characters are sadly ordinary. Still, their petty greed, their lust, and their hunger for love are less threatening than the heroic.

AEGISTHUS
If for ten years the gods have not meddled with our lives it is because I kept the heights empty and the fairground full ... our poor neighboring cities betray themselves by erecting their gallows on the top of the hill. I crucify at the bottom of a valley [148].

Safety lies in anonymity, in not tempting fate. Here there is no heroic struggle and no transformation into manhood. Orestes, the avenging hero, is not roused to passion by means of any communal incantations or libation to the gods, as in Aeschylus. He is not a man of action, craft and noble purpose as in Sophocles, nor is he a man torn between filial love and duty, as in Euripides. He is merely a soft-spoken stranger with no particular commitment, but with a nostalgia for his hometown and a feeling of affection for his sister. There is no passion in his matricide. It is merely the logical consequence of Electra's inquisition. It constitutes the un-heroic deed of an un-hero, an undifferentiated youth.
The closest we come to a masculine form of heroism, in Giraudoux' Electra, is in the practical leadership ability that suddenly develops at the end of the action in the character of Aegisthus, the repressive figure of masculine authority:

AEGISTHUS

Electra, you're in my power. Your brother too. I can kill you. Yesterday I should have killed you. Instead of that I promise as soon as the enemy is repulsed, to step down from the throne and place Orestes on it. ...Tomorrow, before the altar where we celebrate our victory the guilty man shall stand, for there is only one guilty man in a patricide's coat. He'll confess his crime publicly and determine his punishment himself. First let me save the city (198).

In the low "fair-ground" of our un-classical reality, it is not "the purest, the handsomest, the youngest" hero in whom Electra places her trust, that saves the city (191).

If there is any form of idealization in this play, we might find it in the practical man-of-action, the rational politician who does not allow himself to be swayed by passion; in the common sinner with potential for good.

AEGISTHUS

Do you doubt my sincerity?

ELECTRA

I don't doubt it. I recognize in it the hypocrisy and malice of the gods. They change a parasite into a just man, an adulterer into a husband, a usurper into a king. They thought my task not painful enough, so they made a figure of honor out of you, whom I despise! [192].

This is the opposite of the "heroic" so admired by the Greeks. The beggar foresees that Electra will reveal herself as Electra and that the king will "reveal himself as Aegisthus." At the moment Electra emerges as the avenger of objective truth and universal justice, the king grows from a petty tyrant to a man capable of delivering the city into peace. Truth has emerged as an abstraction, an ideal that is antithetical to peace, and Aegisthus begs Electra to delay her truth for the sake of his city. But "the beautiful and cruel thing about truth is that she is eternal, but is also like a flash of lightning" (196). Such is the nature of Electra. Aegisthus, the harbinger of peace, has blood on his hands, and he placates the crowd with half-truths pretending he is already married to Clytemnestra. Electra, the voice of the absolute, cannot brook such compromise. For her, peace can come only after the total eradication of the present order. Despite the deliberately anti- classical episodic structure of the play, Electra's tunnel vision reveals itself to us in the traditional form of the tragic heroine. Her moral vision is contradictory to our own.

The nasty little Furies have grown to the stature of Electra. They are Electra. As such they will leave Argos and hound Orestes who, far from being the newly matured youth on his heroic journey to manhood, is merely an innocent vehicle of death.

SEC. FURY
Satisfied Electra? The city ... is dying.

ELECTRA
I am satisfied. I know that it will be born again.

For the tragic heroine who knows only extremes, life can be resumed only after total destruction.

THIRD FURY
And the people killing each other in the streets, will they be born again?

ELECTRA
I have my conscience. I have Orestes.
I have everything [203].

Electra, ruthless voice of Physis and remembrance, has a morality true only to herself.

The Olympian vision of the relentless and unalterable cosmic order, and the need that Greek tragedy had to bring man into harmony with the forces of nature, have no place in the modern world.

Giraudoux has untied the knot that once bound man to heroism. The lofty but willful gods of the ancient Greeks are reduced to two dramatic elements:

(1) A single meddlesome beggar who sits, essentially off-center stage, observing the suffering of his fellow characters with callous objectivity, and
(2) a pathetic band of outcasts who come as a Deus ex machina to deliver Orestes and Electra not from murder, but for murder. The tragedy wends its way from episode to episode with little regard for character plausibility, tragic flaws, recognition or reversals. All aspects of Aritotelian tragedy are somehow suggested—but missed.

We are familiar with the Aristotelian necessity that the tragic hero fall from a lofty and admired position, as with the fact that only the particular circumstances of a hero's life/character make him commit the tragic deed. Yet here Electra lives on in the palace of her dead father, and remains throughout Electra—fiery element that wields clarity and destruction and accepts no compromise. The heroic is in question, and tragedy, the heroic form, has fallen. Aegisthus challenges Electra's classical justice:

AEGISTHUS
And you dare call this justice that makes you burn your city, damn your family; you dare call this the justice of the gods?

And Electra replies:

ELECTRA
There are criminals we love, murderers we embrace. But when the crime is an
assault on human dignity, infects a nation, corrupts its loyalty, then—
no pardon is possible [195].

Electra is condemned for her extremism. Yet how would we respond today? How would we have reacted, just 25 years after World War II, to the appointment of Kurt Waldheim as Foreign Minister of Austrian Foreign Affairs—or as Secretary General to the United Nations? What if Giraudoux had written this play a few years later, after World War II? Would the supreme moral voice of Physis have seemed more plausible? What about our own twenty first century? How would Electra's extremism react to the rampages of Isis across the globe?

Giraudoux' use of irony is his means of raising, in physical form, the ambiguity that bourgeois audiences have toward their own ideals. It is by means of the poet's use of images, of the sensual, the passionate and the empathic, that he stimulates the humanity of spectators. David Cole writes, "[We] recognize the images which the theatre depends upon our recognizing because, to be human is to recognize them." [103] Again, theater has become the raising of issues between players and spectators in such a way as to form a concentration, a focal point of attention. The reactions that are provoked on a particular stage, at a particular moment, as the direct result of all the combined elements of the performance, constitute the theatrical event.

Robinson Jeffers: The Tower Beyond Tragedy (1937)

Robinson Jeffers was born in Pittsburgh, Pennsylvania, of Anglo-Irish parents on January 10, 1887, but moved with his family to the West Coast while still quite young. He has been described as an individualist, as somewhat of a recluse, as gentle, reserved and meditative. He was raised in a strict Calvinist home and educated by his father in the classics. On August 2, 1913, he married Una Cull, an extremely beautiful and well-educated woman with whom he had been in love for several years. The newlyweds intended to settle in England, but were forced, because of the outbreak of World War I to make Northern California their home. Jeffers wrote:

> the August news turned us to this village of Carmel instead; and when the stage- coach topped the hill from Monterey, and we looked down through the pines and sea-fogs in Carmel Bay, it was evident that we had come without knowing to our inevitable place. [104]

It was in the isolation of these mountains that Jeffers found his true purpose. He loved the mists, the sunsets, the low clouds and the mystical wildness of the ocean. For five years, this solitary, introverted man, became a land-mark for passers-by who saw him daily extracting massive boulders out of the rocks of the shoreline and lugging them to his home on a kind of primitive pulley which is believed to have been used by ancient Egyptians in the construction of their Sphynx. The erection of his tower, which became famous as Tor House, granted Jeffers a profound sense of peace and when it was completed, he'd climb to its summit at nightfall and meditate. He described the scenery around his home in the following war:

> The Santa Lucian hills overlook the Carmel River and extend Southward along the coast. Their northernmost slopes are pine-crested; the valleys beyond are forested with redwoods (sequoias) and oaks and Santa Lucian Firs. This region, and the peninsular are made aerially beautiful by cloud play and the frequent ocean-mists.

The clouds most often hang long, half veiling the hill; and the atmosphere is singularly transparent, and I have been astonished by the brilliancy of the sky during thunderstorms, in heavy and starless nights. [105]

Perhaps during the war years this view atop the human landscape provided the poet his own Private "tower beyond tragedy."

In an interview, Una Jeffers talked with Lawrence Clark Powell about the ambivalence her husband felt regarding America's involvement in the war. "He disliked the cant of neutrality, followed by the cant of our belligerency." She said that he'd been torn between a feeling of obligation to enlist in the military forces and his obligation to stay in Carmel and support his young family. She elaborated: "The conflict of motives on the subject of going to war or not was probably one of several factors that, about that time, made the world and his own mind much more real and intense to him. Another factor was the rebuilding of Tor House. As he helped the workers shift and place the wind and wave-worn granite, I think he realized some kinship with it, and became aware of strengths in himself unknown before. Thus, at the age of thirty-one there came to him the kind of awakening such as adolescents and religious converts are said to experience." [106]

Louis Adamic was a close friend and biographer of Jeffers. He wrote:

The human breed is degenerating (no doubt about it and no way to stop the process,) and viewing it in the mirror of his own mind, his cosmic consciousness, and in relation to his universe, he finds it offensive. America is a "perishing Republic" and will have "centuries of increasing decadence." There is a limited sort of salvation only for the individual. One can crawl into his cave and stay there. A heron a-wing "over the black ebb" is dearer to him than "the many pieces of humanity ... gathering shellfish" and dropping "paper and other filth" on the beach, heedless of the sign warning them against it which has stuck by the road that winds through his place. Indeed, "humanity is needless." He warns his young boys to be moderate in their "love of man" and goes on singing of points Lobos and Sur, of his own hopelessness and violence ... of the elements in their dramatic moods, of Time and Space. [107]

We cannot help regarding the elitist isolationism of this American poet as a rare luxury. No doubt many in Europe, at this time, would also have relished the opportunity to escape the ravages of war.

The "awakening" that Una had attributed to her husband bears an uncanny similarity to the one we've observed so far as that of the prophet, the adolescent, and the hero, returning from their own isolation. It is the awakening that constitutes the starting point of the Electra plays, and perhaps, in general, that of the tragic form.

Jeffers bases his song of matricide, incest and madness on the already familiar context of the Electra myth. From the perspective of the twenty-first century, the myth itself has become as timeless as the eternally recurring cycle of passion and violence it depicts. The characters are fated to an endless chain of emotional torture because they are deprived of any psychological or emotional movement other than what is allotted them in their story so far.

Accordingly, the larger-than-life characters in Jeffers' dramatic poem are spun of a human intensity that will never be disentangled from the context of the myth. In a Lévi-Straussian understanding of tragedy, they suffer from being too close to one another.

ORESTES
...I saw a vision of us move in the dark:
all that we did or dreamed of Regarded each other,
the man pursued the woman, the
woman clung to the man, warriors and kings
Strained at each other in the darkness, all loved
Or fought inward, each one of the lost people
Sought the eyes of another that another should
Praise him; sought never his own but another's;
The net of desire
Had every nerve drawn to the center,
so that they writhed like a full draught of fishes,
all matted In the one mesh...
It is all turned inward, all your desires incestuous,
the woman the serpent, the man the Rose-red cavern
Both human, worship forever. [108]

In this context, the theme of incest becomes emblematic of the introverted and convoluted relationships that suffocate the hero and prevent him from realizing the potential of the greater world of which he is a part. In this context, also, the hero becomes he who can liberate himself from the suffocation of emotional, social and political ties. Orestes is such a hero:

As for me, I have slain my mother.

…
And the grave's open,
The gray boils over the mountain,
I have greater Kindred than dwell under a roof…
…
I have cut the meshes
And fly like a freed falcon [138].

Jeffers' medium is poetry, language of myth, passion and madness. With her own naked body, in the ultimate act of sexual antagonism, Clytemnestra masters and holds at bay the savage, hungry men-of-war that surround her. The queen, a figure of hypnotic, mythic stature, manipulates ritual in a desperate attempt to control her environment and transform her murderous ecstasy into order and acceptance.

CLYTEMNESTRA
I rule you, I
The Gods have satisfied themselves
in this man's Death; there shall not one drop of the
blood of the city Be shed further. I say the high
gods are content; as for the lower.
And the great ghost of the King: my slaves will
Bring out the king's body decently before you
And set it here, in the eyes of the city:
spices the ships bring from the south
will comfort his spirit;
Mycenae and Tiryns and the shores
will mourn him Aloud; sheep will be slain for him;
a hundred Beeves Spill their thick blood into the trenches
Captives and slaves go down to serve him, yes all These captives
Burn in the ten-day fire with him, unmeasured wine Quench it, urned
in pure gold
the gathered ashes Rest forever in the sacred rock; honored; a A
conqueror…
…
A woman among lions! Ah, the king's power, ah the
King's victories! Weep for me, Mycenae!
Widowed of the king! [97–8].

Agamemnon's death has turned into a veritable feast of the gods who, as Clytemnestra puts it, "love what men call crime"(110). [109] There is a distinct hierarchy here between the indifferent gods, the beautifully white-skinned and treacherous aristocracy, and those "dogs," the common men with their "poor brown and spotted women"[110] who serve as fodder for the appetites of their masters. The

Greek plays were aristocratic not only in tone, but also by virtue of the enormous distance that existed between the lives of aristocracy and those of the peasants. In this modern work, there is a sinister closeness between the victims and the victimizers of society. As with Hoffmannsthal's play, suffering here is relentless and perpetual specifically among the masses—the "slaves" of those in power. In an interesting twist to of the theme of ritual as the play of death and rebirth, these slaves must go down with the assassinated ruler in order to guarantee the life and security of the vanquishing head of state.

In *Violence and the Sacred*, Rene Girard describes the sacrificial rites of primitive communities, much as Freud does in Totem and Taboo, as an experience in which all participants are united in a blood-bond with the sacrificial victim. He maintains that communities, in their effort to establish a lasting civilization, held to rigid laws of status and position, that so long as everyone adhered to his or her rank in society, things ran smoothly, but as soon as one member was dislodged from his or her appointed status, the rest of the social pyramid began to crumble. Girard writes:

> The sacrificial crisis can be defined, therefore, as a crisis of distinctions—that is, a crisis affecting the cultural order. This cultural order is nothing more than a regulated system of distinctions in which the differences among individuals are used to establish their "identity" and their mutual relationships. [111]

He claims that

> When the religious framework of a society starts to totter, it is not exclusively or immediately the physical security of the society that is threatened, rather, the whole cultural foundation of the society is put in jeopardy. The institutions lose their vitality; the protective façade of the society gives way; social values are rapidly eroded, and the whole cultural structure seems on the verge of collapse.
> A single principle is at work in primitive religion and classical tragedy alike, a principle implicit but fundamental. Order, peace, and fecundity depend on cultural distinctions; it is not these distinctions but the loss of them that gives birth to fierce rivalries and sets members of the same family or social group at one another's throats. [112]

According to Girard, such a society, under threat of disintegration, needed to sidetrack its destructive intentions from members of its own community, and project its hostility onto some objective scapegoat.

Only in such a way, could all the members of the community regroup harmoniously in a collective hostility against one common enemy. With a clear-eyed scrutiny of that kind of victimization that has characterize Western civilization from the time of Oedipus and Electra to the twenty-first century, Girard claims

> When a community succeeds in convincing itself that one alone of its number is responsible for the violent mimesis besetting it, when it is able to view this member as the single "polluted" enemy who is contaminating the rest; and when the citizens are truly unanimous in this conviction—then the belief becomes reality, for there will no longer exist elsewhere in the community a form of violence to be followed or opposed.

Girard defines such an "event" as the sacrificial victim, as one who has to be of sufficient stature to attract the attention of the entire community. Regicide is the most extreme example of the corrosion of state-hierarchy yet here, in an act of will that surpasses that of the gods themselves, Clytemnestra transforms the king into the sacrificial offering, and forces the community of savage men into a ritual of obeisance and reorientation.

In this theater, the knot of ambition, passion, love, and hatred draws increasingly in on itself in an ever tighter hold of desire and incest to a point of total narcissism. If there are any Eumenides in this poem, elements of the "feminine"—at once a blessing and a curse, we might recognize them in the passion with which Electra attempts to hold her brother, and which represents the cloying, parasitical, human need that she has of him. Just as the repeated crimes of passion in the trilogy of Aeschylus had ended with a break from primal law for the more objective space of public order, so Jeffers frees his hero from the blood knot of human relationships for the emancipation of the individual mind. Orestes, the insane adolescent, breaks from the lure of the sister-lover and wanders alone in a "cloud upon the feasting gods, lightning and madness" (107). Again, this myth becomes the drama of the adolescent's liberation from primal ties as represented by the passions. Again, the hero reaches ultimately for the lone and dangerous regions of the spirit.

This Orestes is a hero, not an Aeschylean representative of the community of spectators, not even the reluctant bearer of the human burden (as we will see when reading Sartre), but he who can free himself from the fetters, the suffocation and the myopia of social demands and emotional ties. With sharp psychological insight, the modern poet has lifted the dramatic screens of "justice," "vengeance" and "heroism" and discovered a frighteningly personal, authentic motive for matricide, the most heinous of human crimes.

For here, the hero's murder of his mother is not an act of revenge. It is a personal emancipation. Murdering, Orestes—and perhaps also Jeffers the poet—liberate themselves from domestic and political ties. With murder, they become emancipated for those broader regions of the poetic, that are associated with inspiration and madness, and which here represent the ultimate of human goals. It would seem that in his Tower Beyond Tragedy, the poet has come full circle to the amoral, Homeric idealization of heroic man and his pursuit of excellence in valor. However, because social intercourse is regarded by him as violent and destructive, the poet's isolationist stance here becomes the one remaining moral alternative in an otherwise immoral world.

Perhaps the most obvious difference between Aechylus' Oresteia and this poem by Jeffers, is that, in the former, Electra was escorted and encouraged by her chorus of women attendants, while, in the latter, she returns to Mycenae as a silent, scheming, beggar girl in pathetic isolation. Her filthy, ragged clothes represent the ugliness of her situation: a girl of such tender age, yet of such murderous hatred, able to dissemble with such finesse.

The destructive dependence that typifies human relationships and that so impedes individual freedom in this work, combined with the readiness of mother and daughter to use their sexual favors as barter, are the results of a society that is not mutually supportive. It is a society that preys on its members, and it results in a violence which tears the individual, like some besieged citadel, from his or her sense of self. These citizens need to dissemble, to attack and defend. This then, is Jeffers' ironic vision of the singleness of purpose characteristic, in earlier works, of the tragic hero. The ritual of communion that had typified the world and the theater of ancient Greece, and which had provided the protagonist with a sense of belonging, is transformed in

Jeffers' poem, into the cloying neediness of human relationships. It is a perverse, cruel closeness that forces the hero into flight.

As in Hofmannsthal's version, this violent world is one of women. Clytemnestra is virulent and powerful as murderess, ruler and lover. She has the full force of Aeschylus' demonic heroine and the same measure of justification for her act. She also has the sad realism of the twentieth century:

ORESTES
This, a god in his temple
Openly commanded.

CLYTEMNESTRA
Ah, child, child, who has mis-taught you, and who has
Betrayed you? What voice has the god?
How was it different from a man's and did you see him?
Who sent the priest presents? They fool us.
And the gods let them [125].

And the tragic, intuitive knowledge of the psychological torment that violence will cause:

CLYTEMNESTRA
...this much I pray, for your sake,
not with your hand, not with your
hand, or the memory
Will so mother you, so glue to you, so
embrace you,
Not the deep sea's green day, no cleft
of a rock in the bed of the deep sea,
no ocean of darkness
Outside the stars, will hide nor
wash you [125].

What she does not know is that this hero is capable of freeing himself, once and for all, from the emotional trap of mother and sister, from the emotional trap of the myth itself, by simply walking away.

As in the Hofmannsthal version of the myth, Electra is here the prime schemer and motivator who goads a reluctant youth into an act of murder. Unlike the Sophocles version, in which it was Orestes, the hero, who'd epitomized cunning and action, here it is Jeffers'

Electra who warns: "Brother, though the great house is silent, hark the city" (126).

Cassandra, the final female character around whom this poem was built, provides the dramatic function of the chorus and is the spiritual medium by means of which the now familiar patriarchal judgment is heard:

THE BODY OF CASSANDRA
I say if you let this woman live,
this crime go unpunished, what man among you
Will be safe in his bed?
The woman ever envies the man,
his strength, his freedom, his loves.
Her envy is like a snake beside him, all his
life through, her envy and hatred:
law tames that viper:
Law dies if the queen die not: the viper is free then.

This is the expression of the male fear of female entrapment that had been so dramatically brought home to us in Clytemnestra's first scene: the brazen manner in which, with her naked body, she had taunted and defied the surrounding host of hostile men. It is also the suggestion that patriarchal law has been instigated for the specific end of emancipating man from her strangulating, emotional and sexual hold. The audience again recognizes the masculine need to master the female when the spirit of the murdered king violently takes possession of the body of Cassandra and, in so doing, forces her into the expression of his will:

BODY OF CASSANDRA
and having tasted
The toad that serves women for heart.
From now on may all bridegrooms
Marry them with swords.
Those that have borne children
Their sons rape them with spears.

Cassandra stands on the steps of the city, stalwart guardian of Agamemnon's place of murder and watchdog of the future. She is the medium through which the mighty powers of European history flows, a history of repeated acts of acquisition, violence and destruction.

CASSANDRA

Curse Athens for the joy and the marble, curse Corinth
For the wine and the purple, and Syracuse
For the gold and the ships; but Rome, Rome,
With many destructions for the corn and the laws
and the javelins, the insolence, the threefold
Abominable power: pass the humble
And the lordships of darkness, but far
down Smite Spain for the blood on the
summer gold, curse France
For the fields abounding and the running
rivers, the lights in the cities,
the laughter, curse England
For the meat on the tables and the terrible gray
ships, for old laws, fat dominions, there remains
A mightier to be cursed and a higher
for malediction
When America has eaten Europe and takes tribute of
Asia, when the ends of the world grow aware of
each other
And are dogs in one kennel, they will tear
The master of the hunt with the mouths of the
pack: new fallings, new risings, O winged one
No end of the fallings and risings?
An end shall be surely,
Though unnatural things are accomplished,
they breathe in the sea's depth,
They swim in the air, they bridle the cloud-leaper lightning to carry their
messages [114].

It is an endless account of the meaningless suffering and violence
of humanity.

CASSANDRA

Make me air to wander free between the stars and
the peaks, but cut humanity
Out of my being, that is the wound that festers in me [115].
The years flow through Cassandra's unflinching body until Orestes
and Electra return to complete the cycle of murder and revenge.

CASSANDRA

Eight years I have seen the phantoms
Walk up and down this stair, and the rocks groan in the night…
…
… I am not Cassandra
But a counter of sunrises, permitted to live
because I am crying to die [116].

Jeffers' choice of language and dramatic structure reinforce his theme of idealized distancing. His dramatic poem is set in the mythical past; his poetic form is itself a kind of alienation, and the highly ritualistic style of his poem produces the opposite effect to that which community-ritual had on Aeschylus' audience. This is because ritual in the 1930s deliberately separated the actors from their community, allowing spectators to embark on their own imaginative voyage of inspiration and reflection.

---

76 Lilian Feder, Madness in Literature (Princeton, N.J.: Princeton University Press, 1980).
77 See Carl E. Schorske, Fin de Siecle Vienna (New York: Vintage, 1981).
78 Schorske, p. 186.
79 Quoted in Schorske, p. 194.
80 Schorske; the quotations are from pp. 196, 197, 197, 199, and 203, respectively.
81 Oscar Wilde, Salome, in The Complete Works of Oscar Wilde (New York: Harper & Row, 1966), p.
319. Hereafter, quotations of this edition are indicated with page number references in parentheses or brackets.
82 Wilde, p. 328.
83 Schorske, p. 19.
84 Schorske, p. 19.
85 Schorske, p. 19.
86 Schorske, p. 21.
87 Hugo von Hofmannsthal, Electra, trans. Carl Richard Mueller, in The Modern Theater, ed. Robert
W. Corrigan (New York: Macmillan, 1964), p. 110Hereafter, quotations from this edition are indicated by page number references in parenthesis or brackets.
88 David Cole, The Theatrical Event (Middletown, Conn.: Wesleyan University Press, 1975).
89 Hofmannsthal, p. 114.
90 Suzanne E. Bales, "Elektra: From Hofmannsthal to Strauss," doctoral dissertation, Stanford, 1984.
91 Lévi-Strauss, p. 215.
92 Bales, p. 126.
93 Slater, p. 91.
94 Slater, p. 91.

95   Northrop Frye, Anatomy of Criticism (Princeton, N.J.: Princeton University Press, 1957), p. 217.

96   Hofmannsthal, p. 108.

97   Hofmannsthal, p. 90.

98   Hofmannsthal, p. 97.

99   Euripides, Orestes and Other Plays (Middlesex, England: Penguin, 1983), p. 310.

100   Eugene O'Neill, "Mourning Becomes Electra," in Nine Plays (New York: Modern Library, 1959), p. 739. Hereafter, quotations from this edition are indicated by page number references in parentheses or brackets.

101   Jean Giraudoux, Electra, in Orestes and Electra, in Nine Plays (New York: Modern Library, 1959), p.739. Hereafter, quotations from this edition are indicated by page number references in parentheses or brackets.

102   Robert Cohen, Giraudoux: Three Faces of Destiny (Chicago: University of Chicago Press, 1968), p. 116

103   Cole, p. 142.

104   Lawrence Clark Powell, Robinson Jeffers: The Man and His Work (Los Angeles: Primavera, 1934).

105   Powell, p. 14.

106   Powell, pp. 16–7.

107   Louis Adamic, Robinson Jeffers: A Portrait (Seattle: University of Washington Chapbooks, 1929).

108   Robinson Jeffers, "The Tower Beyond Tragedy," in The Selected Poetry of Robinson Jeffers (New York: Random House, 1959), p. 138. Hereafter quotes from this edition are indicated by page number references in parentheses or brackets.

109   Jeffers, p. 110.

110   Jeffers, p. 107.

111   Rene Girard, Violence and the Sacred, trans. Patrick Gregory (Baltimore: John Hopkins University Press, 1977), p. 49.

112   Girard, pp. 81–2.

CHAPTER 6

JEAN PAUL SARTRE: LES MOUCHES (1942)

T he deeper the essentially male "hero" sinks into the war-ravaged world of the twentieth century, the more removed he becomes from his original "heroic" persona, the less masculine his characteristics, and the weaker his ties with the establishment: with tradition and history; with community as well as with the precepts of church and state; with the particular ideology of his "personal" as with his "collective" father. In this new antihero, we recognize a representative spirit, one that questions—alone—a world into which he has been thrust and which is not of his making.

World War II plunged Western culture into an open-eyed acknowledgment of its appetite for evil, death and destruction. The shrunken world of today's mass media is bombarded daily by the reaffirmation of its own violence. Where does the "hero" go from here? What effect does his knowledge of history, education, and religion, have on his actions? Modern man is no longer a hero. No longer can he—an anti-hero—find safe haven in the sanctuary of humankind. Each person stands alone, naked and terrified before the responsibility of his actions.

Sartre was mobilized into the French Forces in 1939 and taken prisoner in 1940. He played an active part in the French Resistance and devoted many years, after the war, to questions of patriotism, loyalty, commitment and personal freedom, all of which are issues we have encountered repeatedly in the myth and the plays of Electra. *Les Mouches* (The Flies) was written in 1942 under German occupation.

It was appropriate therefore, for Sartre to raise the figures of Electra and Orestes to question, yet again, archetypal issues of freedom, slavery, vengeance, collaboration, violence and the extremely tainted human soul— this time under the occupation of Vichy France.

In this play, Sartre presents us with a chorus of the citizens of Argos— repulsive, groveling, un-washed men, women, and children, riddled with guilt and self-negation, and void of any last vestige of human dignity. By virtue of their self-hatred, their eternal black garb, their obsequious whining and wailing—and more than anything— their absolute inability to think or take action for themselves, they have become a city of dead souls. The ugly shame of these people hangs in a flee-riddled haze over Argos, a city made intolerable by its scorching temperatures and its permanent plague of black, stinging flies (Furies). This Argos is a city burdened by the ugly shame of its oppressors, a guilt foisted upon them by Aegisthus, their king, as a means of control; as a way of preventing them from ever turning against him for his murder of Agamemnon.

The one beautiful element in Argos is Electra who, though Cinderella-like, reduced to the position of scullery-maid in the palace, is young, pretty, and innocent. Electra's spirit rebels against Clytemnestra and Aegisthus. She rebels against the entire city, its ugliness and its mourning. She dreams only that Orestes is alive somewhere and will come to deliver her. Most particularly, she cries out for vengeance. Yet, Sartre questions whether this Electra can handle vengeance. More even than Euripides' heroine, the female principle in Sartre's "hero" becomes the unheroic, eternally impotent voice of Physis. Perhaps this is because, being innocent, she has no actual concept of what vengeance is, or what it will entail.

In Sartre's play, only the emancipated "masculine" soul, he who guards his personal freedom as his secret (and only) weapon; he who is capable of assessing the more feminine qualities of guilt, superstition and history—only he can survive a reality as horrendous as the Nazi occupation. Because Sartre's Orestes is that of Viche France—an oppressed Europe. Orestes' emergence necessitates the shattering and shredding of what he terms, "Christian guilt." Heroism of the Second World War years demanded clear- eyed action, not emotion. Once again, it is important to remember that the hero has always been depicted in masculine form. My insistence on broadening the general definition of "hero" to include the female, might be an error. We might discover that women, whose development has been neither sufficiently understood, nor recorded, might not have the personality structure, the drive, impulses, or the appetites to fit into the "heroic" mold as defined until now. I will leave this to the reader to question.

Sartre's Orestes is no longer a member of a community. He has no necessary affiliation to the gods, God, or his own human lineage. On the contrary, as an "enlightened" human being, he is free of the beliefs, legends, histories, and superstitions that entangle most of us. For all that—and because of it, he is alone and desperately lonely in his freedom. Why has he come to Argos? What has he come for? Why did he choose to leave a pain-free existence (in what he first claimed was Corinth, but later declared was Athens, telling Electra he was raised by enlightened Athenians,) for Argos, a hell-hole that is unbearably hot, riddled with flies, and infested with the most wretchedly repellent and hostile people on the planet?

Setting:
A public square in Argos, dominated by a statue of Zeus, god of flies and death. The image has white eyes and blood-smeared cheeks. A procession of old women in black, carrying urns ... they make libations to the statue...

ORESTES
Listen, my good women.
(The women swing around, emitting little squeals.)

TUTOR
Would you kindly tell us?
(the old women spit on the ground and move back apace.)

TUTOR
...We are travelers and have lost our way (Dropping their urns, the women take to their heels.)

TUTOR

Stupid old hags! You'd think I had intentions on their virtue. (Ironically,) Ah, young master, and how well-inspired were you to come to this city of Argos, when there are hundreds of towns in Greece and Italy where the drink is good, the inns are hospitable, and the streets full of friendly, smiling people...

ORESTES

This is my palace. My father's birthplace. And it's here a whore and her paramour foully butchered him....
...I was nearly three when that usurpers' bodyguards carried me away....
I had my eyes wide open, and no doubt
I was crying. And yet I have no memories. None whatever.
...I am looking at a huge, gloomy building.... I am looking at it, but I see it for the first time.

TUTOR

No memories, master?...
...Palaces, shrines and temples, with so many of them is your mind peopled...

ORESTES

Palaces—that's so. Palaces, statues, pillars—stones, stones, stones! Why with all those stones in my head am I not heavier?
...Why, an old mangy dog warming himself at the hearth, and struggling to his feet
... to welcome his master home— why, that dog has more memories than I! At least he recognizes his master. His master, but what can I call mine? [pp. 60–61]. When I was seven, I know I had no home, no roots ... I can never make them my memories. For memories are luxuries reserved for people who own houses, cattle, fields and servants.

Despite the incredible places he has visited, and despite the advanced and open city he claims to have come from; despite his freedom to go wherever he likes, do what he wants, and stay as long as he desires, Orestes feels isolated, poorer than any dog with a master. Without family, a home and hearth, our hero feels alone and lonely, belonging nowhere. Despite the vast wealth of philosophy his tutor has taught him, without a history of his own, Orestes is on his own. This is why Orestes has journeyed to this hateful place. Here, a story awaits him. Here he has a sister. Perhaps even more: Perhaps, here he has purpose.

Orestes is young and handsome. We are told he has lively, laughing eyes and curls that cascade round his shoulders. He arrives with the "slave" that was once his tutor, now his guide and traveling companion. His tutor has raised him to the power and thrill of objective thinking, Motivations that determine his actions are his and his alone. Orestes has come to Argos to commemorate the fifteenth anniversary of his father's murder at the hand of Aegisthus; and he has come to find his sister, to discover whether she is alive and how she is living. Initially, his choice might have been whether to identify with his sister and his hometown, or to visit and leave. But Orestes's talk makes the tutor anxious:

TUTOR
...I wondered if you weren't hatching some wild scheme to oust Aegisthus and take his place.

ORESTES
To oust Aegisthus. Ah—(A pause.) No my good slave, you need not fear; the time for that is past. True, nothing could please me better than to ... drag him from my father's throne. But what purpose would it serve? These folks are no concern of mine. I have not seen one of their children come into the world, nor been present at their daughter's weddings; I don't share their remorse, I don't even know a single one of them by name.... A king should share his subjects'memories. So we'll let them be and be gone on tiptoe.... But...if there were something ... to give me the freedom of the city; if, even by a crime, I could acquire their memories, their hopes and fears, and fill with these the void within me, yes, even if I had to kill my own mother—[*Flies*, p. 63]

Orestes'vision of a community; his understanding that belonging means people sharing each other's joys and the rituals of each other's life-cycles might be the most poignant of anything said in this work. Wouldn't it be wonderful if Sartre's story would end that way? But no, we had rather fix our attention on the harsher ruminations that follow.

Just as Orestes is summoning his horses to journey on, Electra appears. This Electra is spunkier than most. She has come, not to offer libations to the statue of Zeus, but to empty her trashcan of refuse over it.

She doesn't see Orestes until she turns:

ELECTRA
Oh!

ORESTES
Don't be alarmed.

ELECTRA
I'm not alarmed. Not a bit. Who are you?

ORESTES
A stranger.

ELECTRA
Then you are welcome. All that's foreign to this town is dear to me. Your name?

ORESTES
Philebus. I've come from Corinth.

ELECTRA
Ah? From Corinth. My Name's Electra.

ORESTES
Electra. (to the Tutor) Leave us. (Exit Tutor)

ELECTRA
Why are you looking at me like that?

ORESTES
You are very beautiful.
Not at all like the people in these parts.

ELECTRA
I? Beautiful? Can you really mean it?
As beautiful as the Corinthian girls?

ORESTES
Yes.

She tells him her story. She tells him how she prays each night that Orestes will come to avenge her father's murderer and liberate her. They chat. After a while,

ELECTRA
How strange! (A short silence.) Please tell me something else; I want to know it because of—of someone I'm expecting. Suppose one of the young fellows you've been telling me about, who walk and laugh with girls in the evenings—suppose one of these young men came home after a long journey and found his father murdered, and his mother living with

the murderer, and his sister treated like a slave—what would he do, that young man from Corinth? Would he just take it for granted and slink out of his father's house, and look for consolation with his girl friends? Or would he draw his sword and hurl himself at the assassin, and slash his brains out? ... Why are you silent?

ORESTES
I was wondering—

ELECTRA
What? You can't say what he'd do?

At this point, Clytemnestra arrives from the palace full of moans, threats, and foreboding regarding Electra's future; so we don't get to know what Orestes was wondering. Instead:

CLYTEMNESTRA
...wait, my girl, one day you too will be trailing behind you an inexpiable crime. At every step you will believe you are leaving it behind, but it will remain as heavy as before ... you will realize that you staked your life on a single throw of the dice. For that is the law,
just or unjust, of repentance.

Crime begets crime, guilt begets guilt, murder begets suffering. Nothing has changed.

The anniversary of the dead king's murder is commemorated as the Day of the Dead. For twenty-four hours, the citizens indulge in a veritable orgy of guilt and self-abasement. The spirits of the dead are released from hell to roam the city, to sit at the table of those relatives who wronged them while they were alive, to eat the food their living relatives have cooked for them, to sleep in their beds, to hold them in their skeletal arms, to make their day a living hell.

The moment he meets Electra, Orestes changes his earlier decision to leave Argos. The Day of Death and its aftermath become increasingly charged with threat to their existence. Consequently, Orestes offers to take her away, to deliver her, as a good hero would, from Argos and everyone in it, to show her other cities where people live gently, joyously, among peace-loving human beings. Electra won't leave. She is adamant. She demands from him nothing short of her nightmares, i.e., that he avenge the murder of Agamemnon with those of Aegisthus and Clytemnestra.

Orestes has found what he came for: Electra. She is his family. With her, for the first time, he would belong; the pangs of loneliness that have afflicted him since earliest childhood would be assuaged. His place as her brother, he tells her, is by her side. It is his chance of happiness.

He doesn't want to murder his mother and her lover, because he knows himself. Despite the emancipated education his tutor has given him, this Orestes is not the avenging brother of his sister's nightmares. He feels no hatred. Neither had he felt love—until he met Electra.

Electra has no room for a peace-loving brother. She tells him to leave.

ORESTES
I want to be a man who belongs to some place, a man among comrades.
Only consider. Even the slave bent beneath his load and staring dully at
The road ... can say he's in his own town.

Electra appears defiantly at the ceremony for the Day of the Dead. Dressed in white, she dances the dance of life over the cavern of the dead hoping the living hags of the town will turn on Aegisthus and follow her. She fails. Aegisthus' cruel hold over this city is too strong for her. Electra's life is in danger now. Again, Orestes offers to rescue her. Again, she refuses. Argos is her destiny.

Orestes is desperate to be with Electra. On an impulse, looking at the city below them, he bids farewell to the city of his youth and all he has left behind. What he wants is to be by Electra's side. What he needs is to belong. He knows what he must do:

ORESTES
Come, Electra, look at our city. There it lies,
rose-red in the sun
buzzing with men and flies., drowsing its doom away....
It fends me off with its high walls ... locked doors. And it's
mine for the taking; I've felt that since this morning. You too,
Electra, are mine for the taking—and I'll take you too.
I'll turn into an axe and hew those walls asunder, I'll rip open the
bellies of those
stolid houses.... I'll be an iron wedge driven into the city.

Then:

Listen! ...
Supposing I set out to win the name of "guilt-stealer,"
and heap
on myself all their remorse...
...Argos, surely then I shall have earned the
freedom of your city.
Shall I not be as much at home within your
red walls as the red-
aproned butcher in his shop,
among the carcasses of flayed sheep
and cattle?

For Orestes, belonging and becoming an integral part of Electra's life and city, means liberating all the citizens of their problem: their guilt. The single, united force holding this city back is the tyranny of Aegisthus and Clytemnestra. Kill them—and the sickness of the city will evaporate. It is a practical decision.

Of course, nothing is that simple. This is the story of Electra, where Furies relentlessly attack the murderer. And so it is. Electra, the innocent, could not have known the extent to which guilt and remorse would beset her once Orestes assumes the responsibility of murder. In fear and horror, she runs form Orestes to the protection of Zeus.

Aware that the Furies and armed towns-people are waiting outside, Zeus forces the tutor to open the doors of the sanctuary.

ORESTES
You see me, men of Argos, you understand that my
crime is wholly mine; I claim it as my own, for all to
know; it is my glory, my life's work, and you can neither punish me
nor pity me. That is why I fill you with fear.
And yet, my people, I love you, and it was for your sake
that I killed.... Now I am your kind ...
there is a bond of blood
between us, and I have earned my kinship over you.
...
As for your sins and your remorse,
your night-fears and the crime Aegithus committed—
all are mine, I take them upon me.
Fear your dead no longer; they are my dead.
And, see, your faithful flies have left you
and come to me.... I shall not sit on my victim's throne or take the
scepter in my blood-stained hands....
Farewell, my people. Try to reshape your lives.

All here is new ... must begin anew.
...
Listen now to this tale.
One summer there was a plague of rats in Scyros.

And, not unlike the Pied Piper, "Orestes strides out into the light. Shrieking, the Furies fling themselves after him." This play might have been called, "Orestes Becomes Orestes," for in a most unexpected, and ironic, almost Christ-like ending, Orestes realizes his destiny. In so doing, he becomes the savior. It is hard for me to believe that that is what Sartre had in mind.

It would be equally hard for us to miss the (again ironic) romantic quality of the ending. Young Orestes, no more than a teen-ager, has saved the city, liberated its people—and has walked off into the sunset. All without guilt, fear, superstition, or religion. With this play, for sure, we have left the Greeks behind us.

As we have noted, in 1942, Europe was still mired in war. What a fond fantasy this must have been at that time: to free our world of guilt.

Sartre's Orestes has made his choice intelligently, guiltlessly and free of superstition, for he is free of the burdens of guilt and history. Yet, his identification appears emotional, perhaps romantic, and heroic.

As we have seen, Sartre's Orestes arrived on stage from a separate space, from a guiltless, outer region, and he brought with him his own, separate perspective: his need to belong. His need of a purpose. Again, players and spectators are caught up in the theatrical event, in this ritual reenactment of issues: commitment versus freedom, patriotism, personal conscience, heroic action, murder and the renewal of life. Any Brechtian-style reflection, (i.e., any social awareness we might gain), grows directly out of the action. Nothing is brought to the theatrical experience other than innate conflicts within the human soul. Electra, Orestes, and the citizens of Argos constitute the agons (oppositions) of a moral dilemma that surfaced under Nazi occupation. They are the invisible made visible. They provoke thought and questioning. They are live theater.

As one who was raised in the twentieth century, I need to question Sartre's motives in portraying such an Orestes. The protagonist murders out of his personal need to belong, to be accepted, to be admired—perhaps even loved. His newfound aim is to win the admiration of the beautiful sister/princess no matter how evil his means. Is this then a romantic play? Is Sartre's Orestes a hero? Or is he a fascist? At the end of this play, we see him Pied Piper–like running off into the sunset, emptying the town, like a foul odor from a room, of its disgusting citizens. No. There are no fairy tales here. Heroism does not exist in the shattered world of World War II.

We might consider this the opposite stand to the one taken by the hero of Robinson Jeffers' play. Sartre's choice is not a moral one. Morality bears no weight on his stage. His Orestes makes his choice consciously, guiltlessly, and free of superstition, for he espouses emancipation from the burden of history. In consequence, he has chosen to assume, as his own, the crime of liberation, to be hounded forever by the furies of the 20th century, and move beyond the society he so longed for. In so doing, he has defined himself and his existence.

Ezra Pound: Elektra (1951)

Ezra Pound's adaptation of the Sophoclean Electra was produced in 1987 under the artistic directorship of Carey Perloff at the Classical Stage Company Repertory Theater, 13th Street, New York. [113]

Pound had become convinced that "Usura" or "credit capitalism" lay at the root of the evils of society and he integrated this conviction into his own anti–Semitic, pro–Fascist ideology. During the war, he gave a series of pro- Fascist broadcasts over Rome radio service for which the American Military Government charged him with treason in 1945.

As a result of his plea of insanity, Pound escaped the death penalty, and was incarcerated in Washington for thirteen years at the St. Elizabeth's Hospital for the criminally insane. It was in this setting, in 1949, that Pound began his interpretation of Sophocles' *Electra* with the collaboration of Rudd Fleming, at that time a faculty member at the University of Maryland. The work was completed in

1951 but was never published for fear, it is believed, that it might prove the author's sanity.

Pound was notorious for his aggressive use of rhythm, and for the way in which he combined formal and colloquial language styles. Perloff claims:

> In Pound's world there is no separation between past and present: as long as the poet can travel there, all times are present. Nor is there separation of languages: Pound took hold of the chiseled, precise, highly rhythmic language of ancient Greece with both hands and planted it firmly in Twentieth Century America. [114]

We have identified the Electra theme as the confrontation of the old by the herald of the new. As such, Electra is a particularly suitable theme for this poet. In addition, although Fleming claims that Pound never specifically mentioned any personal reasons for his manipulation of this theme, it seems likely that he recognized the similarity, both between the devastation of postwar Europe and that of ancient Greece, and that of his own situation with that of the Classical Greek heroine: both are incarcerated, both rage against the injustice of their plight, and both await their liberation from impending insanity and death.

Pound's language vacillates drastically between the classical and the lyrical of the majestic heroine and rough, inner-city colloquialisms, which reflect the naked squalor of a girl, trapped, rejected and maligned.

Elektra is isolated from the other characters by means of the poetry of her language and her tragic situation. She, alone, speaks in poetic form.

Pound's play becomes somewhat of a diatribe against the European forces for having sacrificed their sons, their greatest hopes, to war:

ELECTRA
All that is left me
My hope was Orestes
Dust is returned me
In my hands nothing, dust that is all of him
Flower that went forth
Far from my homeland
Died far in exile

No hand was near thee
To soothe thy passing.
Corpse un-anointed
Fire consumed thee,
All now is nothing
Strangers have brought thee
Small in this urn here
Sorrow upon me
Fruitless my caring. [115]

And

It's the end of the line
We're all there together
Ashes [71].

He seems to regard the war and the present devastation, not as the victory of Good over Evil, but more as the destructive, nihilistic force of history itself and, in so doing, he transforms the death-whish of the Greek heroine, her desperate need to be buried alive with the ashes of her brother, into a modern, postwar image of destruction:

ELECTRA
Dead Agamemnon, dead now my brother,
I am dead also, the great wind in passing
bears us together, mirth for our foeman [73].

To Pound, the enormous heroic potential of the Orestean youth has been reduced to a fistful of ashes. The poet seems even to doubt his nation's ability to recognize the significance of the European destruction:

ORESTES
...All that is of him
is this little jug, as you can see if you want to [70].

And so it is that the horrendous authority which had once represented the fountainhead of spiritual inspiration and the centering force of community ritual is reduced here to a single image of loss, loss which is of questionable interest. The dead of our own time hold no momentous significance, for they have no souls with which to possess us. Death here merely signifies emptiness and ashes. There is, however, an interesting twist to the theme of death and rebirth in the idealization of the revolutionary that emerges. In this twentieth-century, Poundian rendition of the myth, contrary to that of the Sophoclean play, life and vitality lie in the hands of whoever is willing to counter the power of the Establishment with his own daring. Orestes walks onto this stage with the readiness, the bluntness and the sensibility of the proverbial rough diamond and, in so doing, he stands in the same dramatic opposition to Elektra, as did his Sophoclean counterpart.

ELEKTRA
Don't defraud me
Of the pleasure of seeing you here

ORESTES
Damn well let anyone else try it [84–5].

ELEKTRA
Oh dearest friends
if now's to ear
a voice I ne'er
had hoped to hear
if joy shall not burst
forth at this
then ever dumb in wretchedness
should one live on in deep distress.
Now thou art here
in full daylight
shall I not pour
forth my delight,
who ne'er in deepest woe
had forgot thee [85–6].

The Athenian man of action and heroic cunning has been transformed here into a blunt but likeable next-door neighbor, The Greek hero, whose sanity had existed in the fact that he represented the law and order of the patriarchy, however new or revolutionary, has here become the anti-establishment; his sanity exists in his ability to think and act outside the box, independently of the corrupting ideology of the state. He stands in stark dramatic opposition to the oppressive figure of the establishment. Aegisthus, on the other hand, remains the personification of the establishment and its necessary oppression, so it is still he, Aegisthus, who appears on stage "flanked by body-guards." Orestes, by virtue of his own revolutionary activity, becomes the hero for, by means of his independence, his separateness, he infuses new life into old ideals (regardless of what they might represent for Pound):

CHORUS
Aah!
Curses work out. They live who lie under ground,
The blood of the dead, long dead
Overwhelms their slayers.
And the dead hands
Drip Mars, and the slain
Blood, blood. I can't blame 'em.

The chorus reinforces this theme, which seems to fall just shy of terrorism: It's justification of a "few polite words," of cunning and hypocrisy with which to mask the necessary deed of violence. Here, murder and patricide have lost all sense of mystery, while violence is a matter of expediency, merely the function of the liberator.

ORESTES
You don't have to tell me how that bitch and
Aegisthus are running all dad's place to ruin ...
no time for all that
got to get on with the job.
Tell me the best way to get to it.

One cannot help wondering if, and to what extent, Pound is still influenced by his earlier Fascist convictions. In this play, Orestes, though not as invested in the violent emotional needs or experience of Electra, is as willing as she to do the deed; in fact, he is full of zeal for his act of retribution:

ORESTES
It's a pity you can't all of you die like this
and as quickly, every one like you [102].

Far from experiencing pangs of remorse, this Orestes, with reservations that are characteristic of his age, merely records an obligation well executed.

ORESTES
All right, the house is clean again, if what Apollo said is right [95].

174

Unlike his Sophoclean model, Pound's play leaves no unspoken questions hanging over the audience, no guilt, no horror, only that sense of freedom that comes with a quiet conscience:

CHORUS
Delivered, delivered
Swift end
So soon
Te Nun teleothen

In her production, Carey Perloff boldly brings Pound's play into the inner city of New York, side by side with many of the problems of squalid, inner- city life. The set is a large, fenced-in area reminiscent, at one and the same time, of the imprisoned physical and mental states that characterize both Pound and Electra, and also of a basketball court, which typically serves as recreation-center and jail for the urchins of downtown areas. These, it has been noted, are suggestive of a sordid kind of "Greek Side Story." [116] The costumes are evocative but timeless. Electra is dressed in the shapeless black shift that we associate with homelessness and tragedy. Her shock of white hair contrasts with the blackness of her dress thereby accentuating the extreme polarities of her essentially tragic outlook on life. Electra has been described as crow-like in her inwardness and her resolute sense of purpose. [117]

Clytemnestra appears on stage armed from top-to-toe in the crude, pushy sexuality and false youthfulness of an upper middle class, Manhattan, homemaker. In such a manner, the gaping distance that exists between mother and daughter, the disparity in their social and economic situations is dramatized for the audience. With chilling dignity, Electra reveals the full horror of her situation:

ELECTRA
They say she is my mother [77].

At the same time, there are definite insinuations, in the text, of child molestation:

ORESTES
How? Beats you? Starves you?

ELECTRA
Yes, and everything else [77].

The chorus consists of a black woman and a white woman, two powerfully strong females who seem to vacillate between mother figures and prison matrons, who knit and do their paperwork as they guard over this inner-city scene.

In contrast to them, the tutor speaks throughout in the heavy Irish brogue with which, once and for all, he demystifies Sophocles;

PYLADES
You BLOODY fools, shut up.
Ain't you got ANY sense whatever
no more care for your lives? [88].

Orestes is a black avenging hero and deliverer of the victims of city- squalor. It takes the combined efforts of all these aspects of the city, each so disparate from the other, to save it from destitution and insanity.

Electra is the ruined child of her city desperately waiting for deliverance. Again, she is sharply contrasted to her sister: Chrysothemis lives on half- truths while Electra represents the uncompromising voice of an American ideal that has been swept under the rubble, under the savagery of the sprawling metropolis. Again, she is the tragic hero who willingly sacrifices her personal happiness in her single-minded pursuit of the moral ideal.

In a dramatic reversal of the black and white symbolism of good and evil, customary in the Western tradition, this production plays on the concept of vitality, equally a cliché, associated in western literature with dark skin. Here, Electra's diminutive figure, her white hair and her rasping voice which is at times drained of all energy, stand in sharp dramatic contrast to the dark vitality, the new blood, the fresh perspective of her brother. Electra's is the energy of true grit, of an indomitable spirit. She makes her first entrance by literally crawling onto the stage, and she clings to the sides of her cage with the will of the survivor. In this sense, again, Electra becomes Orestes: clinging with the last vestiges of her strength and sanity to the solid values of an ideal which no one but she can remember. Orestes, as a new life-force, a new vitality, is the savior of his city.

Jack Richardson: The Prodigal (1960)

So far, the Electra myth has been defined as the meeting of the old with the new. As such, the myth seems to recur at times of changing ideologies when it becomes necessary to rethink established precepts and institute new ones.

Perhaps one of the reasons there was such a prevalence of Electra plays in the twentieth century is that it was characterized as a period of particularly rapid changes in ideology. It was appropriate therefore, to find such a play in the 1960s, a period that epitomized a reevaluation of the old. And so we arrive at *The Prodigal*, by Jack Richardson.

In this rendition of the Electra theme, the prodigal son has been raised under the myth of his father, a hero, a warrior, and a tyrant; and, like so many sons of the 1960s, the son wants to escape the destiny of the father.

But the father sailed victoriously back into the harbor in what can only be described as an archetypal image of resurrection. He arrived with "golden shields" that "reflected the sun into Electra's pained eyes." [118] He is the sun- god, the sky-god, image of the traditional conquering, masculine hero. The issue here becomes that of separating the legend from the man, for, on this stage, the myth of the father becomes the reality of Orestes. He, and perhaps we of the audience, have related all these years, not to the individual, but to the abstraction; not to Agamemnon the man, but the myth. Any possibility of Orestes having a personal relationship with his father has been shattered by the cruelty of the reputation that has preceded his father's homecoming, i.e., that the war hero had sacrificed his daughter and thousands of innocent lives for the questionable virtue of Helen. Again, masculine heroism implies aggression and the victimization of women. Given Agamemnon's reputation, how can the son come to personal, human terms with the father?

ORESTES
Can laughter, can intimacy, can touch tell more about a man ... than the personal myth he bequeaths to us in death or absence [213]?

Orestes tells Electra:

ORESTES
We both have a legend and now we must undergo the often, painful experience of seeing it turn into a man [226].

This is what The Prodigal does for us, what it did for the audiences of the 1960s. It turned the myth into reality, the hero into the anti-hero and the tragic form into a tale of a man trapped by the ethics of those who preceded him.

In this play, Clytemnestra, mythically the cause of the Electra/Orestes tragedy, is fearful, uncomplicated and relatively un-vindictive. She plays no part in a myth that is the product of an essentially masculine culture. Like Aegisthus, in the play by Giraudoux, this Clytemnestra is not made of the stuff of heroism; but wants only to inhabit the low ground. She justifies her disloyalty to her husband with the words:

CLYTEMNESTRA
I was never strong enough to stand beside you on mountain peaks and gaze with an impersonal eye at the world which you molded to suit your great ideas.... I belong on lower ground where seasons change and where small desires and thoughts are shared and understood. I belong to one who knows the love of this earth [231].

Agamemnon's virility and ambition frighten Clytemnestra because she recognizes in them their acquisitiveness and their destructive tendencies:

CLYTEMNESTRA
I pass by a pear tree.... I suddenly remember how he once climbed it to bring me the fruit from the highest branches. And the pool in front of the palace ... I recalled how Agamemnon used to enjoy throwing pebbles at its oversized fish [223].

Aegisthus seems to recognize the distinction made in the first chapter of this work between himself as what we had termed the "personal father" and Agamemnon as the "transpersonal," for he acknowledged the essential difference between them:

AEGISTHUS
You love a man for what he might be; I for what he is. You glory in his potential…. I sympathize with his existence as it is now … you cry for the heroic; I have tears of verse for the weak [236].

Do these two men represent the ideologically alienated generations of the 1950s and '60s? Do they represent the different political parties that comprised the American government at that time? For his part, Orestes, as the product of a decade in which nothing is certain, admits to his father:

ORESTES
It could be that I, who believe nothing I would ask a dog to miss a meal for, envy you who are certain to the point of a thousand deaths [246].

Ultimately, myths are constructed from authentic human attributes, and Richardson's Agamemnon withstands the challenge of his son. In this play, Agamemnon's courage and humanity prove richer than his reputation to the extent that Orestes is forced, against his better judgment, to acknowledge the nobility—and even the humor—of his father's spirit.

Richardson's Agamemnon brings home no fiery-eyed visionary, no untamed prophetess of doom as in the original known version of the myth, but a homely, middle-aged woman who works a wicker basket (reminiscent of the archetypal female weavers of human destiny from Homer to the present). There is no doubt that, in this play, Richardson has diminished the mythical power of prophesy. This Cassandra sprouts sage little predictions. She is a mother goddess who is comforting in her familiar aunt-like guise, and a seer who instinctively guesses the outcome of events. The diminished dramatic stature she holds on this stage provokes questions regarding the power that modern woman wields over man's destiny, and the position she holds, in general, in the twentieth and twenty-first centuries of Western society. The archetypal image of "visionary" that Richardson's ironic figure suggests makes us question the power of the instincts in general, and their place in modernity. It provokes us to question whether—and to what extent— the opinions of women are heeded in our own rational, equitable society. In this play, as in modern times, prophecy constitutes little more than female intuition.

As Martin Luther King, Jr., would have said, Agamemnon has "slept through a revolution." He is a hero in a changed world; yet, true to his "heroic" character, Agamemnon predicts the tragic fates of himself and his son, and recognizes in them the crucial turning point in every son's life:

My death will be a fact—there in front of you and you will step neither around nor over it [248].

For Richardson's Agamemnon, self-realization means identification and responsibility. Masculine heroism is a struggle against nature and nature does not guarantee its continuance. Agamemnon needs Orestes' promise of help, for his son is his only guarantee that his "heroic" vision will be carried into the future.

But, in this play, the son is no early Shakespearean Hal who runs from responsibility and seeks to hide his youth and innocence; while Pylades is a Falstaffian character who encourages his friend's desire for freedom. Orestes is tempted to sail over the ocean (an image suggestive of death, the unconscious mind and, perhaps, baptism into a better life) with Praxithia, thereby escaping responsibility into fantasy. Cain-like, the prodigal son is exiled from mankind, though this time, ironically it is because he refuses to murder. Richardson's Orestes is prevented from pursuing his own vision of the simple and un-heroic life. Neumann writes:

The absence of father identification prevents the eternal youth from ever obtaining his kingdom. His refusal to become the father and assume power seems to him a guarantee of perpetual youth, for to assume power is to accept the fact that it must be passed on to a future son and ruler. The individualist is essentially non-archetypal— that is to say, the eternal revolutionary, as he grows older, turns out to be a neurotic who is not prepared to "be his age" and accept his limitations. To negate the Isaac complex is not to get beyond it. [119]

From dramatic and mythical perspectives, the withdrawal of Orestes from society constituted the precursor of the birth of the hero, an element of tragedy that we have recognized in all the previous expressions of the myth. Traditionally then, Orestes' tragedy consisted in his inability to free himself from the tethers of his masculine, hero-oriented culture. Not so with Richardson's Orestes.

ORESTES
The world demands that we inherit the pretensions of our fathers, that we go on killing in the name of ancient illusions about ourselves [261].

This pacifist is trapped in the vise of the classical world. The question is: Does he have the degree of tenacity required to loosen its hold?

We might remember that, in his Electra, Giraudoux had not allowed the tragic form to pull the audience under its emotional spell. Apart from his alienating characters of the beggar and the Furies, Giraudoux had the gardener step completely out of the action and chat with members of the audience. Similarly, here in Richardson's play, public opinion is no longer the expression of the chorus, but of us—the audience. Each of us is forced to become judge, not only of the particular crimes of Clytemnestra and Aegisthus but, of tragedy and heroism as a whole. Talking directly to us Cassandra says:

CASSANDRA
Let us suppose the sea is our audience...
(S)ome ... would have Orestes
return ... to curse in public the back-stairs
activities of his mother....
(I)n the cheaper seats (they) think that progress must go on ...
(but) for the
majority, dramatic justice ...
can be simply solved by death.
They speak with Electra's voice [262].

Here, the unconscious, associated with the ocean waves that Cassandra is addressing, no longer represents the furies of Orestes, but the conscience of the spectator. The moral dilemma of meaningless revenge (tragedy) versus the simple life of men and women in nature has become our own struggle; and the struggle of the prodigal son is that he is forced, against his will, into a weltanschauung that is no longer his own. Richardson might also be referring, in this play, to the dilemma that the modern poet has vis-à-vis the classical form.

And what of Electra? Electra has remained throughout the intemperate voice of the past. She is the natural offspring of the heroic, Western ideal that regards reality in stark terms of black and white. Hers is her father's ideal. The "golden shields" of her father are reflected in the pain of her eyes. For her there are innocent and criminals, and the criminals must be condemned. In this version of the myth, hers is the intransigent world of the fathers.

Ideally, there should be two parallel playing areas here, one for the stage- action, and one for the spectators who, as the play progresses, become as much a part of the action as the players. In fact, the spectators become players by virtue of their vital roles in assessing the archetypal questions of Orestes: questions of honor, family loyalty, personal morality and integrity; public versus private vision, duty versus impulsivity, heroism versus anti-heroism, murder versus guilt, and the tragic form versus the anti-tragic form. Does Orestes' flight from the heroic constitute the betrayal of the father, his country and his honor? This is not a "tragic" stage; it should be constructed in such a way as to reflect the equal balance between the old heroic ideal and the new ideal of acceptance and pacifism. It should reflect the equality that exists between the actors and the spectators and the dialectics that is encouraged between them during the performance.

Adrienne Kennedy: Electra and Orestes (1980)

In her free translation of these two plays, Adrienne Kennedy transforms Euripides' realistic use of language and his set, which had emphasized the humble dignity of the Athenian peasant, into a stark, presentational repetition of the myth. The action in Kennedy's version is not introduced by the peasant in such a way as to reveal his character, but by the chorus, as yet another record of ancient oral lore.

CHORUS
Our ancient city of Argos. The river Inachus.
It was here that King Agamemnon led his army forth and with ships Of war set sail for Troy.

And having killed the King of Troy and sacked that noble city he returned here to Argos. And on our temple walls hung high his trophies. [120]

Kennedy's rendition of the play is a record of masculine conquest and violence. The language is impoverished, as is her version of the myth. The style, it seems to me, calls for as bare a stage as possible. The sum of all its parts represents the end of a civilization of which it is characteristic. As such this modern rendition reverts to the ritualistic; its language stylized and atonal.

In Kennedy's interpretation, Electra loses her neurotic features and becomes what is by now a stereotype of female determination and strength of character. Unlike her Euripidean counterpart, Electra here rejects the finery offered by the chorus of women, not out of self-pity, but out of a genuine sense of mourning:

ELECTRA
I cannot come. Fine dresses and necklaces of gold my dear friends, make my heart sadder. I could not bear the sight of the girls of Argos dancing, nor would I want to dance with them [E 108].

Yet, after her liberation, she is ready to rejoice:

ELECTRA
Set your feet dancing Dance like the light.
…
My finery that I possess that is stored in the cottage I will bring out.
Too I will bring the crown
for my brother's head [E 131]).

This, in a manner similar to that of Hofmannsthal's play, is a fiery and savage dance of victory. Yet, the tone is as dead as the soul that is capable of such an act of liberation. The beautiful robes that she has stored for this occasion are reminiscent of the deadly finery that Euripides' Medea (431 BCE) wore when she murdered her two little boys in her own heinous act of revenge:

MEDEA
They say the gods themselves
Are moved by gifts, and gold does more with men than words.
…
And give her the dress, for this is of great importance, That she should take the gift into her hand from yours. [121]

183

The implication of Kennedy's translation is that heroism in our culture is synonymous with violence and that the gods are Western man's assurance that violence will be perpetrated:

ORESTES
Some monster disguised as a god has commanded me, but I can't believe that what the god told me is right.

ELECTRA
You cannot lose your nerve and be the coward now. You must use the same deception she used when with Aegisthus' help she struck our father down.

ORESTES
I'll go in. Every step is dreadful and the deed before me still more dreadful, yet if heaven so wills, let it be done [E 133–4].

Religion is an excuse for murder. Violence is perpetrated at every religious ceremony:

ELECTRA
Will you do this for me? Offer the tenth day sacrifice for a son?

CLYTEMNESTRA
Well, as a favor, I'll go in and pay the gods the respect for your son. And then I must go to where my husband is sacrificing to the nymphs out in the pasture [E 136].

Sorrow is also God-given.

CHORUS
Happiness is brief.
It will not stay.
God batters at its sails,
sorrow strikes,
and happiness goes down,
and glory sinks. [122]

European history is the history of the Electra myth. Western culture perpetuates itself by means of religiously sanctioned violence and grief:

CHORUS
Glory decays, and
greatness goes
from the happy house of Atreus.

Beneath the proud façade
the long stain spread
as the curse of blood began—
strife for a golden ram,
slaughter of little princes,
a table laid with horror,
a feast of murdered sons.
And still corruption swelled,
murder displacing murder,
to reach at last
the living heirs of Atreus [O 155–6].

Matricide is the natural culmination of such a history:

CHORUS
What terror can compare with us?
Hands of a son,
stained with his mother's blood [O 156].

Here, In Kennedy's version of the myth, the "hero" is not horrified when confronted by his sister's savagery. On the contrary, despite his qualms, he comes specifically to recruit his sister for the act of matricide:

ORESTES
I must see her and get her help in executing our
revenge [E 107].

In such a way, the women of the Troy/Electra myths are subsumed into our violent male ideology. They are victims of our own, all-encompassing, essentially alien, masculine culture, one that was founded on violence and that guarantees its future by means of the manipulation and victimization of its women:

ORESTES
How could he be avenged?

PYLADES
Listen: We will avenge him by murdering Helen [O 159].

Here the hero is he who is brave enough to murder innocent women and children:

ORESTES
Seize her and stop her screaming. Let Menelaos learn
what it is to fight with men, not cowards from Troy [O 166].

The gods are a projection of the male ego, created by men to legitimize their victimization of women:

APOLLO
Cease Menelaos. It is I Phoebus Apollo.
Helen is here with me. Orestes did not kill her.
Helen, being born of Zeus, could not die
and now will sit enthroned forever, a star for sailors.
It is Orestes' destiny to leave Argos and journey to the city of Athena
and givejustice for his mother's murder. The gods on the hill of Ares
shall be his judges and acquit him in a sacred verdict. Then Orestes will
marry Hermione.
Electra shall marry Pylades as promised.
Happiness awaits him.
Menelaos will be king in Sparta and I shall give Argos to Orestes ...
for it was I who commanded his mother's murder. I compelled him to
kill [O 171].

This ending is the stuff of fairy tales. The men are guaranteed eternal happiness, while the beautiful Helen is transformed from a woman into the abstraction of masculine ambition.

On the subject of male projection of the female onto objective reality, Simone de Beauvoir points out that:

Not only are cities and nations clothed in feminine attributes, but also abstract entities such as institutions: the Church, the Synagogue, the Republic, Humanity, are women. [123]

In fact, she is repeating the Freudian principle that such institutions, being receptacles, are symbols of female-sexuality. Simone de Beauvoir continues:

So ... are Peace, War, Liberty, the Revolution, Victory. Man feminizes the ideal he sets up before him as the essential Other, because woman is the material representation of alterity; that is why almost all allegories, in language as in pictorial representation, are women. Woman is Soul and Idea, but she is also a mediatrix between them; she is the divine Grace leading the Christian toward God, she is Beatrice guiding Dante in the beyond, Laura summoning Petrarch to the lofty summits of poetry.... The gnostic sects made wisdom a woman, Sophia, crediting her with the redemption of the world and even its creation. Here we see woman no longer as flesh, but as glorified sub-stance; she is no longer to be possessed, but venerated in her intact splendor ... through all the tradition of gallantry, woman is no longer an animal creature but is rather an ethereal being, a breath, a glow. [124]

Beauvoir also says of man's regard for women: "If he is anxious to believe her pure and chaste, it is less because of amorous jealousy than because of his refusal to see her as a body." The male abstraction of the female, as we see in the myth of Helen is, then, nothing more than the manifestation of his fear of her maternal nature.

Beauvoir quotes from medieval litanies to illustrate the idealization and de- sexualization of women in Christianity:

Most high Virgin, thou art the fertile Dew, the Fountain of Joy, the Channel of pity, the Well of living waters which cool our fervors. Thou art the Breast from which God gives orphans to suck... Thou art the marrow, the tiny Bit, the Kernel of all good things, Thou art the guileless Woman whose love never changes...
Thou art the subtle Physician, whose like is not to be found in Salermo or Montpellier...
Thou art the Lady with healing hands.... Thou makest the paralized to walk, thou reformest the base, thou revivest the dead.

With this, we have come full circle to the prehistoric, Egyptian representation of the all-encompassing and all fecundating cow-Goddess and goddess of the sky; yet ironically, it is against this reduction of the real woman into an abstraction that Adrienne Kennedy, as a modern woman, is struggling.

The other predicament of woman in a male society is that of Hermione, the trusting young girl who is so easily bartered by her father into the hands of her would-be assassin. The subject of this myth is, probably always has been, the questioning of the ambiguous role that women hold in this otherwise perfectly ordered, consciously destructive society. Beauvoir says:

Representation of the world, like the world itself, is the work of men. They describe it from their own point of view, which they confuse with absolute truth.

And what of the Amazon-like Clytemnestra and Electra? How, in the final analysis, do we come to terms with their violence? On the question of woman in myth, in Greek theater, and in theater in general, Sue-Ellen Case writes:

She definitely feels excluded from the conventions of the stage, bewildered by the convention of cross-gender casting, which is only practiced for female characters. Mimesis is not possible for her. Perhaps the feminist reader will decide that the female roles should be played by men, as fantasies of "Woman" as "other" than man, as disruptions of a patriarchal society and illustrative of its fear and loathing of the female parts. In fact, the feminist reader might become persuaded that the Athenian roles of Medea, Clytemnestra, Cassandra, and Phaedra are properly played as drag roles. The feminist reader might conclude that women need not relate to these roles or even attempt to identify them. Moreover, the feminist historian might conclude that these roles contain no information about the experience of real women in the Classical world. Nevertheless, the feminist scholar must recognize that theater originated in this kind of cultural climate and that the Athenian experience will continue to provide a certain paradigm of theatrical practice for the rest of Western theatrical and cultural history. By linking practice, text and cultural background in this new way, she may enhance her understanding of how the hegemonic structure of patriarchal practice was instituted in Athens. [125]

It is one thing to question whether women characters, as male creations, bear any similarity to their silent, off-stage counterparts. Another, and, to my mind, more acute requirement is to question the extent to which real women force themselves into these masculine models of femininity: Perhaps it is time to turn our male and female backs on the way in which the "hegemonic structure of patriarchal practice was instituted in Athens." Can we relinquish the myth and liberate Electra? Can women extricate themselves from an alien theatrical legacy that has been foisted on them? Or, have women already learned their own movements, their own dance, their own story, their own theater? Perhaps when the truly female principle is released, it will give rise to an entirely new and different Western civilization.

With this, Electra has become a theater that challenges the moral right of the dominant culture to impose its myths on its subjects. Far from the Aeschylean dependence on a shared worldview, writers of the 1980s and 1990s advocated diversity and decentralization as the democratic mode.

This theater exposes the lie inherent in the myth that the hero is an excuse for the perpetuation of masculine control. It exposes the god as tool of the male power structure. In Kennedy's theater, maturation can take place only on the part of individual spectators as they distance themselves from the controlling mechanisms of the Establishment.

Heiner Muller: Hamlet-Machine (1984)

The final Electra play that we will read as one that conforms to the deep- structure of the myth, as we have defined it, is the *Hamlet-Machine* by the East German playwright Heiner Muller.

I am aware that there are many readings and theories of Hamlet that are not included in this study as Electra plays, and I feel satisfied in including this play as such because of the specifically schizophrenic treatment by which Muller deals with the characters of Hamlet and Ophelia, and because of the way in which he ultimately reduces the Hamlet theme to a dialectic between the masculine and feminine, in the persons of these two characters.

Muller's work is filled with violent, surrealistic and macabre images, expressions both of the turmoil, destruction ad schizophrenia of his immediate German experience under Nazi rule, and the product of German history as a whole. It is theater torn between the conflicting emotions of a Marxist ideology to which he adheres and the experience of Communist brutality which became a reality in 1956. With the invasion of Soviet forces into Hungary, Khrushchev revealed the worst excesses of Stalinism.

Muller is the quintessential German writer. His national ad personal experiences have made him acutely conscious of himself as both victimizer and victim, as Hamlet, the citizen who supports the brutality of oppressive regimes:

HAMLET
LET ME HELP YOU UP, UNCLE, OPEN YOUR LEGS, MAMA. [126]

and Ophelia, eternal image of despair:

OPHELIA
I am Ophelia. The one the river didn't keep. The woman dangling
from the rope. The woman with her arteries cut open. The woman with
the overdose. SNOW ON HER LIPS. The woman with her head in the
gas stove [54].

He is also the poet (Orestes)—guilty because he is a passive
witness to the horrors that have been perpetrated against his country
(Electra):

HAMLET
I'M GOOD HAMLET GI'ME A CAUSE FOR GRIEF AH THE WHOLE
GLOBE FOR A REAL SORROW RICHARD THE THIRD I THE PRINCE-
KILLING KING OH MY PEOPLE WHAT HAVE I DONE UNTO THEE I'M
LUGGING MY OVERWEIGHT BRAIN LIKE A HUNCHBACK CLOWN
NUMBER TWO IN THE SPRING OF COMMUNISM SOMETHING IS
ROTTEN IN THIS AGE OF HOPE
LET'S DELVE IN EARTH AND BLOW HER AT THE MOON [53].

And Electra, the eternal female land that now, Gaia-like, rejects
her children-lovers:

OPHELIA
Yesterday I stopped killing myself. I'm alone with my breasts my thighs
my womb. I smash the tools of my captivity, the chair the table the bed.
I destroy the battlefield that was my home. I fling open the doors so the
wind gets in and the scream of the world. I smash the window. With my
bleeding hands I tear the photos of the men I loved and who used me on
the bed on the table on the chair on the ground. I set fire to my prison.
I throw my clothes into the fire. I wrench the clock that was my heart out
of my breast. I walk into the street clothed in my blood [54–5].

Ophelia-Electra is Armageddon. She is the new order that, in
this instance, smashes idols of the old order. She is A-Lektra, the
unmated, because, in her bitterness, she declares:

OPHELIA
I eject all the sperm I have received. I turn the milk of my breasts into
lethal poison. I take back the world I gave birth to. I choke between my
thighs the world I gave birth to. I bury it in my womb. Down with the
happiness of submission. Long live hate and contempt, rebellion and
death. When she walks through your bedrooms carrying butcher knives
you'll know the truth [58].

Ophelia appears on stage as the inversion of the Virgin Mother.
In the form of the Madonna with breast cancer, she rejects the

world of male-domination to which she as given birth. Horatio and Hamlet "freeze under the umbrella, embracing. The breast cancer radiates like the sun" (55).

In Oscar Wilde's Salome, the Electra-character was identified with the moon, symbol of beauty, madness, dangerous changeability, and erotic female sensuality. But by the time we arrive at Muller's play, the violence of Western culture has transformed the entire archetype of the female as we have known her. Here, in self-defense, in rage and in protest, the female breast—universal image of love and nurture—has become a source of poison, a fire equal to that of the sun (image of the male, and of masculine power) in its potential for destruction.

Are the capitalized male speeches quoted above contrasted to the small letters of Ophelia's speeches in a deliberate demonstration of their relative roles in society? And should they be understood as such by the actors?

I am tempted to digress, for a moment, from our Electra theme, in order to add yet another element to our expanding definition of theater. To this end, I quote from the words of the famous director of political theater, Erwin Piscator, as he reminisces about his experiences in the first world war:

Ypres—Belgium.
The shells whistle around our heads. The order is DIG IN! I am Lying on the ground, my heart beating madly, and like the others I Try to use my spade and dig into the earth.
The sergeant arrives, cursing,
    "Dig in, Piscator!" "I can't."
Sergeant: "Why not?"
"I can't."
Sergeant (howling!):
What's your profession?" "Actor."
I looked at the sergeant helplessly as I pronounced the word.
What a fraud, what false ecstasy and elusive life of dreams! Suddenly, I felt less afraid of the falling shells around me than ashamed of being an actor. Something was shattered forever: illusion. The curtain separating. Life from stage was torn away. Theatre, yes, but a different kind—not a stage, but a platform—theatre as instrument to probe life and to come to grips with reality—not an audience, but a community. [127]

Muller also questions the validity and purpose of the artist in face of battle. His theater brings dead philosophers on stage lecturing behind tombstone- lecterns. As they philosophize, women— metaphors for the victims of a savage society—dangle on the stage from a rope, expose themselves to the spectators with lacerated and bleeding arteries while Hamlet the poet, together with the audience, looked on as visitors in a theater or a museum. Muller realizes that, as in life so in theater, pain cannot be romanticized; it is personal and immediate:

The author can't ignore himself anymore.... If I don't talk a about myself I'll reach no one. [128]

Hamlet is Muller. He is every citizen in a regime of violence and oppression. As such, he rips Muller's portrait apart on stage:

HAMLET
Somewhere bodies are torn apart so I can dwell in my shit.
Somewhere bodies are opened so I can be alone with my blood. My thoughts are lesions in my brain. My brain is a scar. I want to be a machine [57].

Machines of our domestic lives—a refrigerator and three television sets— become repositories for our emotions. The refrigerator hums and the televisions play silently on stage until the moment life ceases. Then the refrigerator bleeds and the television sets go blank.

Like Piscator, Muller dedicates his art of exposing to his audience the horrors and ambiguities of society. However, in contrast to Brecht, his mentor, solutions to the political problems do not interest him. Like Herbert Blau, he claims that art consist of raising the issues. As such, all aspects of the Electra-Orestes question are granted equal validity. Muller is equally horrified by the Hamlets as by the Falstaffs of society and, though ashamed of the passive intellectual stance, he would rather be victim than aggressor, an attitude which is, ironically, quintessentially intellectual:

OPHELIA
Do you want to eat my heart, Hamlet?

HAMLET
I want to be a woman [55].

According to Carl Weber in his Introduction to this play, Muller considers Hamlet's dilemma:

> The German "split"; the "two souls dwelling in my breast" the archetypal German Dr. Faustus agonizes over; Hamlet—"this 'very German' character, as Muller once said—torn apart by the contradictions of existence; the divided Germany of today's political map—no other German writer represents these schisms as boldly and clearly in his life and work [15].

Muller is the Hamlet that berates himself for his effete intellectualism in the face of a violent reality.

There are shades of Büchner's Woyzeck in Muller's play, of a nightmarish reality in which Hamlet becomes the victim of his own mind. Indeed, Muller's theater might be viewed as the logical extension of Büchner's:

> Claudius—now Hamlet's father—laughs without uttering a sound, Ophelia blows Hamlet a kiss and steps with Claudius/Hamlet's father back into the coffin [55].

The ritual of this theater is, again, the gathering of disparate members of the community for a raising of issues common to all. Yet the post Fascist mentality is wary of mass ideology. In this world, there are no answers. Hope for the survival of human values consists in honestly confronting the question, not by means of a shared world-view, but by the unflinchingly independent assessment of the individual. As such, this theater of alienation, a theater that labels its scenes (perhaps with placards) in order to keep the spectators on guard and distanced from the performance. More than anything perhaps, it is the theater of Jean Genet, theater of violent images which, in this instance, represent the victims of political horror as fellow perpetrators in an inescapable dance of death. It is a theater which depicts the divorce of the masculine from the feminine as the macabre fallout of that violence:

> An angel, his face at the back of his head: Horatio. He dances with Hamlet. The dance grows faster and wilder. Laughter from the Coffin. On a swing, the Madonna with breast cancer [55].

In this theater we recognize the age-old Hippolytus style misogyny, yet here man's horror of the female has become an expression of his desire to escape the guilt of his own violence:

HAMLET
I would my mother had one less when you were still of flesh: I would have been spared myself. Women should be sewed up—a world without monsters. We could butcher each other in peace and quiet and with some confidence, if life gets too long for us or our throats too tight for our screams [53].

We have defined the Orestean story as the journey of the individual toward manhood. However, in no version of the myth have we encountered the hero actually inheriting his kingdom. All versions end with the horror that is the consequence of such an experience. When talking about Brecht, Muller says,

Out of revolutionary impatience with the immaturity of the conditions stems the trend to substitute the proletariat, a trend that leads to paternalism, the disease of all Communist parties. In defense against the anarchic-natural matriarchy, the re- construction of the rebellious son into the father-figure begins [Weber's Introduction, 18].

Muller is acutely aware of the regression that automatically occurs when the son becomes the father, when the revolutionary becomes the Establishment, and when the poet achieves success and is raised to the comfortable ranks of society. Consequently, this Hamlet-Orestes refuses manhood. To Muller, the heroic stance manifests itself in the refusal to pick up the gauntlet. "I want to be a woman" is his way of refusing adulthood and the price it exacts, of maintaining his integrity at the expense of experience.

113   Peter Brook, The Empty Space (New York: Atheneum, 1984).
114   "Electra: Theater, Downtown," 2 Dec. 1987.
115   Ezra Pound, Elektra, trustees of the Ezra Pound Literary Property Trust, 1987, p. 72. Hereafter, quotations from this edition are indicated by page number references in parentheses or brackets.
116   "Electra," rev. of Elektra, by Ezra Pound, dir. Carey Perloff, Theater, 2 Dec. 1987.
117   John Peter, "Why Broadway's Fairy-Tale Lacks a Happy Ending," rev. of Elektra by Ezra Pound, dir. Carey Perloff, The Sunday Times, 8 Nov. 1987.

118 Jack Richardson, The Prodigal, in Orestes and Electra, ed. William M. Force (Boston: Houghton Mifflin, 1968), p. 211. Hereafter, quotations from this edition are indicated by page number references in parentheses or brackets.

119 Neumann, p. 190.

120 Adrienne Kennedy, Electra, in One Act (Minneapolis: University of Minnesota Press, 1988), p.105. Hereafter, quotations from this edition are indicated by an "E" and by page number references in parentheses or brackets.

121 Euripides, The Medea in Euripides 1, ed. David Grene and Richmond Lattimore (Chicago:University of Chicago Press, 1955), p. 92.

122 Adrienne Kennedy, Orestes in In One Act (Minneapolis: University of Minnesota Press, 1988.) p.147. Hereafter, quotations from this edition are indicated by an "O," and page number references or brackets.

123 Simone de Beauvoir, The Second Sex, trans. and ed. H.M. Parshley (New York: Vintage, 1974), p.202.

124 The Beauvoir quotations are, respectively, from pages 202, 165, 203, and 161.

125 Sue-Ellen Case, Feminism and Theater (New York: Methuen, 1988), p.

126 Heiner Muller, Hamlet-Machine, ed. Carl Weber (New York: Performing Arts Journal Publications, 1984), p. 53. Hereafter, quotations from this edition are indicated by page number references in parentheses or brackets.

127 Maria Ley Piscator, The Piscator Experiment: The Political Theatre (Edwardsville: Southern Illinois University Press, 1967).

128 Muller, p. 55.

CHAPTER 7

T.S. ELIOT: THE FAMILY REUNION (1939)

I n all the plays we have studied so far, the masculine and the feminine have been represented as dramatic metaphors for contradictory impulses that rage in the deepest parts of the human soul: impulses of creativity, passion, and freedom versus the drive of "civilized" man toward control, reason and order. In all the above instances, the playwrights have challenged accepted notions of justice, honor, patriotism; and the public versus the private conscience from inside the deep structure of the myth. In this chapter, I will present two examples of what I consider are Electra plays in which the playwrights deliberately deviate from the deep structure of the myth, and I will question possible reasons for these playwrights' motivations.

In this 1939 version of the Electra myth, Eliot provides his audience yet again with alternative realities, for, in the same text, he juxtaposes realism with ritual, and the poetic with the mundane. The directions state that "the scene is laid in a country house in the North of England" in a "drawing room, after tea" and we are presented with the genteel family scene, maidservant and butler, which constitute the traditional paraphernalia of realistic theater. Yet in this structure there is a chorus of family members which, despite the realism of the situation, introduces on stage both a modern sense of meta- theater, and an almost classical sense of the unknown:

CHORUS

Why do we feel embarrassed, impatient, fretful, ill at ease, assembled like amateur actors who have not been assigned their parts?
Like amateur actors in a dream when the curtain rises, to find themselves dressed for a different play, or having rehearsed the wrong parts. [129]

These characters have been gathered for a simple dinner party, yet they sense a subtext for which they are not prepared. The uneasy sense of alienation that the members of this chorus feel toward their assigned roles mirrors, perhaps, those of the members of such a society, roles that are assigned at birth, but which don't quite fit as they should.

There is an atmosphere of foreboding here, a suggestion of the uncanny and the unknown. The subtext of the chorus differs greatly from the surface text of social decorum, and we soon realize that the chorus, though ignorant of the fact, is in a liminal space not unlike the one in which Aeschylus' chorus had conjured up the spirit of the dead, or that in which Hamlet had confronted the spirit of his father:

CHARLES

I might have been in St. James's Street, in a comfortable chair rather nearer the fire.

IVY

I might have been visiting Cousin Lily...

GERALD

I might have been staying with...

VIOLET

I should have been helping...

CHORUS

Yet we are here at Amy's command, to play an unread part in some monstrous farce, ridiculous in some nightmare pantomime.

AMY

What's that? I thought I saw someone pass the window. What time is it? [22].

The audience expects a play of domestic problems in a comfortable setting. Instead, it is exposed to a re-examination of the structure of its society, and a suggestion that reality exists not in the familiar but in an entire, untapped world of spiritual opportunity. As such, it is Charles—specter from another world, not the expected Arthur or John—who passes the window in this scene, conjured up by this very chorus of unsuspecting household guests. The modern chorus differs from the classical one in that it is unaware that there is an alternate, and perhaps more satisfying, reality beyond their window. As such, spirits are not here to comply with the wishes of the protagonists, but as some objective, arbitrary force, a force that is silent and unseen.

HARRY
How can you sit in this blaze of light for all the world to look at?
...
Do you like to be stared at by eyes through a window? [23].

Throughout the performance the characters, and no doubt the spectators, are driven to the wrong conclusions because they are unable to conceive the unfamiliar. As Agatha says:

AGATHA
Men tighten the knot of confusion
Into perfect misunderstanding,
...
Neglecting all the admonitions
From the world around the corner
The wind's talk in the dry holly-tree
The inclination of the moon
The attraction of the dark passage
The paw under the door [21].

And so, with alternate styles of poetry and prose, alternate modes of reality are suggested—and missed—by the limited vision of the characters in this play. It is unfortunate that Eliot's characters vacillate between the poetic and the prosaic to such an extent that they destroy the intrinsic integrity of the play and thereby disrupt the receptiveness of the audience. Mary, for instance, totters precariously from the sublime to the ridiculous:

MARY
...I should have known it;
It was all over, I believe, before it began;
But I deceived myself. It takes so many years
To learn that one is dead! So you must help me.
I will go. But I suppose it is much too late Now, to try to get a fellowship? [117–8].

The immediate, almost petty practicality of the last one-and-a-half lines of this quotation jars as badly with the tone of the earlier lines as an opera singer singing off-tune.

In this version of the myth, Eliot cuts directly to the attraction-repulsion of the mother-son relationship. As such, the mother is not portrayed in the traditional role as the murderess of her husband and the mother who banishes her son from the maternal bosom. Rather, here, Amy is the deserted wife and the devoted mother who, Electra-like, arrests all signs of the passage of time in her dedication to his return. The return of the son constitutes the life of the mother:

> **AMY**
> I do not want the clock to stop in the dark.
> If you want to know why I never leave Wishwood
> That is the reason. I keep Wishwood alive
> To keep the family alive, to keep them together,
> To keep me alive, and I live to keep them.

By now the all-too-close ties, the almost suffocating proximity and interdependence of relationships in the family constellation are recognizable to us as characteristic of the Electra motif.

Amy's only crime is the willful, Clytemnestra-like tenacity, which Agatha recognizes in her:

> **AGATHA**
> ...But you are just the same:
> Just as voracious for what you cannot have because you repel it [113–4].

As we have noted, the mythical characters in this play are not clearly defined, independent personalities; rather, they overshadow, stint, and cling parasitically to each other, each usurping the space of the other and, in so doing, suggesting that there is no possible room for the individual. The chorus of Ivy, that plant which lives and climbs on the success of others, and Violet, which blooms only in the shade of others, is emblematic of the plight of the characters in their dependency and lack of differentiation. Harry's life bears the stamp of Agamemnon and Paris, of their inordinate fear of, and dependency on, the female. He had run from the misty, northern air of intellectual blindness and stifled emotions (represented by

Wishwood,) and from the overbearing will of his mother under the spell of a woman who— before long, in fantasy, if not in reality—he was compelled to murder.

It is Agatha who grants Harry a means of transcending the myopic claustrophobia of domestic materialism, who gives him some insight into that other realm, a realm that lies always beyond the socialized grasp. It is she who shows him that reality is more expansive, more multifaceted than it seems. Harry responds to Agatha with:

HARRY
I think I see what you mean,
Dimly—as you once explained the sobbing in the chimney
The evil in the dark closet, which they said was not there,
Which they explained away, but you explained them or at least, made me
cease to be afraid of them.

Are we to understand the "sobbing in the chimney" and the "evil in the dark closet" from a Freudian perspective, as the pain of human intercourse and as Harry's fear of the female, a fear which is denied by society but regarding which Agatha had reassured him, thereby enabling him to leave Wishwood and marry?

The traditional plights of Agamemnon, Orestes, and Paris, merge into that of Harry in such a way as to emphasize that the domestic situation always constitutes a trap for the hero:

AGATHA
...I mean that at Wishwood he will find another Harry.
The man who returns will have to meet
The boy who left...
And it will not be a very jolly corner.
When the loop in time comes—and it does not come for Everybody—
The hidden is revealed, and their specters show themselves.

The hero recognizes that

...the last apparent refuge, the safe shelter,
That is where one meets them.
That is the way of Specters [110].

However far and long the hero runs ultimately, he is bound to return and confront himself and his personal destiny in the mirror of his own nature. However long and arduous the Electra-struggle has pitted itself against social structures and mores of Western civilization, a moment of final reckoning with it does arrive, as it seems to do in this play. With the final reckoning comes the suggestion that perhaps, after all is said and done, the deep structure of this civilization fails to adhere to the needs of its individuals.

Agamemnon and Orestes are both destroyed when they return home. So is Harry, but Harry is not a hero for his community. Moreover, the seven-year absence from which Harry returns is more reminiscent of the undifferentiated experiences of Paris and Menelaos in the Trojan war than the pre-heroic state of Orestes. Amy says of Harry's former wife:

AMY
She never wished to be one of the family,
She only wanted to keep him to herself
To satisfy her vanity. That's why she dragged him
All over Europe and half around the world
To expensive hotels and undesirable society
Which she could choose herself [20].

Again, it is appropriate to note that relationships overlap in Eliot's play; that the names of mythical heroes, of heroism itself, are muddled and unclear. Amy has the strength and the pathos of Clytemnestra, yet the sense of loss she has suffered for her husband and the devotion with which she waits for the return of her son are characteristic of Electra. Agatha is undoubtedly a Cassandra figure in her ability to see beyond the materialism of everyday life and in her opposition to Amy; yet she is also Electra, for it is she who is responsible for having saved and exiled Orestes. Observe the similarity between Agatha's blurring the sentiments of love, closeness, and death, and what we had noted earlier in Sophocles' Electra:

AGATHA
I didn't want to kill you!
You to be killed! What were you then?
Only a thing called "life"—
something that should have been mine, as I felt then.
...
... But I wanted you!
If that had happened, I knew I should have carried death in life, death through lifetime, death in my womb [100–1].

Mary is also Electra. She has been held against her will in this house. She is a servant tied to the indomitable will of Amy. Yet Amy holds Mary captive not in order to prevent her from marriage or to bar her access to the Orestean figure, but for the specific purpose of marrying her to him. The horror of this Orestes is not that he is divorced from his beloved sister/lover, but that he is destined to be confronted by her at every turn. Most strange of all, perhaps, is that here the Clytemnestra figure does not murder her husband; rather it is— at least symbolically—the reverse. In addition, in this play, it is not Electra's two sisters who epitomize the alternative fates of women in an aggressive, masculine world; but rather it is Arthur and John, (the reckless and the docile) younger brothers of Harry. Here, it is the young boys who are unable to find themselves in a world forever dominated by their mother. What is more, here, Mary—the Electra figure—is not the tragic heroine whom we have recognized so far as she who sacrifices life and love for the correction of a moral imbalance in nature; she does not goad Harry into murdering his mother; rather she pleads with him to stay and protect himself from the ravages of his own mind. Here, in Eliot's play, she is Mary, a Christianized Electra, gentle and asexual. Yet the fact that she is planted in this house as bait for Harry makes us question her true nature. Is she harmless, or simply another tool of the domestic ideology and, as such, a cloaked dagger? Could this represent— despite Eliot's much publicized conservatism and his initiation into the Anglican Church—the poet's personal suspicions regarding the function of Christianity in Western culture?

Whatever our interpretation, Eliot is surely taking a stand against the typecasting of his characters and for the multifaceted nature, the many possible roles, the diversity and complex potential in each and every one of us.

The major similarity between the traditional versions of the myth and this is, it seems, that Harry comes from a separate physical and emotional space than that of the other characters. Throughout his life, he has been persecuted by Eumenides, a fear, even a terror (perhaps of himself,) that has driven him from traditional situations.

A clarification of Harry's dilemma and the turning point of this action seem to lie in his confrontation with Agatha:

AGATHA
There is a deeper
Organization, which your question disturbs (97).
…
A curse is like a child, formed
To grow to maturity:
O my child, my curse…
You shall be fulfilled:
The knot shall be unknotted
And the crooked made straight [107].

I suppose that this play is a deliberate inversion of the myth in its original form for the purpose of untying the knot in which the social structure of Western society binds its members.

At the beginning of this work, we had noted that the original use of the term "virgin" referred not to a woman who had never experienced sexual intercourse, but to one who, while utilizing of the physical sperm of a man, conceived by inspiration, by imbibing into her being a godly spirit. Here we have such a situation, but the genders are reversed. Harry's mother is nothing more than a physical vessel, a carrier for a son who is the spiritual child of Agatha:

HARRY
Tell me now, who were my parents?

AGATHA
Your father and your mother.

HARRY
You tell me nothing [98].

Agatha reveals her intimacy with Harry's father:

AGATHA
I remember
A summer of unusual heat
For this cold country [99].

and her feelings for his child:

AGATHA
I felt that you were in some way mine!
And that in case I should have no other child [100].

Agatha, the spiritual mother, tells Harry that she has had to "fight for many years to win" her "dispossession." It is her revelation to him that sets him off on his own "heroic" journey toward "dispossession." In this sense, Harry bears a remarkable similarity to the hero of Robinson Jeffers' *Tower Beyond Tragedy*. Here, for the first time, and true to the inverted tone of this version of the myth, the hero's separation from the maternal does not, in and of itself, prepare him for manhood in society; rather, by relinquishing the maternal, he prepares himself for an alternate reality, a reality that necessitates the distancing of himself from society as he has known it:

HARRY
The things I thought were real are shadows, and the real Are what I thought were private shadows. O that awful
privacy
Of the insane mind! Now I can live in public.
Liberty is a different kind of pain from prison [103].

The turning point of this work is Agatha's revelation to Harry that his father had wanted to murder his mother. With this revelation Harry recognizes the feelings that he had harbored toward his own former wife and, perhaps, to women in general.

HARRY
...Family affection
Was a kind of formal obligation, a duty
Only noticed by its neglect. One had that part to play.
After such training, I could endure, these ten years, Playing a part that
had been imposed upon me;
And I returned to find another one made ready—
The book laid out, lines underscored, and the costume
Ready to be put on [103].

Perhaps what frees Harry from his sense of obligation is his sudden realization that the woman's role in domestic society is as vulnerable and as circumscribed as the male's:

HARRY
When other people seemed so strong, their apparent strength

Stifled my decision. Now I see
I might even become fonder of my mother—
More compassionate at least—by understanding.
But she would not like that [103].

The world of this play is not the patriarchal one that we have observed so far, but a domestic world that is dominated by the female and that allows for no spiritual space. As such, sexual roles are reversed. This Agamemnon murders his Clytemnestra in an act of ultimate frustration. The hero's siblings are boys whose growth has been stunted by an overly dominant mother, and the hero himself is forced into flight by the claustrophobic hold that the female has over him. In this play, it is the rape of the male by the female that causes the hero to seek an alternative. Amy admits to Agatha, her spiritual counterpart, so attractive to her husband and her son:

AMY
You knew that you took everything
Except the walls, the furniture, the acres;
Leaving nothing—but what I could breed myself
…
… What of the humiliation,
Of the chilly pretenses in the silent bedroom,
Forcing sons upon an unwilling father? …
I would have sons, if I could not have a husband:
Then I let him go. I abased myself [113; emphasis added].

With this we have come almost full circle to the stark, modern version of the queen bee—a mother-goddess who is disempowered, who simply relinquishes her mate after a forced and loveless coitus. Ironically, with this conversion of the myth from a patriarchal to a matriarchal society, we arrive, again, at man's most primordial dilemma: can the male wrench immortality from the female by means of his intellectual or spiritual activity? Is he able to move beyond the traditional and the socially prescribed, beyond the female and the domestic—and relinquish himself to a new way of life?

Sam Shepard: Curse of the Starving Class (1978)

We have defined the deep-structure of the Electra myth as one in which the Orestean figure is forced to take a stand against the establishment; in which the focal point of action is always the meeting of the old (Agamemnon) with the new; where the play is propelled into action by the meeting of the male (Orestes) with the female (Electra); where Electra represents filial loyalty; the Clytemnestra figure is "tainted" and always a mother manqué; the figure of Aegisthus is characterized by a lack of idealism or any sense of the spiritual; and the Orestean figure approaches the action from a separate physical or psychological space than that of the other characters.

We have noted that, in this myth, the figure of Aegisthus has usurped the position of the Agamemnon figure both in the political arena and in the affections of the Queen; that the figure of Clytemnestra is one whose affections are diverted from her children, directed rather toward the one who is presently in power; that the Electra figure is, by definition, the unmated, the imprisoned and the vengeful; and that the Orestean youth is the son and heir of Agamemnon and the would-be avenger of his father's murder.

In Curse of the Starving Class, royalty of the classical world is reduced to a Californian family characterized more by its painful obscurity and lack of gainful employment than by any positive social quality. Its members belong to a recognizable tribe of American nomads who migrate to the West in the hope of instant, free, fame and fortune. From this perspective, Weston's alcoholic bouts away from home and his futile attempts to buy cheap land in Palm Springs represent the last gasp, the final, threadbare, American vestige of classical heroism:

WESTON
I just went off for a little while. Now and then. I couldn't stand it here. I couldn't stand the idea that everything would stay the same, that every morning it would be the same. I kept looking for it out there somewhere. I kept trying to piece it together. The jumps. I couldn't figure out the jumps. From being born, to growing up, to dropping bombs, to having kids, to hittin' bars, to this. It all turned on me somehow. It all turned around on me. I kept looking for it out there somewhere. And all the time it was right inside this house. [130]

Could it be that for us moderns, in contrast to the above, the ability of ancient Greek heroes to leave their families for ten years of heroic warfare appears easy? Indeed, to us it might seem that, in the context of Classical Greek culture and its definition of heroism, there was not as great a need to "figure out the jumps." Or perhaps the distance that divides us from the ancients has erased our empathy. We might believe that, for the ancient Greeks, "dropping' bombs"— or the ancient equivalent of bombs—was their way of ensuring a manhood worn thin in the narrow confines of domesticity; that warfare was their way of maintaining control, of ensuring that life did not "turn on them." Despite differences—whether real or imagined—it seems that neither the modern, nor the ancient Greek hero is able to withstand the deadliness that awaits him back home. Is this what Aristotle was referring to when he claimed that tragedy affects us most acutely, most forcefully, is most poignant, when it occurs between close family members?

What of the home? Ella is a far cry from the Greek Clytemnestra. Though a mother manquée, she does not consort with Taylor as a means of maintaining control over an abandoned kingdom, but rather as a way of escaping responsibility. Here, the lights go up on a battered house. There is no front door, and within the first few sentences we learn that the door was burst from its hinges in a confrontation between the drunken man of the house who was trying to enter, and his wife who had bolted it against him. Like Clytemnestra, Shepard's Ella resented her husband's desertion. Now she resents his return, resents his assumption of authority over her. The home we are watching has been destroyed from within and is now vulnerable, literally and symbolically, to any passing predator.

The broken house has potential. It has land, an orchard, even some livestock, yet all the images associated with them are images of devastation and neglect. The avocadoes are rotten, the livestock diseased, the tractor in disrepair. The land is neglected and the sheep castrated and diseased.

The family congregates in the kitchen. Ella is the epitome of female alienation and maternal neglect. It is the kitchen, "the warmest part of the house," that has assumed the qualities of the hearth and, in so doing, represents the female nurturing center of the home. Within the kitchen, the central shrine of this home is the refrigerator, symbol of the excruciating, indefinable pangs of hunger from which this family suffers. What is more, it is the refrigerator—this sterile and mostly empty machine—that constitutes the mother-substitute in a family that has alienated itself from any understanding of community; that has no roots, no center, and no sense of self. Indeed, the major activity throughout the play is the constant opening and shutting of the refrigerator door:

WESTON
Slams all day long and through the night. SLAM! SLAM! SLAM! What's everybody hoping for, a miracle! IS EVERYBODY HOPING FOR A MIRACLE? [157].

The poverty of this family is not that of the dignified peasant whom we encountered in Euripides' Electra; rather it is a source of shame. Emma begs the refrigerator:

EMMA
Any corn muffins in there? Hello! Any produce? Any rutabagas? any root vegetables? Nothing! It's all right. You don't have to be ashamed. I've had worse. I've had to take my lunch to school wrapped up in a Weber's bread wrapper. That's the worst. Worse than no lunch [150].

The dishonor lies in the family's insensitivity to the promise of life that lies in their grasp. Their home, their land and their family abound in images of potential fruitfulness from the lambs which they castrate to Emma, the daughter with "the curse," the ability to give birth "the first time around" (155). Yet they neglect the fertile land on which they live, preferring to set their dreams on arid desert in the vague hope of instant, unearned wealth. Weston's family hungers for the most basic commodities: food, identity, a sense of belonging, a feeling of worth and purpose, yet he brings home artichokes from the desert. Like Agamemnon, he spurns the immediate for the intangible, the material for the dream. Ultimately, this family falls victim to the Taylors, the Ellises, the Emersons and the Slaters because they want to, because they buy into the sterile materialism of nameless, rootless strangers:

TAYLOR
Of course, it's a shame to see agriculture being slowly pushed into the background in deference to low-cost housing, but that's simply a product

of the times we live in. There's simply more people on the planet these days. That's all there is to it. Simple mathematics. More people demand more shelter. More shelter demands more land. It's an equation. We have to provide for the people some way [153].

The absurdity, of course, is that they are not providing for the people.

Ella is a mother manquée in the fullest sense of the word because, like Euripides' Phaedra, she has assumed, as her own, a dominant ideology that runs counter to her own nature:

ELLA
Now I know the first thing you'll think is that you've hurt yourself. That's only natural. You'll think that something drastic has gone wrong with your insides and that's why you're bleeding. That's only a reaction. But I want you to know the truth. I want you to know all the facts before you go off and pick up a lot of lies. Now, the first thing is that you should never go swimming when that happens. It can cause you to bleed to death. The water draws it out of you. ...The next thing is sanitary napkins. You don't want to buy them out of an old machine in any old gas station bathroom. I know they say "sanitized." They're filthy in fact.... You don't know whose quarters go into those machines.... They're not hospital clean that's for sure. Any you should know that anything you stick up in there should be absolutely hospital clean [138–9].

The "zombies" that dupe Weston and Ella out of their home are agents of the dominant ideology. It is an ideology that rejects the life-cycle represented by the land, the orchard, the sheep, and Emma's menarche in preference of the plastic sterility of urban life.

Emma's own fear of sexuality bears an uncomfortable similarity to that of Euripides' Hippolytus:

EMMA
Suddenly everything changed. I wasn't the same person anymore. I was just a hunk of meat tied to a big animal. Being pulled [148].

In the thousands of years that elapsed from Classical Greece BCE to the twentieth century CE human dependence on its own nature did not change. Indeed, it has not changed in our own twenty-first century. Neither has the human struggle against its own nature. The only means Emma has of transcending her mother's hold over her and of escaping the trap of this unsavory family environment lies in her direct confrontation with her greatest fear, and in her manipulation of it toward her own ends.

EMMA
I got out.

WESLEY
I know, but how?

EMMA
I made sexual overtures to the sergeant. That's how. Easy [196].

As we have seen in all the forms of this myth so far, it is the divorce of A- Lektra—the unmated from the natural cycle of life and the repression of her own sexuality that force her into violence. Ironically, in this case, that violence is achieved by means of an explosion of sexuality that is entirely commensurate with the degree of repression which she has suffered.

EMMA
I'm going into crime. It's the only thing that pays these days....It's the perfect self- employment. Crime. No credentials. No diplomas. No overhead. No upkeep. Just straight profit right off the top [196–7].

Financial profit, after all, is the goal of all the characters in Shepard's play.

Freedom from the demands of nature is the ultimate goal of all the characters, even of Wesley who, at least for the present, fights for the preservation of the home. Even in this play there is a suggestion of the brother-sister-lover relationship, a proposal on the part of Emma that, if the feuding parents would disappear, she and her brother would be able to live harmoniously together. Wesley, however, wants to remove himself as far as possible from the complications of nature and from the human bond:

EMMA
Maybe they'll never come back, and we'll have the whole place to ourselves. We could do a lot with this place.

WESLEY
I'm not staying here forever.

EMMA
Where are you going?

WESLEY
I don't know. Alaska, maybe.

EMMA
What's in Alaska?

WESLEY
The frontier.

EMMA
Are you crazy? It's all frozen and full of rapers.

WESLEY
It's full of possibilities. It's undiscovered.

EMMA
Who wants to discover a bunch of ice? [163].

Like Harry in *The Family Reunion*, it is on his final return that this hero is forced to confront what, in Jungian terms, would be called his "shadow," his dark, unconscious self, and his ultimate needs. But, in this play, it is the father, not the son, who attempts to find himself. Here, the Eumenides of the hero's conscience do not drive him from his home. Rather, they reveal to him the promise of self-cultivation. Tragically, it is a promise he is unable to realize.

For Weston and Ella, the table at center-stage represents the altar of the dead hero we had witnessed in classical Greek theater. Both characters are emotionally and spiritually dead—dead to their needs as human beings and their obligations as members of family and community. In relinquishing responsibility, they have exposed their vulnerabilities. Consequently, in their separate moments of symbolic death, others close in over their bodies. Around these anti-heroes, in their figurative deaths, predators congregate. We, the audience, are witness to a macabre dramatization of the relentlessness of time, and of the anonymity of an existence that has staked no claim on the living. Chaos and violence take over, drowning-out, obliterating the space that our anti-heroes had held in life.

In the absence of the father, the alienated mother comes into her own. It is Wesley, the son, who comes to the defense of Weston:

WESLEY
I wouldn't wake up if I were you

ELLA
He can't hurt me now! I've got protection! If he lays a hand on me, I'll have him cut   to ribbons! He's finished!

WESLEY
He's beat you to the punch and he doesn't even know it.

ELLA
Don't talk stupid! And get this junk out of here! I'm tired of looking at broken doors every time I come in here.

WESLEY
That's a new door.

ELLA
GET IT OUT OF HERE!

WESLEY
I told you, you'd better not wake him up.

ELLA
I'm not tiptoeing around anymore. I'm finished with feeling like a foreigner in my own house. I'm not afraid of him anymore [173].

Wesley, the Orestean figure of this play, is the one character who fights throughout to protect the family home. When the play opened, we saw him picking up the shards of the open door, remnants of the battle of the sexes that had raged between his parents. Now, as the play ends, Wesley remains on stage, protecting Ella from the knowledge of her daughter's death. He stands in stark opposition to the narrow materialism of Taylor (Aegisthus), loyal rather to a love of the living, which Weston really represents but which has been buried beneath the temptation of a "quick and easy buck."

WESTON
What's the matter with the lamb?

WESLEY
Maggots.

WESLEY
Poor little bugger. Put some a' that blue shit on it. That'll fix him up [159].

For Wesley, although he might dream ultimately of reaching the icy regions of Alaska, there has been no radical denial of nature. On the contrary, it is he who has tried to restore the maggot-infested lamb to life. But he is as conditioned by biological and social factors as the other members of his family, because ultimately, the "nitroglycerine" that courses through his father's veins ignites him too into madness. The curse, the madness that is upon him is that he is destined to become his father, and it is his recognition of this that causes him to salvage, as his own, his father's discarded clothes and to murder the sacrificial lamb that he had brought on stage as symbol of both men:

WESLEY
And every time I put one thing on it seemed like part of him was growing on me. I could feel him taking over me....
I could feel myself retreating. I could feel him coming in and me going out. Just like the change of the guards.

EMMA
Well, don't eat your heart out about it. You did the best you could.

WESLEY
I didn't do a thing.

EMMA
That's what I mean.

WESLEY
I just grew up here [196; emphasis added].

The pathos of Wesley's situation lies in this play's deviation from the deep structure of the Electra myth. Ultimately, Wesley does not come from another space. It is possible that his parents were just like him when they started out in life; that, as their son, his future is as determined as theirs. As he puts on the old, soiled clothes his father has discarded, he grows into their curse, their spiritual poverty and their foul smell.

The pathos of Wesley's life lies in the fact that he is not a hero, that he does not challenge the values of his parents and that he does not entertain any vision of his own. For him there has been no rupture with the female, no rebellion against the maternal. Only acceptance.

The play closes with Wesley and his mother on stage, sole survivors of their family. If this had been any other version of the Electra myth, one might claim that the mother-son togetherness depicted here represents the ultimate desire of the son to be bonded with his mother. But in this play—Shepard's play of myopic vision—it represents nothing more than the final remnants of Western society's crumbling family structure. Wesley, on stage with his mother, does not realize the much sought after heroic struggle or the heroic ideal, because this Oresteian figure, like his father, is no more than the sum and victim of social factors.

The sleep of the parents might also represent their separate dreams. This scene might, in fact, be directed as their stepping back and finally taking account of their lives, as their way of recognizing, within their respective personalities, the potential for that meaning and that sense of belonging for which they have so much hungered. Perhaps, on awakening, Weston starts anew and Ella assumes, albeit momentarily, her responsibility to her daughter. But no. It is at this moment of awakening that both are cruelly confronted by "fate," by the hereditary curse of their family and of the human, social condition. It is the curse that Ella had recognized when first confronted with the fact that Weston had beat her to the sale of their house:

ELLA
Do you know what this is? It's a curse. I can feel it. It's invisible but it's there. It's always there. It comes onto us like nighttime. Every day I can feel it. Every day I can see it coming. And it always comes. Repeats itself. It comes even when you do everything to stop it from coming. Even when you try to change it. And it goes back. Deep. It goes back and back to tiny little cells and genes. To atoms. To tiny little swimming things making up their minds without us. Plotting in the

womb. Before that even. In the air; We're surrounded with it. It's bigger than government even.
It goes forward too. We spread it. We pass it on. We inherit it and pass it down, and then pass it down again. It goes on and on like that without us [173–4].

This is the curse of the House of Atreus. It is the curse of accumulated deeds that do not recognize a change of heart; but that come, relentlessly, to exact retribution.

WESTON
YOU UNDERSTAND ME? IT'S ALL OVER WITH BECAUSE I'VE BEEN REBORN.
I'M A WHOLE NEW PERSON NOW! I'm a whole new person.

WESLEY
They're going to kill you.

WESTON
Who's going to kill me? What're you talking about! Nobody's going to kill me!

WESLEY
I couldn't get the money.

WESTON
What money?

WESLEY
Ellis.

WESTON
So what?

WESLEY
You owe it to them.

WESTON
Owe it to who? I don't remember anything. All that's over with now.

WESLEY
No. It's not. It's still there. Maybe you've changed, but you will still owe them…

WESTON
I can't run out on everything.

WESLEY
Why not?

WESTON
'CAUSE THIS IS WHERE I SETTLED DOWN! THIS IS WHERE
THE LINE ENDED. RIGHT HERE! IMIGRATED TO THIS SPOT! I GOT
NOWHERE TO GO TO. THIS IS IT!

WESLEY
Take the Packard [192–3].

It is the curse of a world of predators in which all are interlocked,
not in a sense of community for the common good, but in a deathly
struggle for personal, separate survival.

WESLEY
And that eagle comes down and picks up the cat in his talons and
carries him screaming off into the sky.

ELLA
...And they fight. They fight like crazy in the middle of the sky. That cat's
tearing his chest out, and the eagle's trying to drop him, but the cat won't
let go because he knows if he falls he'll die.

WESLEY
And the eagle's being torn apart in mid-air. The eagle's trying to free
himself from the cat, and the cat won't let go.

ELLA
And they come crashing down to the earth. Both of them come crashing
down. Like one whole thing [200].

The characters in *Curse of the Starving Class* make desperate
attempts to free themselves from the mundane, only to be ultimately
dragged back into the bog of their everyday struggle. As a reflection
of this, the text makes repeated attempts at poetry but is inextricably
governed by the depressing prose, and by realism, so characteristic
of an un-heroic age. This style reflects the particular deviation from
the deep structure of the Electra myth that most characterizes *Curse
of the Starving Class*. For the deviation consists precisely of the
protagonist's inability to reach new vistas and the fact that Wesley
has never, and can never, reach a separate physical or psychological

space from those of the people who share his house—the house he loves so much.

In action, on stage, *Curse of the Starving Class* can be hilariously funny. It is a humor born of pain so deep it cannot be addressed directly, and as such it constitutes comedy in its truest form. Because comedians are rarely, if ever, complacent members of the establishment. Their humor is an expression of pain felt by the disenfranchised—the fringe members of society. It is the language kids banter around when they have to say what hurts but are too proud to show their pain.

Theater of all kinds creates the "empty space" of the playing area and the masks, as a unique meeting place for players, audience, and issues relevant to human awareness.

---

129 T. S. Eliot, The Family Reunion (New York: Harcourt Brace, 1939), pp. 21–2. Hereafter, quotations from this edition are indicated by page number references in parentheses and brackets.
130 Sam Shepard, Curse of the Starving Class, in Seven Plays (New York: Bantam, 1986), p. 194. Hereafter, quotations from this edition are indicated by page number references in parentheses or brackets.

Conclusion

The ritual of theater constitutes a raising of issues, a giving of physical form, to those intangible realities of our lives that we'd prefer to sweep under the rug. Theater "makes the invisible visible" in such a way as to enable us to examine our values, our nature, and our judgment. It is the constant return of spectators to the sacred center of performance; and each performance necessitates, like the final return of Harry in *The Family Reunion*, the confrontation of ourselves with our Eumenides, our conscience, or our "shadow."

As in Jack Richardson's The Prodigal, we, the audience, constitute as integral a part of the action as the actors, for the conflict of theater, once it has been granted form, is recognized as our own human struggle. Do we reject the values that have been handed down to us and attempt to establish new ones, as did the prodigal in Richardson's play or Harry in the play by Eliot; or do we passively accept the dictates of the past with the subjection and victimization that this entails *(Curse of the Starving Class)*? Are we as indifferent to the issues as the hero of Giraudoux' play, or do we take up the gauntlet of human concerns, as did Sartre's Orestes and suffer, from that moment on, from the pain of human history and social concerns?

What of the issue of ritual in the twentieth and twenty-first centuries? We have made mention of the concern of modern dramatists to counteract the passivity of an estranged, bourgeois audience. It has taken the contradictory geniuses of Artaud and Brecht to provoke modern spectators and to stimulate live, meaningful theater in our time. But neither writer's theory stands alone. Artaud's theater stirred emotions and passions, though, as Michael Mclain (UCLA) said when speaking about the stimulating succession of

218

images in television's rock video, "Does this vivid succession of images really substitute for the meaningful grappling with a story?" Does the pricking of one's emotions, one's passions, even one's sensuality constitute the total theatrical event? On the other hand, is it not generally recognized that, despite the unchallenged validity of Brecht's intellectual theater of alienation, Brecht's own theater works best when one is (as one undoubtedly is) pulled emotionally into the soul striving, the very human dilemmas, of his characters? For the modern audience which is no longer tied to the action in the manner of the ancient Greeks by means of a shared religious belief, successful theater makes visible on stage an energy that is at once intellectual and emotional. It is this that draws the audience repeatedly from the cinema houses and the television screens. It is this return and bonding of the audience with the actors that constitutes the ritual of live theater for the modern (as for any) age.

Pirandello forced the underlying, authentic issues of human nature onto his stage by lifting the mask of language (that rationalizing, regulating, deadening mechanism) from our actions and by revealing beneath the essential chaos of our human condition. In fact, men and women have attempted to stratify chaos since their first attempts to utter sound. Language—the human longing for order and communication—is by now as legitimate an aspect of our natures as is the chaos in our minds. The Nietzschean conflict between the Apollonian and the Dionysian, the rational and the instinctual, has raged for as long as we can trace the human line, and theater is the presentation of that conflict. Theater is the play of life itself: Chaos and order, images and words, emotions, ideas and themes—the sensual, the sexual and the spiritual—all claim equal hold on the theatrical platform. The actor, as the messenger of his or her community, seeks out all the polarities and complexities of the human condition. It is these things that the emerging hero confronts, and it is with these that the spectators have to grapple. Theater is the ritual sacrifice of the actor for the creation of something meaningful in the minds of the spectator-community. [131] The actors create violence and conflict on stage in order, shaman-like, to give body to the spiritual or emotional subtext of our existence. As such, theater is still the sacred round of the original Greek amphitheater and, as such, the spectators of today's theater constitute as much a community as did those of ancient Greece.

Tout ca change, tout c'est la meme chose—the more things change, the more they stay the same. Throughout the many variations of the Electra myth that we have studied in this work, even that of *The Family Reunion* in which Electra was not rebellious against the mother-figure; or that of *Curse of the Starving Class*—which deviates from the deep-structure of the myth in that there is no significant break from the maternal on the part of Wesley the Orestean figure—the issues have remained consistent. Throughout, it has questioned the artificial divorce of the male from the female and the relationship of that estrangement to the human being's alienation from nature. Throughout it has questioned whether such an alienation constitutes the cause of violence and destruction in our culture.

This study has questioned whether or not the primal deed of heroism—the slaying of the maternal dragon by the adolescent and his attempts to combat the restraints of the repressive, all-too present Aegisthean father-figure while claiming as his own the vision of the heroic spirit—becomes the legacy of the male adolescent as he emerges into manhood. If one is to read these Electra plays in the way we have presented them here, we might come to believe that the western human struggle so far has been a masculine one, fated to reoccur in each successive generation. It is a struggle that has constituted—and still constantly shatters—the bedrock of our civilization; it has twisted our history into a record of masculine violence.

What about the voiceless nature of authentic women throughout this history? If our culture had recorded equally the emotional needs, the social development, the struggle and the dreams of women and men and not regarded men as the personification of all people-kind; if the male had allowed the feminine a balanced, sane place in his personal, psychological structure and his political outlook; if men had not wrenched themselves so ruthlessly from the female, would the narration of Western history be different?

From our present-day perspective, we might question the absurd: Does our own hard-driving, masculine, and still sexist Western society derive its nature from the unconscious fears experienced by Classical Greek males in earliest childhood? If so, will we ever rid ourselves of its violence?

---

131   Michael McLain, "The Directorial Challenge in New Technology," New Theater, 1985, p. 8½.

Chapter Notes

INTRODUCTION

1   Joseph Campbell, Primitive Mythology: The Masks of God (New York: Penguin, 1987), p. 4.
2   Claude Lévi-Strauss, "The Structural Study of Myth," in Structural Anthropology (New York: Basic, 1963), pp. 207–31.
3   Lévi-Strauss, p. 217.
4   Theodor H. Gaster, "Myth and Story," in Sacred Narrative (Berkeley: University of California Press, 1984) pp. 110–36
5   Gaster, p. 112.
6   T.S. Eliot, "The Perfect Critic," in The Sacred Wood (New York: Methuen, 1920).
7   Gaster, pp. 125–128.
8   Lévi-Strauss, pp. 206–31.
9   Mircea Eliade, The Myth of the Eternal Return, or, Cosmos and History, trans. Willard R. Trask (Princeton, N.J.: Princeton University Press, 1974).
10   Geza Roheim, The Gates of the Dream (New York: International University Press, 1952) p. 401.
11   Lévi-Strauss, pp. 207–31.
12   Peter Brook, The Empty Space (New York: Atheneum, 1984), p. 42.

I

13   Erich L. Neumann, The Great Mother (Princeton, N.J.: Princeton University Press, 1974), p. 18.
14   Carol Gilligan, In a Different Voice (Cambridge, Mass.: Harvard University Press, 1982), p. 6.
15   Erich L. Neumann, The Origins and History of Consciousness (Princeton, N.J.: Princeton University Press, 1973), p. 131.
16   Anderson, Myths and Legends of the Polynesians, pp. 367–8, quoted in Neumann, p. 103.
17   Isaiah Tishby, "The Doctrine of Evil and the 'Klipah' in the Lurian Cabala," quoted in Neumann, The Origins and History of Consciousness, pp. 119–20.

18 Barbara G. Walker, The Woman's Encyclopedia of Myths and Secrets (San Francisco: Harper & Row, 1983), p. 1049.
19 Neumann, p. 132.
20 Aeschylus, The Oresteia (New York: Penguin, 1977), p. 161. Hereafter, quotations from this edition will be indicated by page number references in parentheses or brackets.
21 Jan Kott, The Eating of the Gods (Evanston, Ill.: Northwestern University Press, 1987) p. 254.
22 William Ridgeway, The Origin of Tragedy (New York; Benjamin Blom, 1966).
23 Eliade, p.34
24 Homer, The Odyssey: The Story of Odysseus, trans. W.H.D. Rouse (New York: New American Library, 1937), p.36.
25 Lévi-Strauss, p. 217.
26 Eliade, p.35.
27 Eliade, p. 35.
28 Herbert Blau, Take Up the Bodies: Theater at the Vanishing Point (Chicago: University of Illinois Press, 1982), p. 83.
29 Northrop Frye, Anatomy of Criticism: Four Essays (Princeton, N.J.: Princeton University Press, 1973), p. 217.
30 Homer, The Odyssey: The Story of Odysseus, trans. W.H.D. Rousee (New York: New American Library, 1937), p. 39.
31 Aristotle, Poetics, trans. Gerald Elese (Ann Arbor: University of Michigan Press, 1970), p. 27.
32 Michael Grant, The Rise of the Greeks (New York: Macmillan, 1987), p.
33 Grant, pp. 30–1.
34 Euripides, Orestes and Other Plays (Middlesex, England: Penguin, 1983), p. 333.
35 Grant, p. 31.
36 Euripides, Hippolytus in Ten Plays, trans. John McLean (New York: Bantam, 1985), pp. 80–1. Hereafter cited as Hippolytus.
37 Hippolytus, pp. 78–9.
38 Grant, p. 31.
39 Philip E. Slater, The Glory of Hera (Boston: Beacon, 1968).
40 Slater, p. 25.
41 Slater, p. 103.
42 Slater, pp. 16 and 13.
43 Slater, pp. 186–7 and 187.
44 Slater, pp. 13 and 25.
45 Slater, p. 31.
46 Slater, pp. 91 and 89.
47 Edward Tripp, The Meridian Handbook of Classical Mythology (New York: New American Library, 1970), p. 248.
48 Arnold van Gennep, The Rites of Passage (Chicago: University of Chicago Press, 1960), pp. 92–3.

II

49 Sophocles, Electra, in Electra and Other Plays, trans. E.F. Watling (New York: Penguin, 1978), pp. 87–8. Hereafter, quotations from this edition will be indicated by "Watling," and a page number reference, in parentheses or brackets.

50 Thomas Woodard, "The Electra of Sophocles," in Orestes and Electra, ed. William M. Force (Boston: Houghton Mifflin, 1968), p. 281. Hereafter, quotations from this edition will be indicated by "Force," and a page number reference, in parentheses or brackets.

51 H.D.F. Kitto, The Greeks (New York: Penguin, 1986), p. 89.

52 Kott, p. 267.

53 Blau, p. 4.

III

54 Euripides, Electra, in David Greene and Richmond Lattimore, Euripides V (Chicago: University of Chicago Press, 1959), p. 53.

55 Force, p. 96.

56 Force, p. 124.

57 Joseph Campbell, Primitive Mythology: The Masks of God (New York: Penguin, 1987), p. 4.

58 Euripides' Orestes, pp. 310 and 313.

59 William Shakespeare, Hamlet, ed. Louis B. Wright (New York: Washington Square Press, 1958), p. 29.

60 Euripides' Orestes, p. 337.

IV

61 L.C. Knight, Drama and Society in the Age of Jonson (London: Chatto and Windus, 1977).

62 Woodbridge, p. 55.

63 Woodbridge, p. 56.

64 Woodbridge, p. 61.

65 Woodbridge, p. 67.

66 Woodbridge, p. 68.

67 William Shakespeare, Hamlet (New York: Washington Square Press, 1958), p. 82. There are numerous editions of Shakespeare. This edition was convenient for the author. However, for the convenience of the reader, quotations are accompanied by act, scene and line indications.

68 Susan Lettzler Cole, The Absent One (University Park: Pennsylvania University Press, 1985), p. 51.

69 Peter Brook, The Empty Space (New York: Atheneum, 1984), p. 56.

70   Cole, pp. 46–7.
71   Cole, pp. 51, 46–7.
72   Cole, p. 5.
73   Kott, pp. 252–3 and 257–8.
74   Kott, pp. 254 and 253.
75   Cole, p. 11.

V

76   Lilian Feder, Madness in Literature (Princeton, N.J.: Princeton University Press, 1980).
77   See Carl E. Schorske, Fin de Siecle Vienna (New York: Vintage, 1981).
78   Schorske, p. 186.
79   Quoted in Schorske, p. 194.
80   Schorske; the quotations are from pp. 196, 197, 197, 199, and 203, respectively.
81   Oscar Wilde, Salome, in The Complete Works of Oscar Wilde (New York: Harper & Row, 1966), p. 319. Hereafter, quotations of this edition are indicated with page number references in parentheses or brackets.
82   Wilde, p. 328.
83   Schorske, p. 19.
84   Schorske, p. 19.
85   Schorske, p. 19.
86   Schorske, p. 21.
87   Hugo von Hofmannsthal, Electra, trans. Carl Richard Mueller, in The Modern Theater, ed. Robert W. Corrigan (New York: Macmillan, 1964), p. 110 Hereafter, quotations from this edition are indicated by page number references in parenthesis or brackets.
88   David Cole, The Theatrical Event (Middletown, Conn.: Wesleyan University Press, 1975).
89   Hofmannsthal, p. 114.
90   Suzanne E. Bales, "Elektra: From Hofmannsthal to Strauss," doctoral dissertation, Stanford, 1984.
91   Lévi-Strauss, p. 215.
92   Bales, p. 126.
93   Slater, p. 91.
94   Slater, p. 91.
95   Northrop Frye, Anatomy of Criticism (Princeton, N.J.: Princeton University Press, 1957), p. 217.
96   Hofmannsthal, p. 108.
97   Hofmannsthal, p. 90.
98   Hofmannsthal, p. 97.
99   Euripides, Orestes and Other Plays (Middlesex, England: Penguin, 1983), p. 310.

100 Eugene O'Neill, "Mourning Becomes Electra," in Nine Plays (New York: Modern Library, 1959), p. 739. Hereafter, quotations from this edition are indicated by page number references in parentheses or brackets.
101 Jean Giraudoux, Electra, in Orestes and Electra, in Nine Plays (New York: Modern Library, 1959), p.739. Hereafter, quotations from this edition are indicated by page number references in parentheses or brackets.
102 Robert Cohen, Giraudoux: Three Faces of Destiny (Chicago: University of Chicago Press, 1968), p. 116
103 Cole, p. 142.
104 Lawrence Clark Powell, Robinson Jeffers: The Man and His Work (Los Angeles: Primavera, 1934).
105 Powell, p. 14.
106 Powell, pp. 16–7.
107 Louis Adamic, Robinson Jeffers: A Portrait (Seattle: University of Washington Chapbooks, 1929).
108 Robinson Jeffers, "The Tower Beyond Tragedy," in The Selected Poetry of Robinson Jeffers (New York: Random House, 1959), p. 138. Hereafter quotes from this edition are indicated by page number references in parentheses or brackets.
109 Jeffers, p. 110.
110 Jeffers, p. 107.
111 Rene Girard, Violence and the Sacred, trans. Patrick Gregory (Baltimore: John Hopkins University Press, 1977), p. 49.
112 Girard, pp. 81–2.

VI

113 Peter Brook, The Empty Space (New York: Atheneum, 1984).
114 "Electra: Theater, Downtown," 2 Dec. 1987.
115 Ezra Pound, Elektra, trustees of the Ezra Pound Literary Property Trust, 1987, p. 72. Hereafter, quotations from this edition are indicated by page number references in parentheses or brackets.
116 "Electra," rev. of Elektra, by Ezra Pound, dir. Carey Perloff, Theater, 2 Dec. 1987.
117 John Peter, "Why Broadway's Fairy-Tale Lacks a Happy Ending," rev. of Elektra by Ezra Pound, dir. Carey Perloff, The Sunday Times, 8 Nov. 1987.
118 Jack Richardson, The Prodigal, in Orestes and Electra, ed. William M. Force (Boston: Houghton Mifflin, 1968), p. 211. Hereafter, quotations from this edition are indicated by page number references in parentheses or brackets.
119 Neumann, p. 190.
120 Adrienne Kennedy, Electra, in One Act (Minneapolis: University of Minnesota Press, 1988), p. 105. Hereafter, quotations from this edition are indicated by an "E" and by page number references in parentheses or brackets.

121 Euripides, The Medea in Euripides 1, ed. David Grene and Richmond Lattimore (Chicago: University of Chicago Press, 1955), p. 92.

122 Adrienne Kennedy, Orestes in In One Act (Minneapolis: University of Minnesota Press, 1988.) p. 147. Hereafter, quotations from this edition are indicated by an "O," and page number references or brackets.

123 Simone de Beauvoir, The Second Sex, trans. and ed. H.M. Parshley (New York: Vintage, 1974), p. 202.

124 The Beauvoir quotations are, respectively, from pages 202, 165, 203, and 161.

125 Sue-Ellen Case, Feminism and Theater (New York: Methuen, 1988), p.

126 Heiner Muller, Hamlet-Machine, ed. Carl Weber (New York: Performing Arts Journal Publications, 1984), p. 53. Hereafter, quotations from this edition are indicated by page number references in parentheses or brackets.

127 Maria Ley Piscator, The Piscator Experiment: The Political Theatre (Edwardsville: Southern Illinois University Press, 1967).

128 Muller, p. 55.

VII

129 T. S. Eliot, The Family Reunion (New York: Harcourt Brace, 1939), pp. 21–2. Hereafter, quotations from this edition are indicated by page number references in parentheses and brackets.

130 Sam Shepard, Curse of the Starving Class, in Seven Plays (New York: Bantam, 1986), p. 194. Hereafter, quotations from this edition are indicated by page number references in parentheses or brackets.

CONCLUSION

131 Michael McLain, "The Directorial Challenge in New Technology," New Theater, 1985, p. 8½.

Annotated Bibliography

Ackerman, Roberts. *The Myth and Ritual School*: J.G. Frazer and the Cambridge Ritualists: New York: Garland Publishers, 1991.

Adam, Peter. *Art of the Third Reich*. (20th century German Art.) New York: H. N. Abrams, 1992.

Aeschylus. *Aeschylus* 1, Oresteia, trans. David Grene and Richmond Lattimore. Chicago: University of Chicago Press, 1970.

_____. The Oresteia, trans. Robert Fagles. New York: Penguin Books, 1977.

_____. The Orestes Plays of Aeschylus, trans. Paul Roche. New York: New American Library, 1962.

Ahlberg-Cornell, Gudrun. *Myth and Epos in Early Greek Art: Representation and Interpretation*. (Studies in Mediterranean Archeology.) Jonsered: P. Astoms Forlag, 1992.

Approaches to Greek Myth. Edited and introduced by Lowell Edmunds.Baltimore: Johns Hopkins University Press, 1990.

Aristotle. Poetics, trans. Gerald F. Else. Ann Arbor: University of Michigan Press, 1970. Authoritative modern reading, chosen for its clarity of language and its scholarly, yet independent interpretation of Aristotle's definition of theater.

Armstrong, Robert Plant. Wellspring: *On the Myth and Source of Culture*. Berkeley: University of California Press, 1975. Art, mythology, and psychological aspects of art.

Artaud, Antonin. The Theater and Its Double. New York: Grove Press, 1958. Artaud's theory of theater as a play of the volatile and the dangerous, as a magical and violent attack of theatrical images on an audience, is suggested in this work as part of its emerging definition of theater.

Auerbach, Erich. *Mimesis: The Representation of Reality in Western Literature.* Trans. Willard R. Trask. Princeton, New Jersey: Princeton University Press, 1974.

Auerbach, Erich. *Mimesis*, trans. Willard R. Trask, Princeton, New Jersey: Princeton University Press, 1974.

Auerbach, Nina. Women and the Demon: The Life of a Victorian Myth. Cambridge, Mass: Harvard University Press, 1982. Feminism in the literature of 19th century England.

Ausband, Stephen C. *Myth and Meaning, Myth and Order.* Macon, Ga.: Mercer University Press, 1983.

Bachofen, Johan Jakob. *Myth, Religion, and Mother Right: Selected Writings of J. J. Bobofen.* Translated from the German by Ralph Manheim. Preface by George Boas. Introduction by Joseph Campbell. (Bollingen Series, 84.) Princeton, N.J.: Princeton University Press, 1967.

Bales, Susan E. "Elektra: From Hofmannsthal to Strauss." Diss. Stanford University, 1984.

Baring, Anne. *The Myth of the Goddess: Evolution of an Image.* Harmondsworth, England: Penguin, 1984.

Barish, Jonas. *The Anti-Theatrical Prejudice.* Los Angeles: University of California Press, 1981. A scholarly, detailed record of the antipathy toward theater that has been held by guardians of morality within Western history. This book is a record of the fear that the rational and the political have always felt for the passionate, the emotional, and the theatrical.

Barksdale, E.C. *Cosmologies of Consciousness: Science and Literary Myth in an Exploration of the Beginnings and Development of Mind.* Cambridge, Mass.: Schenkman, 1980. Covers creative psychology and mythology.

Barnes, Wesley. *Existentialism, the Philosophy and Literature of.* New York: Barron's Educational Series, 1968.

Bassnet-McGuire, Susan. *Luigi Pirandello.* New York: Grove Press, 1983.

Beauvoir, Simone de. *The Second Sex*, trans. and ed. H. M. Parshley. New York: Vintage Books, 1974. Beauvoir's work was the first and most important work on the psychology and nature of women within feminist literature. In a woman's voice, it studies the historical, biological, psychological and sexual forces of femininity.

Beitl, Sheldon Jerome. "Hofmannsthal's 'Elektra' and O'Neil's 'Mourning Becomes Electra': The Nature of Life." Diss. California State University, 1977.

Bentley, Eric. *The Classic Theatre: Six Italian Plays*, ed. Eric Bentley, New York: Doubleday Anchor Books, 1958.

_____. *The Life of the Drama.* New York: Atheneum Press, 1983.

Authoritative study of the dynamics of theater written by one of the giants of modern theater criticism.

_____. *The Pirandello Commentaries.* Evanston, Ill.: Northwestern University Press, 1986. A series of essays on the theatricality within the plays

of Pirandello.

_____. *The Theory of the Modern Stage*, N.Y.: Penguin Books, 1983.

_____. *What Is Theatre? Incorporating the Dramatic Event.* New York: Limelight Editions, 1984.

Biological Woman—*The Convenient Myth: A Collection of Feminist Essays and a Comprehensive Bibliography*, ed. Ruth Hubbard, Mary Sue Henifin and Barbara Fried. Cambridge, Mass.: Schenkman, 1902. Deals with feminism, discrimination against women, and sex roles.

Black, Katherine C. "Direct Address in Sophocles: A Study in Dramatic Convention." Diss. Catholic University of America, 1985. Covers a variety of topics, including stagecraft, marked and unmarked words, power and solidarity, and vocatives.

Blau, Herbert. *Blooded Thought*. New York: Performing Arts Journal Publications, 1982. One of the most authoritative theater-scholars of the 20th century, Blau combines academic inquiry with the practical experience of the director. This book is a dynamic study of theater-in- practice and of the risks that it demands.

_____. *Take Up the Bodies*: Theater at the Vanishing Point. Chicago: University of Illinois Press, 1982. Included for its sense that theater is an attempt to capture past dreams and hold them in the present, an attempt to envision a better future based on some half recalled utopia, i.e., theater as the recapturing of myth.

Blundell, Mary Whitlock. "Sophocles: An Ethical Approach. A Study of 'Electra,' 'Philoctetes' and 'Oedipus at Colonus.' Diss. University of California, Berkeley, 1981.

Brecht, Bertolt. *Collected Plays*, ed. Ralph Manheim. New York: Vintage Books, 1971.

Brook, Peter. *The Empty Space*. New York: Atheneum, 1984. Seminal work on theory-criticism by the great director. A definition of "live" theater.

_____. *The Shifting Point*. New York: Harper & Row, 1987. A series of brilliant essays in which Brook talks about his innovative work as director. Includes his dynamic treatment of Shakespeare, opera and film.

Brustein, Robert. *The Theatre of Revolt*. Boston: Atlantic Monthly Press, 1964. A series of essays on theater as the act of rebellion, covering the works of the founders of modern theater: Ibsen, Strindberg, Chekhov, Shaw, Brecht, Pirandello, O'Neill and Genet.

Buller, Jeffrey Lynn. "Sophocles and the Sacred Hero." Diss. University of Wisconsin. Madison, 1981.

Burgess, Dana Livingston. "Late Euripidean Narrative." Diss. Bryn Mawr College, 1984.

Burkert, Walter. Ancient Mystery Cults. Cambridge, Mass.: Harvard University Press, 1987.

Campbell, Joseph. *The Hero with a Thousand Faces*. Princeton, N.J.: Princeton University Press, 1968. This classic work examines the "hero" within myths from all regions of the world and relates their stories to the vision of the prophets of world religions such as Moses, Jesus and Mohammed, and to dreams recorded in clinical studies by modern psychoanalysts. From this the great master of mythology extracts a prototype: the archetypal hero.

_____.*Primitive Mythology*: The Masks of God, New York: Penguin Books, 1987. Authoritative study in which Campbell reads ancient world mythology, its symbols and its meanings, from the perspectives of 20th century archeology, anthropology and psychology.

Case, Sue-Ellen. *Feminism and Theater*. New York: Methuen Press, 1988. In this slim book Case deconstructs male-oriented theater and the male perspective, and introduces the female aesthetic.

Clemon-Karp, Sheila. "The Female Androgyne in Tragic Drama." Diss. Brandeis University, 1980. A redefinition of the "female" and the "feminine" in tragic drama.

Cohen, Sandra Heiman. "The Electra Figure in Twentieth Century American and European Drama." Diss. Indiana University, 1969.

Cole, David. *The Theatrical Event*. Middletown, Conn.: Wesleyan University Press, 1975. A study of theater as an altered state, as one in which the unphysical, i.e., the life within the mind, is encapsulated, for the theatrical moment, within physical form. All aspects of the theater are scrutinized from this perspective.

Cole, Susan Letzler. *The Absent One: Mourning, Ritual, Tragedy and the Performance of Ambivalence.* University Park: Pennsylvania State University Press, 1985. In this erudite examination of classical texts, Cole discovers a similar acting-out of ambivalent impulses in funeral rites and tragic drama.

Corrigan, Robert Willoughby. "The Electra Theme in the History of Drama." Diss. University of Minnesota, 1955.

Crane, Walter. Echoes of Hellas: *The Tale of Troy and the Story of Orestes from Homer and Aeschylus.* London: M. Ward, 1887–1888. Presented in 82 designs with introductory essay and sonnets by George G. Warr.

Diggle, James. *The Textual Tradition of Euripides' Orestes.* New York: Oxford University Press, 1991.

Dinerstein, Norman Myron. "Polychordality in 'Salome' and 'Elektra': A Study of the Application of Reinterpretation Technique." Diss. Princeton University, 1974.

Durry, Marie-Jean. *L'Univers de Giraudoux.* France: Mercure de France Press, 1961. In this slim volume, Durry depicts Giraudoux as a man torn between the conflicting loyalties of France and Germany in World War II.

Eden, Kathy Hannah. "The Influence of Legal Procedure on the Development of Tragic Structure." Diss. Stanford University, 1980. This work studies the origins and development of in drama with an examination of both the literary and critical conditions of fifth-century Athens, B.C., early Imperial Rome and Elizabethan England.

Eliade, Mircea. *The Myth of the Eternal Return,* Princeton, N.J.: Princeton University Press, 1974. Authoritative scholarship on the world of the ancients.

_____. *Shamanism*, Princeton, N.J.: Princeton University Press, 1974. Authoritative source.

Eliot, T.S. *The Family Reunion*. New York: Harcourt Brace Jovanovich, 1939.

Engelsman, Joan Chamberlain. *The Feminine Dimension of the Divine*. Wilmette, Ill.: Chiron Publications, 1987.

Esslin, Martin. *An Anatomy of Drama*. New York: Hill and Wang, 1976. Euripides.

Euripides I, ed. David Grene and Richmond Lattimore. Chicago: University of Chicago Press, 1955.

_____. *Euripides IV*, ed. David Grene and Richmond Lattimore. Chicago: University of Chicago Press, 1958.

_____. *Orestes and Other Plays*, trans. Philip Vellacott. Middlesex: Penguin Books, 1983. Chosen for its reliability and clarity.

_____. *Ten Plays*, trans. Moses Hadas and John McLean. New York: Bantam Books, 1985. Chosen for its modern translation of Hyppolytus and for the clear way in which it illustrates points discussed in the present work.

Feder, Lilian. *Madness in Literature*. Princeton, N.J.: Princeton University Press, 1980. A scholarly questioning of the human propensity for chaos from its first traces in prehistoric times.

Foucault, Michel. *The History of Sexuality*, trans. Robert Hurley. New York: Vintage Books, 1980. A short, incisive discourse on the power and the politics of sexual behavior in Western Civilization.

Freud, Sigmund. *The Basic Writings of Sigmund Freud*, ed. A.A. Brill. New York: Random House, 1966.

_. *Civilization and Its Discontents*. New York: W.W. Norton, 1963. This tiny book (104 pages) contains Freud's most profound theories of human behavior and Western Civilization.

Frost, Christopher Powell. "The European Recognition: A Study in Dramatic Form." Diss. University of Cincinnati.

Frye, Northrup. *The Anatomy of Criticism*. Princeton, N.J.: Princeton University Press, 1957.

Fuentes, Orlitio. "El Teatro de Virgilio Pinera." Diss. City University of New York, 1985.

Gaster. Theodor H. *Sacred Narrative*. Berkeley: University of California Press, 1984.

Gillian, Bryan Randolph. *Richard Strauss' Elektra*. New York: Oxford University Press, 1991.

Girard, Rene. *Violence and the Sacred*. Baltimore: Johns Hopkins University Press, 1977.

Giraudoux, Jean. Electra, *Stuck in zwei Akten*, trans. into German by Hans Rothe. Munich: List, 1959.

Goethe, Johann Wolfgang von. *Faust*, trans. Walter Arndt, ed. Cyrus Hawlin. New York: W.W. Norton, 1976.

Gordon, Bill. Review of Elektra, by Ezra Pound, dir. Carey Perloff. *Town & Village*, 12 Nov. 1987.

Grant, Michael. *The Rise of the Greeks*. New York: Macmillan, 1987. Graves, Robert. *The White Goddess*. New York: Farrar, Straus and Giroux, 1948.

Greenblatt, Stephen. *Tyrant: Shakespeare on Politics*. New York: Norton, 2018.

_____. Will in the World: *How Shakespeare Became Shakespeare*. New York: W.W. Norton, 2016.

Grote, Dale Allan. "Sophocles' 'Electra': Social Document of Late Fifth Century Athens (Greece)." Diss. University of Wisconsin, Madison, 1990.

Grotowsky, Jerzy. *Towards A Poor Theater*. New York: Simon & Schuster, 1968.

Grubb, Kevin. Review of Elektra by Ezra Pound, dir. Carey Perloff. *New York Native*, 30 Nov. 1987.

Gussow, Mel. "Stage: Pound's 'Elektra,' rev. of *Elektra* by Ezra Pound, dir. Carey Perloff. New York Times, 11 Nov. 1987.

Hauser, Arnold. *Mannerism: The Crisis of the Renaissance and the Origin of Modern Art*. Cambridge, Mass: Belknap Press of Harvard University Press, 1986.

Hawkins, Jocelyn Hunter. "'Hoffmannsthal's 'Electra': The Play and the Opera." Diss. 1971.

Hechler, Marilyn E. "Past and Present in American Drama: The Case of Eugene O'Neill and Sam Shepard." Diss. State University of New York at Stony Brook, 1989. (Chapter 3 discusses *Mourning Becomes Electra and Buried Child.*)

Hillman, James. Anima: *An Anatomy of a Personified Notion*. Dallas: Spring Publication, 1985.

_____. *Archetypal Psychology*: A Brief Account. Dallas: Spring Publications,1981.

Hoffer, Stanley. "Audience Expectation in Greek Tragedy: Scenic Structures and Conflicts of Sympathis in Four Plays."Diss. University of California, Berkeley, 1993. Plays by Euripides and Sophocles.

Hofmannsthal, Hugo Von. "Electra," trans. Carl Richard Mueller in The Modern Theater, Robert Corrigan, ed. New York: Macmillan, 1964.

Holt, David. *Theatre & Behaviour: Hawkwood Papers*, 1979–1986. Oxford: Moreton Road, 1987.

Homer. *The Odyssey: The Story of Odysseus*, trans. W.H.D. Rouse. New York: New American Library, 1937.

Jaeger, Werner. *Paideia: The Ideals of Greek Culture*, trans. Gilbert Highet. New York: Oxford University Press, 1965.

Jarry, Alfred. *Nihilism and the Theater of the Absurd*, ed. Maurice Marc Labelle. New York: New York University Press, 1980.

Jeffers, Robinson J. "The Tower Beyond Tragedy," in *Selected Poems*. New York: Random House, 1965.

Jung, C. G. *Four Archetypes: Mother/Rebirth/Spirit/Trickster*. Princeton, N.J.: Princeton University Press, 1959.

_____. *A Primer of Jungian Psychology*. New York: New American Library, 1973.

_____. *Symbols of Transformation*. Princeton University Press, 1956. Kaplan, Howard Gary. "Borderline and Narcissistic Rage and Emptiness: Their Dramatization and Drama Therapy." Diss. Northwestern University Press, 1956.

Kaplan, Richard Andrew. "The Musical Language of 'Elektra': A Study in Chromatic Harmony." Diss. University of Michigan, 1985. A musical investigation of Richard Strauss' *Elektra*.

Kennedy, Adrienne. *Adrienne Kennedy in One Act*. Minneapolis: University of Minnesota Press, 1988.

Kerr, Walter. *Tragedy and Comedy*. New York: Da Capo Press, 1985. Kitto, H.D.F. *The Greeks*. New York: Penguin Books, 1986.

Kling, Vincent. "The Artist as Austrian: Social Principle in Some Early Works of Hugo Von Hofmannsthal." Diss. Temple University, 1990.

Knight, L. C. *Drama and Society in the Age of Jonson*. London: Chatto & Windus, 1962.

Kott, Jan. *The Eating of the Gods*. Evanston, Ill.: Northwestern University Press, 1973.

Lee-Bonanno, Lucy. "The Quest for Authentic Personhood: An Expression of the Female Tradition in Novels by Moix, Tusquets, Matute and Alos." Diss. University of Kentucky, 1984. Feminism in Catalonia.

Lefkowitz, Mary R., and Maureen B. Fant. *Women's Life in Greece and Rome: A Source Book in Translation.* Baltimore: Johns Hopkins University Press, 1977.

Levi, Peter. *The Life and Times of William Shakespeare.* New York: Henry Holt & Co., 1988.

Lévi-Strauss, Claude. *Structural Anthropology.* New York: Basic Books, 1963.

Lindemann, Louise Jeanne. "In Quest of Orestes: A Critical Study of the Figure in Dramas Ancient and Modern Dealing with the Orestes-Electra Legend." Diss. New York University, 1978.

Lois, Mary. "Becoming a Heroine: A Study of the Electra Theme." Diss. University of California, Riverside, 1984.

Maufort, Marc Jean. "Visions of the American Experience: The O'Neill- Melville Connection." Diss. Free University of Brussels, Belgium, 1986.

McDonald, Lawrence Francis. "Compositional Procedures in Richard Strauss' 'Electra.'" Diss. University of Michigan, 1976.

Mclain, Michael. "The Directorial Challenge in New Technology." *New Theater 1* (1987) 7/11–9/13.

Muller, Heiner. *Hamlet-Machine,* ed. Carl Weber. New York: Performing Arts Journal Publications, 1984.

Murray, Gilbert. *Hamlet and Orestes:* A Study in Traditional Types (British Academy, Annual Shakespeare Lecture, 1914.) New York: Oxford University Press, 1914.

Nelsen, Don. "Electrifying 'Elektra,'" rev. of Elektra, by Ezra Pound, dir. Carey Perloff. *Daily News*, 16 Nov. 1987.

Neumann, Erich. *The Archetypal World of Henry Moore*. Princeton, N.J.: Princeton University Press, 1959.

Their Dramatization *Art and the Creative Unconscious*. Princeton, N.J.: Princeton University Press, 1974.

_____. *The Great Mother*. Princeton, N.J.: Princeton University Press, 1963.

_____. *Mimesis: The Representation of Reality in Western Literature*, trans.

Erich Auerbach. Princeton, N.J.: Princeton University Press, 1974.

_____. *The Origins and History of Consciousness*. Princeton, N.J.: Princeton University Press, 1954.

Nietzsche, Friedrich Wilhelm. Ecce Homo, trans. R.J. Holingdale. New York: Penguin, 1982.

_____. *The Portable Nietzsche*, ed. Walter Kaufmann. New York: Penguin Books, 1959.

O'Neill, Eugene. *Nine Plays*. New York: Modern Library, 1959.

Ormand, Kirk, W. B. "The Representation of Marriage in Sophoclean Drama." Diss. Stanford University, 1992. Feminist theory.

Paolucci, Anne. Pirandello's Theater, *The Recovery of the Modern Stage for Dramatic Art*. London: Feffer & Simons, 1974.

Paul, Angus. "World Premiere Focuses Long-Overdue Attention on Pound's Version of Sophocles' 'Elektra,'" rev. of Elektra by Ezra Pound, dir. Carey Perloff. *Chronicle of Higher Education*, 16 Dec. 1987.

Peter, John. "Why Broadway's Fairy-Tale Lacks a Happy Ending," rev. of *Elektra* by Ezra Pound, dir. Carey Perloff. *Sunday Times*, 8 Nov. 1987.

Piscator, Maria Ley. *The Piscator Experiment: The Political Theater.* Edwardsville: Southern Illinois University Press, 1967.

Powell, Brenda Joyce. "The Metaphysical Quality of the Tragic: A Study of Sophocles' Electra,' Giraudoux' Electra and Sartre's 'Les Mouches.'" Diss. University of North Carolina at Chapel Hill, 1981.

Ridgeway, William. *The Origin of Tragedy.* New York: Benjamin Blom, 1966.

Ringer, Mark Justin. "Electra and the Empty Urn: A Study of Sophoclean Metatheatre." Diss. University of California, Santa Barbara, 1983.

Roheim, Geza. *The Gates of the Dream.* New York: International Universities Press, 1952.

Rowse, A.L. *Shakespeare the Man.* New York: St. Martin's Press, 1988. Sanderson, J., and Everett Zimmerman. *Medea: Myth and Dramatic Form.*

Boston: Houghton Mifflin Co., 1967.

Schechner, Richard. *Between Theater and Anthropology.* Philadelphia: University of Pennsylvania Press, 1985.

Schmitt, Patrick E. "'The Fountain,' 'Marco Millions,' and 'Lazarus Laughed': O'Neill's 'Exotics' as History Plays." Diss. University of Wisconsin, Madison, 1985.

Schorske, Carl E. *Fin-de-Siecle Vienna: Politics and Culture.* New York: Vintage Books, 1979.

Shakespeare, William. *Hamlet.* New York: Washington Square Press, 1958. Shepard, Sam. *Seven Plays.* New York: Bantam Books, 1986.

Simpson, Paula. "A Response to the Ironic Reading of Sophocles' 'Electra.' Diss. Dalhousie University, 1991.

Slater, Philip E. *The Glory of Hera.* Boston: Beacon Press, 1968.

Smith, Louise Pearson. "Studies of Characterization in Euripides: The 'Medeia,' 'Elektra,' and 'Orestes.'" Diss. Princeton University, 1976.

Sogliuzzo, A. Richard. *Luigi Pirandello, Director*. London: Scarecrow Press, 1982.

Solmsen, Friedrich. *Electra and Orestes: Three Recognitions in Greek Tragedy*. Amsterdam: Noord-Hollandsche, 1967.

Song, Nina. "Death in the Tragedies of William Shakespeare and Eugene O'Neill." Diss. State University of New York at Albany, 1988.

Sophocles. *Electra and Other Plays*, trans. E. F. Watling. New York: Penguin Books, 1978.

_. *Orestes and Electra*, ed. William M. Force. Boston: Houghton Mifflin, 1968. This edition was chosen for its clarity and because it best illustrates arguments used in the present work.

Soulis, Timothy Charles. "The Double Identity Pattern: Reality and Theatre in the Characters of Sophocles, Shakespeare and Ibsen." Diss. University of Denver, 1980.

Sroka, Elliott Frank. "The Other Side of Experience: The Radical Theater of Euripides." Diss. Stanford University, 1980. This study compares the radical form of Euipides with those of Bertolt Brecht and Eugene Ionesco.

Strauss, Richard. *Elektra*, ed. Derrick Puffett, New York: Cambridge University Press, 1989.

Swart, Gerhardus Jacobus. "The Electra of Sophocles: A Critical Evaluation of the Different Interpretations." Diss. University of Pretoria, South Africa, 1983.

Symanski, Leonard L. "Sign and Symbol in the Theater of Jean Giraudoux." Diss. Middlebury College, 1982. French text. Themes of life-in-death, death-in-love, and love-as-death. Among the plays dealt with in this collection are Hamlet and Mourning Becomes Electra.

Tripp, Edward. *The Meridian Handbook of Classical Mythology*. New York: New American Library, 1970.

Tuck, Susan. "The O'Neill-Faulkner Connection." Diss. University of Indiana, 1984.

Turner, Victor. *From Ritual to Theatre: The Human Seriousness of Play*. New York: PAJ Publications, 1982.

Van Gennep, Arnold. *The Rites of Passage*. Chicago: University of Chicago Press, 1960.

Vernant, Jean-Pierre. *The Origins of Greek Thought*, Ithaca, N.Y.: Cornell University Press, 1962.

Verral, Arthur Woollgar. *Essays on Four Plays of Euripides: Andromache, Helen, Heracles, Orestes*. New York: Cambridge University Press, 1905.

Webster, John. *The White Devil*, ed. John Russel Brown, Manchester: Manchester University Press, 1974.

Wellein, Lawrence Theodore. "Time Past and the Hero: A Suggested Criterion for Sophoclean Tragedy as Exemplified by the 'Ajax,' 'Trahohiniao' and 'Electra.' Diss. University of Washington, 1969.

Wilde, Oscar. *The Complete Plays of Oscar Wilde, New York*: Harper & Row, 1966.

_____. *Plays*. New York: Penguin Books, 1985.

Woodard, Thomas Marion. "'Elektra' by Sophocles: The Dialectical Design." Diss. Harvard University, 1962.

Woodbridge, Linda. *Women and the English Renaissance*. Chicago: University of Illinois Press, 1986.

Yunis, Harvey Evan. "Athenian Polis Religion and Euripides: Fundamental Religious Beliefs in Life and Fiction." Diss. Harvard University, 1987.

List of Names and Terms

Dorian invasions Drake, Sir Francis dramatic opposition
Duchess of Malfi

E
Easter mass
The Eating of the Gods, Jan Kott Eliade, Mircea
Eliot, T.S. Elizabeth I erga facts
Eumenides Euridice Euripides Europe

G
Goethe, Johann Wolfgang von Grant, Michael
Great Mother Greek City States Grotesque

H
Hamlet
Hamlet-Machine Hannibal Hebrews
Hegel, Georg Wilhelm Friedrich Helen
Helenic era Hephaestus Hera
hero Herod
heroic theater hieros gamos Hippolytus Hitler, Adolf holy theater
Homer humanism

I
Ibsen, Henrik
In a Different Voice
incest infant
Ionian people irony
Isis Jacobian James I Jesus
Jewish bourgeoisie John the Baptist

K
Kant, Immanuel Kings, annual Kitto, H.D.F. Klimpt, Gustav
Knight, L.C. Kott, Jan

L
Lévi-Strauss, Claude libations

Schopenhauer, Arthur Schorske, Carl Emil segregation Semonides
serpent
Shakespeare, William shaman
sister sky
Slater, Philip social democrats Socrates
Song of Songs stichomythia symbolism

T
Tasso, Torquato Thun, Count Titans
tombs
totemic practice tree as coffin

U
Uranus uroborus usura

V
vagina dentata Van Gennep, A. victimization Virgin

W
Waldheim, Kurt Walker, Barbara Weber, Carl Webster, John The
White Devil Wiesel, Elie
Wiesenthal, Simon
A Woman Killed with Kindness
Woman's Encyclopedia of Myths and Secrets women
Woodard, T. Woodridge, Linda

Z
Zeus